ADVERTISING MENSWEAR

The bold *Dress and Fashion Research* series is an outlet for high-quality, in-depth scholarly research on previously overlooked topics and new approaches. Showcasing challenging and courageous work on fashion and dress, each book in this interdisciplinary series focusses on a specific theme or area of the world that has been hitherto under-researched, instigating new debates and bringing new information and analysis to the fore. Dedicated to publishing the best research from leading scholars and innovative rising stars, the works will be grounded in fashion studies, history, anthropology, sociology, and gender studies.

ISSN: 2053–3926

ADVERTISING MENSWEAR

Masculinity and Fashion in the British Media since 1945

PAUL JOBLING

B L O O M S B U R Y
LONDON · NEW DELHI · NEW YORK · SYDNEY

Bloomsbury Academic
An imprint of Bloomsbury Publishing Plc

50 Bedford Square	1385 Broadway
London	New York
WC1B 3DP	NY 10018
UK	USA

www.bloomsbury.com

Bloomsbury is a registered trade mark of Bloomsbury Publishing Plc

First published 2014

© Paul Jobling, 2014

Paul Jobling has asserted his right under the Copyright, Designs and Patents Act, 1988, to be identified as Author of this work.

British Library Cataloguing-in-Publication Data
A catalogue record for this book is available from the British Library.

ISBN: HB: 978-1-4725-3343-2
ePDF: 978-1-4725-5811-4
ePub: 978-1-4725-5810-7

Library of Congress Cataloging-in-Publication Data

Jobling, Paul.
Advertising menswear : masculinity and fashion in the
British media since 1945 / Paul Jobling.
pages cm. — (Dress and fashion research)
ISBN 978-1-4725-3343-2 (hardback) — ISBN 978-1-4725-5810-7 (epub) —
ISBN 978-1-4725-5811-4 (epdf)   1. Advertising—Men's clothing—
Great Britain—History—20th century.   I. Title.
HF6161.M38J6195 2014
659.19'687—dc23   2013045221

Typeset by Apex CoVantage, LLC, Madison, WI, USA
Printed and bound in Great Britain

For **Michael F., Jude, Christopher, Bruno, Patrick** and **Max.**

Thanks for the memory.

CONTENTS

LIST OF ILLUSTRATIONS

ACKNOWLEDGEMENTS

As usual, researching, writing and producing a book like this would not be possible without the generous support of others and I owe a debt of gratitude to many people. To the students on the MA History of Design and Material Culture, University of Brighton, with whom over the years I shared my research in illuminating seminar discussions. To all the producers, advertisers and archives that very kindly granted me permission to reproduce the advertisements included. In particular, to Anna Wright and Hannah Crump at Bloomsbury, for helping me to keep faith in the project through thick and thin, and the anonymous peer reviewers of the draft manuscript, for their unstinting words of encouragement and appreciation.

INTRODUCTION

While there have been many changes, it should be recognised that they have had more to do with the structure of the fashion and textile industries, the development of a mass consumer market and new techniques in marketing and retailing than with specific phases of creative activity on the part of individuals. (Anne Gardener, *Did Britain Make It?*, 1986)

People look at ads. They don't necessarily read them . . . It is more likely they are going to be stopped by a visual or a combination of both picture(s) and word(s). (John Hegarty, 'Why Creativity Must Lose Its Straightjacket', *Campaign*, 30 March 1979)

This book is the first study about British advertising for men's clothing since 1945. It encompasses the onset and vagaries of affluence and youth culture after 1955, and what is commonly regarded as the golden age of creative British advertising from the mid 1960s until the global impact of the economic downturn following the Al-Qaeda bombings of the United States of 11 September 2001.[1] During this period, print advertising for the likes of Tern shirts and televisual promotions for jeans brands Levi's, Brutus and Wrangler were often the recipient of Design and Art Directors Association (D&AD) awards, which were introduced in 1963; campaigns for Levi's also won awards at the Cannes and New York film festivals on seven occasions between 1976 and 1994, as well as a Royal Society of Arts Grand Prix in 1994 (see Appendix IV). Consequently, this study deals with print, television and cinema publicity—principally for suits, trousers, jeans, shirts and underwear—and picks up the thread, chronologically and thematically, of *Man Appeal: Menswear, Advertising and Modernism* (2005) in which I examined the period 1900–45.

The overarching objective that I expressed there for undertaking that project was 'to elaborate a dialectical exposition of the material in question . . . such that any technological, economic and social changes in the production and consumption of men's wear and any corresponding changes in the advertising industry can be seen to coalesce in, or give rise to, new forms and styles of clothing publicity'.[2] In common with its companion volume, therefore, *Advertising Menswear* is concerned with two key issues: first, the representation of clothing, or how the material object is translated into words and images; and second, the complex interface between advertising and design issues, the dress preferences and spending patterns of the fashionable male, and gender theory. Yet this is not to argue that the two projects simply tell the same story at different points in time. For, alongside traditional forms of press and poster publicity, after 1945 other channels of advertising came into their own—principally, cinema and commercial television— and, thus, the volume of menswear publicity in circulation increased exponentially. So too, debates about the form and content of advertising and its relationship to the male consumer—in particular, the style-conscious youth culture—intensified both within the professional literature and in academic writing without.

Any study of the rhetoric of menswear publicity, whether print or televisual, inevitably involves an initial analysis of the concomitant tension between 'image-clothing' and 'written clothing' that Roland Barthes evinced in *The Fashion System* (1967).[3] Publicity designed by Ashley Havinden for Daks, for instance, negotiated a balanced integration of copy and illustration and it won the first Layton Advertising Trophy on this basis in 1955 (Figure 6), whereas by the mid 1980s 'image-clothing' began to hold sway and a common stylistic trend in campaigns for jeans and formal attire alike was the postmodern aesthetic of simulation and retro styling (Figure 45). But, as Barthes also insisted in his essay 'The Advertising Message' ([1964] 1994), when it comes to decoding the verbal and visual rhetoric of publicity there is an additional tension to consider between the use-value of the product being promoted and its symbolic or exchange value. Thus, in interrogating how menswear advertising denoted the functional and connoted the symbolic qualities of various items of clothing by 'reconverting function into spectacle',[4] I enlist Jean-Marie Floch's semiotic square as an overarching methodology. Floch elaborated the analytical model of the semiotic square in his assessment of a series of ads for Citroën between 1981 and 1985, postulating that it involved a 'generative trajectory . . . from what is simplest to what is most complex'.[5] Accordingly, he argues that advertising rhetoric elicits the chiastic interpenetration of four types of oppositional but complementary coordinates: a practical valorization, based on utilitarian values, that is diagonally opposed to a ludic valorization, based on 'non-utilitarian values' such as ideas of luxury, escapism and refinement; and a critical valorization, based on 'non-existential values' such as benefits, quality and cost, that is diagonally opposed to a utopian valorization, based on 'existential' values such as the identity and lifestyle of the subjects in the ad, and by implication the spectators of it. In turn, a practical valorization complements a critical one, whereas a ludic valorization complements a utopian one.[6]

As we shall see, the synthesis of the practical and the symbolic that Floch propounds is evident to one degree or another in much of the publicity addressed in this study. However, to illustrate at the outset what the semiotic square entails, it is worth briefly singling out the copy and image of one advertisement here—a 1966 promotion for Byford beach wear, 'Men in Orlon' (Figure 1). In regard to the garment's practical valorization, for instance, the copy informs us that the Orlon shirt 'has minimum upkeep costs', and this message is diagonally opposed to its ludic valorization that states, 'Men in ORLON love life and luxury'. In regard to its critical valorization, the copy relates that the shirt 'looks expensive' but is priced 'about 75s',[7] and this point is diagonally opposed to its utopian valorization,

Figure 1 'Men in Orlon', Byford beachwear, full-page colour advertisement, *Men in Vogue*, 15 March 1966. Permission of Du Pont, USA.

connoted in the way that the copy refers to the south of France as the 'natural habitat' of men in Orlon. The different types of valorization addressed in the copy are also expressed in the colourful photograph of a male model wearing shorts and shirt as, hands on hips, he straddles a canoe at the water's edge. But the overall tone and content of both text and image give emphasis to the ludic and utopian messages of the ad that foreground a playboy lifestyle of untrammelled hedonism to promote Orlon, an acrylic substitute for wool pioneered by Du Pont in 1949; thus, as Floch argues, the ad's tone and content enable a free exchange of associations and fantasies through which 'we dream of joining "what is useful with what is pleasant" '.[8] Accordingly, the semiotic square proffers a general paradigm to analyse the rhetoric of menswear publicity. Yet, it is only a springboard for a deeper examination of the more specific socio-economic and cultural contexts surrounding the creation, circulation and interpretation of the advertisements that I consider in each of the three thematic parts that constitute this study.

In Part 1, 'Going for a Burton', I focus on the period 1945–57, at which time clothing itself and press and poster publicity for it were equally constrained by material shortages, rationing and the Utility scheme. Notwithstanding this situation the British public was still shopping for clothes and, according to government statistics, in 1949 sales of men's and boy's garments totalled £271 million. And yet, as I also argue, there were regional and class differences within this general picture, and it was not until 1953 that household expenditure on clothing, regardless of earnings, levelled at 11 per cent of annual income.[9] (Again in common with *Man Appeal*, I give the contemporary reader some indication of the value of the earnings, prices and currency cited for the period—much of it pre-decimalization—by providing the 2000 equivalents and including such details in the footnotes. These equivalents are not, however, intended to convey actual earnings or cost of any product in 2000.) Amongst the male population the suit in particular remained as popular as it had been before the war. A survey about post-war hardship published in the *Sunday Pictorial* in July 1946, for example, revealed that the majority of men were 'especially put out by not being able to buy a suit'.[10] This meant that tailors across a wide class spectrum—Burton's, John Collier, Austin Reed, and Daks Simpson—were just as keen to continue promoting their wares in the daily newspapers and popular weeklies such as the *Radio Times*, *Punch* and *Picture Post* as they had been during the interwar period, even though the overriding ludic message of their publicity was one of delayed gratification (Figure 5).

Simultaneously, therefore, I trace the efforts of the advertising agents, artists and copywriters who were responsible for generating the rhetoric of such publicity and whose handiwork was often subject to intense critical scrutiny in the trade press. (A representative sample of seventy-three menswear labels and retailers, alongside the advertising agents they employed between 1945 and 2000, is shown in Appendix I, and a sample of artists, illustrators and photographers in Appendix II.) Between 1945 and 1957 there were three methods or styles of pictorialization in print advertising: hand-drawn illustration, scraperboard and photography (Figures 4–6). Illustration was by far the most prevalent, with photography not beginning to make some impact until the mid 1950s; however, of great import in debates of the period was the relationship of advertising to art. In this respect both Milner Gray and Mary Gowing adumbrated Barthes' concern for the intertexuality of copy and image, asserting that 'the art in advertising is the whole advertisement—not just the picture, not just the type, and not just the text, but all three together'.[11]

In the post-war period print advertising was also challenged by cinema and the onset of commercial television, which was enshrined in the Television Act of 1954. In autumn 1952, for example, Pathé screened 'Man About Town', a short fashion advertising feature, and the first television clothing ads appeared on the Rediffusion channel in London in autumn 1955. (Appendix III lists all the menswear retailers and brands that resorted to broadcast advertising between 1955 and 2000 that I could trace.) Consequently, choosing the right medium in which to advertise was strategic and, as C.R. Casson (whose advertising accounts in the 1950s included Peter England shirts) argued, the preparation of any advertising campaign involved three key considerations: 'Will it be seen? Will it be remembered? Will it be "accepted"?'[12] Hence, I ask why and how the new media effectuated audience engagement and identification with the products being advertised in any ways that were different from press and poster publicity. In dealing with these issues, I explore the impact of consumer psychology and motivation research and enlist the handful of quantitative and qualitative surveys that were conducted, such as those by Mass Observation for the Advertising Service Guild in 1949 and by the London Press Exchange in 1953. Although neither of these two surveys was conducted to infer that the psychological impact of advertising could act as an enticement to purchase a particular product, the correlation between reading or viewing and consumption was precisely the concern of Viennese psychologist Ernst Dichter, who in 1951 had exhorted advertising agencies to realize they were 'one of the most advanced laboratories in psychology'.[13]

In British advertising culture the precepts of consumer psychology were promulgated by agencies such as Greenlys Ltd and McCann Erickson, with the research director of the latter, Harry Henry, stressing that the agency's purpose was to realize the difference between promoting needs and promoting wants.[14] Stereotypically, motivation research was conducted to find out what made the female consumer tick, and yet the rhetoric of much menswear publicity is uncompromisingly and exclusively addressed at the male consumer. By this measure, one of the seminal tropes that advertisers relied on to appeal to men was heroic masculinity; witness the designs by F. Whitby Cox, Alexis Delmar and Poul

Sprøgøe (Figures 3 and 9). In particular, Sprøgøe's illustration of an ebullient male gymnast and the caption 'Look good . . . feel good' in a 1954 advertisement for Lyle and Scott's y-front underpants epitomizes this ideal, while also symbolizing the phenomenological pleasure that men would get from simultaneously wearing or 'being touched' by the garment in question and seeing it, or being seen in it. Thus cloth, and in particular cloth worn on the human body, obviously has an instrumental part to play in such an imbrication of touch and sight—not only for the person in the ad who sees and feels him- or herself wearing it, and is seen wearing/feeling it, but for the spectator as well who, in looking at how the cloth is worn, can sense what it would also feel like to be clad in it him- or herself. It is this idea of haptic visuality, through which French philosopher Maurice Merleau-Ponty argued we encounter 'the two "sides" of our body, the body as sensible and the body as sentient',[15] that is further addressed in Parts 2 and 3. There I analyse publicity for Dormeuil, Austin Reed, Viyella and Levi's jeans.

By the early 1950s a new type of consumer—the teenager—had begun to emerge and to be hotly contested in the critical discourse about both fashion and advertising. An editorial in *Men's Wear* in April 1951 stated that 'its [the teenager's] taste is flamboyant, with an eye on colour' and this was the challenge that longstanding and new retailers and brands had to face in the design of both their merchandise and publicity.[16] In 1954, for example, the advertising agency Crawford's introduced a more relaxed attitude in symbolizing male desire in publicity for Burton's, shifting attention from the homosocial space of the shop floor to youthful scenes of flirtation and romance (Figure 7). But, as Frank Mort has aptly argued, Burton's new role model was 'decidedly not a teenager'.[17] Rather the youth market embraced men in both their teens and twenties, and the rise of independent boutiques such as Vince Man's Shop and John Stephen's His Clothes, which originated around London's Carnaby Street, was instrumental in catering to their needs. While Mort also maintains, 'The relationship of affluence to regional and generational change within working-class communities, its effects on women's roles and experience and on the crystallisation of new youth identities, has been studied almost obsessively,' the same cannot be said when it comes to menswear advertising.[18] Accordingly in Part 2, 'Thinking Young', I concentrate on the period 1958–78 and consider the changes that occurred in the marketing and promotion of menswear under the influence of youth culture.

In the first instance, market researchers were preoccupied with finding out how young people spent their income and leisure time. Investigations by Mark Abrams and Stanley Orwell between 1956 and 1961 had indeed revealed that there was considerable affluence among 15- to 24-year-old males, but also that two-thirds of the youth market were working class, belonging to social groups D and E.[19] Although these young men may have had a predilection for more colourful, Italian-styled clothing, nevertheless the suit remained a popular garment with young men of all classes, accounting for 30 per cent of menswear sales in 1964. Thus even clothing chains such as Hector Powe and Austin Reed designated departments for the young male consumer in their Regent Street stores. At the same time, where to advertise and to whom once more challenged menswear retailers and their advertising agents. The latter had long relied on the baseline socio-economic classifications of groups A–E, first formulated in the United States in the 1920s by Paul Cherington for J. Walter Thomson, afterwards espoused and modified by the Incorporated Society of British Advertisers (ISBA) in 1936 and currently adopted by the National Readership Survey (NRS),[20] to help them target both the optimum audience and advertising media (see Table 1). But the appearance of the new colour weeklies *Weekend* (founded 1957) and the *Sunday Times Magazine* (founded 1962) contested the NRS class boundaries, much as the consolidation of affluent youth markets had done. For example, *Weekend* was targeted at class C–D readers and the *Sunday Times Magazine* at classes A, B and C, but campaigns for class C–D retailers like Burton's and class B–C retailers like Sabre leisurewear appeared in both titles. Surveys by Pearl and Dean, Associated Television (ATV) and Target Group Index (TGI) on the nexus of cinema and television viewing to buying habits similarly suggest that there was considerable class permeability; it is tempting to believe, therefore, that cinema and television publicity had democratized the audiences for menswear advertising. By 1960 television publicity was not necessarily more expensive to produce or screen than other forms of advertising, but it was harder for advertisers to know whether audiences paid attention to the commercial breaks. Moreover, as colour advertising on television did not become widely available across Britain until summer 1971, the majority of menswear retailers and brands concentrated their publicity in magazines and posters; in any case, clothing advertising did not come into its own as a televisual event until the widespread promotion of jeans brands such as Levi's and Wrangler from the late 1970s onwards.

In this part, therefore, I propound a modulated assessment of the relationship between advertisers, the media and the public, considering the cultural affiliations of taste of distinct consumers in relation to their age and profession—what Pierre Bourdieu terms *habitus*[21]—and how advertising exploited this. The boutiques themselves did not tend—or even need—to publicize their products, more often relying on window displays and word of mouth for sales. By contrast, mainstream retailers and brands did rely heavily on advertising in men's titles such as *Man About Town* (founded 1954), *Men Only* (founded 1960) and *Vogue for Men* (founded 1965), as well as the dailies, popular weeklies, and colour supplements such as the *Sunday Times Magazine*. As R. Taylor appositely framed the last publication type: 'The Sunday colour supplements have been enormously important to the development of advertising—the understated, the elegant, the urbane, the witty, the pleasantest advertising of all to look at and read.'[22] Flicking through the pages of the *Sunday Times Magazine*, *Daily Mirror* and *Men in Vogue*, it soon becomes apparent not only how much the image of youth culture had seeped into menswear advertising but also how prevalent the pivotal stereotype of the male peacock was in campaigns for the likes of Austin Reed, John Collier and Van Heusen (Figures 15–16 and 19). But it would be misleading to argue that age differences no longer mattered or that menswear advertising managed to appeal seamlessly to new and traditional markets alike. Thus the visual and verbal rhetoric of a press advertisement, 'Is your father stopping you going to Hector Powe?' (*Sunday Times Magazine*, 27 September 1970), pinpointed the dilemma menswear multiples faced in performing a delicate balancing act to build cross-generational brand loyalty while respecting the different needs, tastes, and desires of both young and traditional clienteles at the same time.

Furthermore, many of the men who appear in the advertising of the period are depicted as both spectator and spectacle, and so I interrogate the extent to which such visibility in campaigns for Burton's, John Collier, Lyle and Scott, and Bri Nylon troubles the heteronormative dynamics of (male) looking and (female) being looked at (Figures 16 and 25). Finally, I examine how advertising during the 1960s and 1970s dealt with the practical and ludic valorizations of artificial fibres such as nylon and Terylene in comparison to cotton and wool. In regard to the latter, the centrepiece of my argument is the egregious press campaign 'Cloth for Men' for Dormeuil mohair, which appeared in 1973 and 1974 (Figures 26–9). In them, the German model, Veruschka von Lehndorff, wears 1930s-styled clothing and 'doubles up' to play both 'male' and 'female' parts, while the copy and *mise-en-scène* of the ads evoke a nineteenth-century sensibility. Hence, I take the opportunity to analyse how the gender ambiguities and criss-crossing of time connoted in the rhetoric of the ads perform what Jane Gaines has called a kind of 'homosexual/heterosexual flip-flop',[23] and how the knowing transvestism, style and visual décor they represent overlap with Susan Sontag's notion of camp as 'Being-as-Playing-a-Role'.[24]

To a large extent the relationship between identity and masquerade is also the leitmotiv of Part 3 of this study, 'Leader of the Pack', where I examine advertising for jeans since the 1960s. By 1965 jeans had begun to challenge the clothing hegemony enjoyed by the suit, and sales were in the ascendant well into the 1990s; in 1980, for example, 25 million pairs were bought in the United Kingdom.[25] More than any other item of clothing jeans had also latched onto the potential of cinema and television advertising. Campaigns for most brands were promoted through these channels from 1972 onwards, but the key players were Levi's, Wrangler, Brutus and Lee (Appendix IV lists the details of Levi's cinema and television campaigns). Furthermore, starting in the 1980s and continuing until the early 2000s, these brands tended to represent jeans as male or masculine attire in their publicity, even though they were popular with both men and women, and across generations. There are two related factors that contributed to this gender bias: the promotion of Levi's in a series of award-winning campaigns by the independent advertising agency Bartle, Bogle and Hegarty, which had won the account in 1982; and the epiphany of the style-conscious new man, which had been typologized in McCann Erickson's *ManStudy* Report in 1984. Of course, the 'new man' itself was not a new concept at the time: his advent had been heralded previously in 1919 by Sidney Garland and 1953 by Geoffrey Gilbert. But, in trading on the message 'looking good . . . feeling good', by the mid 1980s he was symbolic of a more sexualized and narcissistic masculinity that appealed to male and female spectators/consumers alike and that was exemplified in the seminal Levi's 501 campaigns first aired in December 1985: 'Bath' and 'Laundrette'.

One of the key issues I examine in Part 3, therefore, is the imbrication of sex and pleasure in objectifying the male body in jeans advertising. But the impact of such publicity—from the revivalism of the 1950s/1960s in 'Laundrette' to that of the 1850s/1860s in 'Settler's Creek'—is attributable also to its mythological, hyperreal image of the past that, according to Dick Hebdige, 'is played and replayed as an amusing range of styles, genres, signifying practices to be combined and recombined at will' and thereby treats history as nothing more than 'a series of masks'.[26] In televisual publicity for jeans this ludic or escapist postmodern historicism is achieved not only through images but also through the use of a pop or classical music soundtrack, which came to replace entirely the jingle, dialogue or voice-over. Accordingly, I consider the extent to which music, such as 'I Heard It Through the Grapevine' (Levi's), 'Crosstown Traffic' (Wrangler) and 'The Anvil Chorus' (Lee), contributes to the narrative arc of the campaigns it orchestrates. And yet, one is left to ask, is such style raiding and the seamless recycling of history merely gratuitous and totally devoid of deeper signification? Janice Winship, for instance, has argued that the period revivalism of 'Bath' and 'Laundrette' resonated with young people in the 1980s because they viewed the 1950s and 1960s as a time of youth rebellion and of opportunities for personal expression denied to them under the Thatcher government. Likewise, the way that both ads engendered the male body as a 'new sex object' can be regarded as a political act challenging the patriarchal values of the gaze.[27] It is not for nothing, then, that Mark Jones cavilled that the striptease performed by Nick Kamen in the 'Laundrette' ad 'gave agencies a charter to demean and exploit men's bodies'.[28] With this point in mind, I address the ambiguous sexual charge of the new man in publicity for jeans and other apparel, and the slippage between straight and gay male identities, which Susan Bordo argues is enacted through a supersession of 'leaners', that is: 'male bodies that do not assert themselves aggressively, but ask to be admired, loved, or sexually dominated'.[29]

At the same time, jeans publicity was among the first to represent non-white subjects, and I take the opportunity in Part 3 to examine also the persistent colour-blindness of the advertising industry in Britain since the Second World War. A significant problem for menswear promotions was the dearth of black models, something that was transcended initially by the use of well-known sportsmen such as boxer John Conteh in the 1970s (Figure 38) and footballer David James in the 1990s. As photogenic role models of dual heritage, however, both men conform to the hegemonic white stereotype of the 'noble savage', and they bolster bell hooks's assertion that '[a]ds are a primary vehicle for the dissemination and perpetuation of white-supremacist and patriarchal values'.[30] Certainly, some jeans advertising can be accused of this objectification; non-white subjects make only a token appearance, for instance, in Levi's 'Tackle' and 'Campfire' campaigns of 1993. But, as we shall see, the treatment of racialized sexuality in 'Taxi' (1995) was singular in comparison and, as I argue, the way that it intertwines the otherness of race and gender identities invites a nuanced analysis of the Manichean ambiguity of being 'the same but not exactly the same'.[31] Consequently, I interrogate here the strategy of mimicry that the ad and publicity for other menswear labels such as Ben Sherman and Hush Puppies mobilize, and the extent to which this proffers a consideration of the pros and cons of non-white representation (Figures 39 and 40).

By extension, the racial mimicry and double-coding of ads such as Ben Sherman's 'A man should be judged by the colour of his shirt' brings us to the final point addressed in this study: the shift from advertising rhetoric intended to appeal to the new man to that for the new lad. In January 1991 a press release for *GQ* announced that 'New Man has officially been laid to rest', and in 1994 the launch of *loaded* seemed to be the last nail in his coffin. As Robert Connell has contended, however, 'To recognise diversity in masculinities is not enough. We must also recognise the relations between different kinds of masculinity: relations of alliance, dominance and subordination.'[32] His perception is a valid one because the two male/masculine stereotypes not only coexisted but there was also considerable overlap between them, not least an intense interest in sex, clothing and appearances. Certainly, an advertisement such as 'No guts, no glory' for Base shoes in 1997 in its depiction of leery heterosexual desire is not dissimilar to scenes of chauvinistic and hedonistic flirtation in Katharine Hamnett's 1988 press campaigns, though it is a world apart from the sensitive portrayal of a man getting dressed in a Russell & Bromley shoes ad in 1986 or the barefooted gigolo represented in a 1998 promotion for Yves Saint Laurent Rive Gauche (Figures 36 and 45). Consequently, if this book achieves anything it is to embrace the sense of diversity and similarity that Connell emphasizes, not just in regard to masculine identities between 1945 and the turn of the millennium but also in the form and content of menswear publicity across the same period as well.

A Note on Sources

Several authors have contributed original and illuminating perspectives on men's fashion in the 1950s and 1960s (Breward, *Fashioning London*, 2004; Cole, *Don*

We Now Our Gay Apparel, 2000; Cohn, *Today They Are No Gentlemen: The Changes in Englishmen's Clothes Since the War*, 1971; O'Neill, *London—After a Fashion*, 2007); style culture and the new man in the 1980s (Mort, *Cultures of Consumption*, 1996; Nixon, *Hard Looks*, 1996); and the advertising profession in the 1960s (Nixon, *Advertising Cultures*, 2003). Yet Mort and Nixon also tend to dwell on a handful of menswear advertisers (to wit Burton's, Levi's and Next), and in this study I wanted to achieve a more rounded and representative analysis of a broad spectrum of promotions for male dress since 1945 in their cultural and socio-economic contexts. This has been a monumental undertaking, not least in regard to the myriad menswear advertisements circulated during the period. To bring a sense of order to such complexity, therefore, I decided it would be necessary to include and exclude certain material.

In the first instance, I wanted to continue the advertising story of some of the retailers and brands I had already initiated with *Man Appeal*, namely, Austin Reed, Simpson Daks, Hector Powe, Burton's, and the Fifty Shilling Tailors, rechristened John Collier in 1954. This led me to trawl through the press media analyses conducted by Legion Publishing until its demise in 1976 and through articles in the trade literature such as *Advertiser's Weekly*, *Outdoor Advertising*, *Campaign*, *Man and His Clothes* and *Men's Wear*; as well as to search for advertisements in a sample of periodicals and newspapers aimed at diverse readerships, chiefly *Picture Post*, *Man About Town*, *Men in Vogue*, *Reveille*, *Weekend*, *Sunday Times Magazine*, *The Face*, *Arena*, the *Daily Mirror*, the *Daily Express* and *The Times*. In the process, I was also pointed in the direction of some other important or interesting advertising campaigns that I have included for analysis here: Burberry's; Rael Brook, Tootal, Rocola and Ben Sherman shirts; Lyle and Scott y-fronts; Terylene and Bri Nylon; C&A; and Dormeuil 'Cloth for Men'. In terms of cinema and television publicity the picture becomes clearer because the lion's share of advertising has been for the different brands of jeans I address in Part 3. To this end, both advertising agents and manufacturers, as well as the History of Advertising Trust, were extremely cooperative in helping me to trace and view television campaigns for Brutus, Lee, Levi's and Wrangler.[33] Overall, then, this research project has proved to be a Sisyphean task, though the opportunity to pore over the kind of ads aimed at my father's generation in the 1950s and 1960s as well as to revisit those aimed at my own in the 1980s was also the source of much pleasure and a certain amount of mirth.

With the notable exception of Emporio Armani underwear and Yves Saint Laurent Rive Gauche (Figures 44 and 45), publicity for designer labels is conspicuous by its absence in this study. This is largely explained by the fact that, for the period under discussion, many of them had comparatively small annual advertising budgets in comparison to mass-market retailers and brands—less than £500,000 per manufacturer in 1997—or did not want to lose their cachet through widespread advertising.[34] Absent also is any consideration of publicity for sports brands such as Nike, Adidas, Reebok and Puma. It is not the case, however, that these companies did not resort to advertising in the period covered by this study. Adidas, for instance, appointed Connell, May and Stevenson as advertising agents for its £250,000 press account in 1979 and in 1982 began to advertise on television during the World Cup; shortly afterwards Nike launched a full range of sportswear in the United Kingdom with a £500,000 advertising campaign by the FCO Agency in 1983.[35] Although trainers and track suits became a popular form of leisurewear and street style from the 1980s onwards, publicity for these brands emphasized their sports pedigree.[36] Thus in spring 1984 the scenario of 'England 10, Italy 0', a 40-second national television ad for Nike shot by photographer Max Forsythe, centred on a group of children playing football in a back alley close to Anfield, Liverpool.[37] And in spring 1996 a national television campaign for Puma football boots, directed by Jon Greenhalgh for K Advertising, represented a man stripping off to get ready for a match to a wistful voice-over by actress Patsy Kensit exclaiming, 'Men. They only think about one thing.'[38]

Finally, in dealing with the print ads included here I reproduced them as they appeared in their original periodical contexts rather than falling back on original artwork. Hence, the back copies of magazines and newspapers became my hunting ground for both press and poster publicity. Many original menswear posters from the period under discussion do not exist in current collections, for example, but were often reproduced photographically by the advertising agencies that commissioned them in titles such as *Outdoor Publicity*, *Advertiser's Weekly* and *Campaign*. As is inevitably the case with this kind of printed ephemera, it is frequently dog-eared and bears the tinted patina of age (few old magazines are, after all, restored to their pristine condition). Nevertheless, I was grateful that records of past advertising could at least be mined from periodical sources, particularly when much of the archival material of advertising agents themselves (whether they are extant or defunct businesses) no longer survives. There are some exceptions to this general rule, however: the History of Advertising Trust houses the archives of W. S. Crawford and the London College of Fashion those for C&A, whereas the work and records of several graphic designers, who were involved in the advertising profession and the promotion of menswear, can be found in various institutional collections. Thus the University of Brighton Design Archives contain much information about F.H.K. Henrion and the Ashley Havinden Archive is held by the Scottish Gallery of Modern Art.

Notes

1   Jeremy Myerson and Graham Vickers, *Rewind: Forty Years of Design and Advertising* (London: Phaidon, 2002), 15.

2   Paul Jobling, *Man Appeal: Advertising, Modernism and Menswear* (Oxford: Berg, 2005), 2.

3 See Roland Barthes, *The Fashion System* [1967], trans. M. Ward and R. Howard (Berkeley: University of California Press, 1990). For Barthes, however, it is written clothing (*le vêtement écrit*) that takes precedence over image-clothing (*le vêtement-image*) because, as he argues, words seem to proffer a purer reading of the fashion text than pictures. As we shall see, such logocentrism is not necessarily the case in many of the menswear advertisements included in this book, which either deploy a more balanced integration of word and image or else give precedence to the visual.

4 Roland Barthes, 'Semantics of the Object' [1964], in *The Semiotic Challenge,* trans. R. Howard (Berkeley: University of California Press, 1994), 190. This volume also contains 'The Advertising Message' (173–8).

5 Jean-Marie Floch, *Semiotics, Marketing and Communication: Beneath the Signs, the Strategies*, trans. R. O. Bodkin (London: Palgrave, 2001), 111.

6 Ibid., 117 and 120.

7 The 2000 equivalent was £52. This and all subsequent monetary figures for 2000 have been calculated by using Lawrence H. Officer and Samuel H. Williamson, 'Purchasing Power of British Pounds from 1245 to Present', MeasuringWorth [Website] (2013). http://www.eh.net/hmit/ppowerbp, accessed 12 January 2013.

8 Floch, *Semiotics, Marketing and Communication*, 117 and 120.

9 *Men's Wear* (9 November 1957), 15.

10 Peter Hennessy, *Having It So Good: Britain in the Fifties* (London: Allen Lane, 2006), 121–2.

11 Cited by James de Holden Stone and Milner Gray, 'In the Case of Art v. Advertising: A Summing Up', *Penrose Annual* (1953), 62.

12 'C. R. Casson Ltd.', *Art and Industry* (May 1953), 149.

13 Cited in Vance Packard, *The Hidden Persuaders* (Harmondsworth: Penguin, 1991), 29.

14 Harry Henry, 'Motivation Research? — It's out of the Swaddling Clothes', *Advertiser's Weekly* (5 July 1957), 26.

15 Maurice Merleau-Ponty, *The Visible and the Invisible*, trans. A. Lingis (Evanston, IL: Northwestern University Press, 1968), 136.

16 'Today's Teenage Male', *Men's Wear* (7 April 1951), 20.

17 Frank Mort, *Cultures of Consumption — Masculinities and Social Space in Late Twentieth-Century Britain* (London: Routledge, 1997), 142.

18 Frank Mort, 'The Commercial Domain: Advertising and the Cultural Management of Demand', in B. Conekin, F. Mort and C. Waters (eds), *Moments of Modernity: Reconstructing Britain 1945–1964* (New York: Rivers Oram, 1999), 57.

19 See Stanley Orwell, 'Survey of the Youth Market', *Advertiser's Weekly* (21 February 1958), 32. Orwell also wrote 'Selling to the 16–24 Market', *Advertiser's Weekly* (3 February 1961), while Abrams contributed two articles titled 'Selling to the Teenager' to *Advertiser's Weekly* (23 January 1959: 31–2 and 12 February 1960).

20 See Jobling, *Man Appeal*, 45–7.

21 As Pierre Bourdieu argues in *Distinction* (London: Routledge, 1992) 172–5, it is through taste, whether of luxury or necessity, and not just high or low income, that 'a system of perceived differences, distinctive properties' is enacted.

22 R. Taylor, '25 Years of the Creative Circle', *Ad Weekly* (30 October 1970), 40.

23 Jane Gaines, 'The Queen Christina Tie-ups: Convergence of Show Window and Screen', *Quarterly Review of Film and Video* II (1989), 43.

24 Susan Sontag, 'Notes on "Camp"', in *Against Interpretation and Other Essays* (London: Picador, 2001), 108.

25 *Campaign* (28 August 1981), 8.

26 Dick Hebdige, 'The Bottom Line on Planet One—Squaring up to THE FACE', *Ten.8* 19 (1985), 47.

27 Janice Winship, 'Back to the Future', *New Socialist* (July/August 1986), 48–9.

28 *Campaign* (19 February 1988), 43.

29 Susan Bordo, 'Gay Men's Revenge', *Journal of Aesthetics and Art Criticism* 57:1 (Winter 1999), 22.

30 bell hooks, 'Doing it for Daddy', in M. Berger, B. Wallis and S. Watson (eds), *Constructing Masculinity* (London: Routledge, 1995), 101.

31 Homi K. Bhabha, *The Location of Culture* (London: Routledge, 1994), 86–9.

32 Robert W. Connell, *Masculinities* (Oxford: Polity, 1995), 37.

33 Many of Levi's television ads may be viewed in the Arrows Archive at the History of Advertising Trust website: http://www.hatads.org.uk.

34 Michele Martin, 'Why Fashion Shuns Adland', *Campaign* (23 May 1997), 36–7.

35 *Men's Wear* (13 May 1982), 2–3. For Nike see *Campaign* (30 September 1983), 64. Between August 1996 and July 1997 Adidas spent £3,843,524 on TV publicity and £274,289 on advertising in men's magazines, and Nike spent £4,144,133 and £757,146 respectively (*Campaign*, 7 July 1998).

36 *Campaign* (3 January 1985), 18. A report by Textile Market Studies stated that sales of tracksuits in 1983 constituted 12.9 per cent of all major branded sportswear. Encouraged by the crossover from sports clothing to leisurewear, in 1983 Levi's launched its own sports line that retailed in Burton's, Foster Menswear, Fenwick, Olympus Sport, and Selfridge. John Flynn, who collaborated on the range, stated that it was aimed at the 15- to 30-year-old male: 'He's a fashion conscious sportsman—and by sportsman we mean active, semi-active or even just a spectator.'

37 *Campaign* (11 May 1984), 4.

38 *Campaign* (3 May 1996), 11.

PART ONE

GOING FOR A BURTON

MENSWEAR ADVERTISING FROM AUSTERITY TO AFFLUENCE, 1945–57

The man who eventually buys the clothes must understand what the tag stands for, and be made aware of clothes as something more than mere necessity. (Bill Taylor, 'Do Style Shows Sell More Men's Clothes', *Men's Wear* 22 December 1951)

The present advertising is designed by subtle methods . . . and it impinges on the subconscious and raises doubts and questions in people's minds as to whether they are correctly dressed. (Sydney Jacobson, 'The Problem of the Demobbed Officer', *Men's Wear* 16 October 1954)

Introduction

The situation facing menswear retailers and advertisers in Britain after the cessation of hostilities in Europe in May 1945 and the landslide victory of Clement

Attlee's Labour Party in the general election of July 1945 was undoubtedly precarious though, as during the war period, not without a glimmer of hope. For instance, the 'Britain Can Make It' exhibition, organized by the Council of Industrial Design and held at the Victoria and Albert Museum in the autumn of 1946, included a representative display by Ashley Havinden of the kind of men's clothing that would soon be made available in the shops (Figure 2).[1] Yet clothing remained subject to rationing until March 1949 and, combined with paper shortages, this hampered the quantity of press and poster advertising for it that appeared between 1945 and 1951. Nonetheless, the British public was still shopping for clothes. In 1948, for instance, the publisher Hulton's 'Men's Wear Trade Readership Survey' recorded the existence of a substantial 17,800 men's outfitters across the British Isles, of which 11,640 were independent and 6,160 multiple concerns,[2] and figures from the Central Statistical Office revealed an exponential rise in clothing sales (for men, women and children) from £178 million between April and June 1947 to £214 million between April and June 1948.[3] Although the majority of small-scale menswear shops did not advertise on a regular basis, if at all, publicity for popular multiple retailers such as Burton's, Austin Reed and the Fifty Shilling Tailors (which was rechristened John Collier in the spring of 1954) and brands like Wolsey and Lyle and Scott underwear,

Figure 2 Britain Can Make It, men's clothing display by Ashley Havinden, 1946. Permission of Design Council/University of Brighton, Design Archives.

Radiac shirts, Daks trousers and Baracuta raincoats continued to appear in all of the mass-circulation national and regional dailies and the best-selling weeklies *Radio Times*, *Punch* and *Picture Post* (Figures 3–9), while the state of the advertising and clothing industries was as keenly debated in the pages of trade journals such as *Advertiser's Weekly* (founded 1913), *Men's Wear* (1902) and *Man and His Clothes* (1926) as it had been in the first half of the twentieth century. Indeed, Frank Bishop went so far as to argue that not only would advertising be imperative to the reconstruction of the post-war British economy but, in sympathy with the consumer capitalism of the United States, that it would also be morally purposeful in countering any drift towards totalitarianism.[4]

Figure 3 'Baracuta', poster advertisement; illustration by F. Whitby Cox, 1947. Permission of BMB Clothing.

Figure 4 'Radiac's that kind of shirt', scraperboard advertisement, *Radio Times*, 4 March 1955. Private collection.

In this part, therefore, I want to deal with the socio-economic, cultural and aesthetic factors that circumscribed the production and circulation of both menswear itself and publicity for it during what are commonly referred to as the 'short post-war' or Age of Austerity of 1945–53 and the burgeoning of affluence between 1954 and 1957. As we shall see, some of these trends had been sedimented in both the interwar and war periods, while by the mid 1950s some others portended the more ebullient, democratic youth culture and the shift to cinema and television advertising that I address more fully in Parts 2 and 3.

Figure 5 Austin Reed, full-page colour advertisement, *The Sphere*, 29 June 1946. Permission of Austin Reed.

Figure 6 'You can always tell . . . Daks', half-page black and white advertisement, *The Times*, 4 July 1954. Permission of Daks Simpson Group.

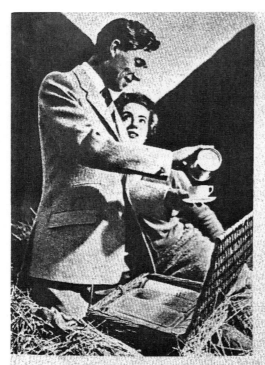

Figure 7 Burton's, 'At times like this . . . You can't beat Burton tailoring!', quarter-page black and white advertisement, *Daily Express*, 20 June 1955.

Figure 8 Rael Brook Toplin shirt, 'The London Look', full-page colour advertisement, *Woman's Own*, 19 November 1958. Private collection.

Figure 9 Lyle and Scott y-front, 'Look good . . . feel good. Be twice the man', full-page black and white advertisement, *Picture Post* 10 April 1954. Permission of Lyle and Scott Ltd.

Notes

1   The menswear display was designed by Ashley Havinden, who created a giant mural and a series of thematic bays featuring day wear, evening wear, formal, town and country wear. The 'Britain Can Make It' (BCMI) exhibition was a huge success, attracting 1.5 million visitors between September–December 1946. On Havinden, see Ashley Havinden, *Advertising and the Artist* (London: Studio Publications, 1956); on BCMI, see Penny Sparke (ed.), *Did Britain Make It?* (London: Design Council, 1986).

2   'Men's Wear Trade Readership Survey', *Advertiser's Weekly* (17 June 1948), 526.

3   *Monthly Digest of Statistics* (London: Legion Publishing, September 1948).

4   F. P. Bishop, *The Ethics of Advertising* (London: Robert Hale, 1949) 35.

1

THE POST-WAR MARKET FOR MEN'S CLOTHING

The most significant hangover from the war effort to affect the production and consumption of clothing was, of course, the continuation of rationing until May 1949 and of the Utility scheme until 1952, the latter having compensated to a certain extent for the shortage of raw materials and democratized to a larger extent the supply of good quality clothing to all classes. As Mass Observation correspondent B. Charles remarked in his diary for 2 July 1948: 'This morning I got a pair of utility [braces] for 2/- . . . It is far better to get utility clothes instead of buying the things that are not controlled.'[1] Although there was a standard issue of coupons to all British citizens, the annual entitlement had diminished successively from 66 coupons per capita between June 1941 and January 1942 to 36 coupons by 1945, in part to deal with the exigencies of clothing the demobilized military. The coupon system was determined according to the amount and quality of cloth used in the making of any garment, such that in 1941 a man's three-piece suit equated to 26 coupons, an overcoat to 16, a sweater to 8, a cotton shirt to 7 and underwear and shoes to 4 apiece, with a man's entire wardrobe requiring the unattainable sum of 223 coupons in 1945.[2] But men from different income groups also began to demonstrate different purchase preferences over the period 1941–44: groups A and B (upper- and middle-class professionals), for instance, cut down on overcoats, footwear, shirts, suits and nightwear, whereas Group E (manual workers, pensioners and the unemployed) reduced their purchases of overcoats, vests, raincoats and pants.[3] Overall, shoes remained the most popular purchase, with men from all class groups using 22 per cent of their coupon allocation on such items, whereas only 19 per cent bought suits.[4]

However, when asked which garment they would most likely have purchased had rationing ended in 1944, some 60 per cent of men from all classes expressed a preference for a new suit. Even by July 1946, the majority of men on the panel of 100 families surveyed about the hardships of post-war living by the *Sunday Pictorial* said they were 'especially put out by being unable to buy a new suit', and in a Mass Observation directive, London civil servant Anthony Heap lamented that, after ordering a suit in grey tweed from his local Burton's branch at the Angel, a North London district, in November 1947, it would probably take about nine months before he could have it.[5] For ex-military, at least, the pressing demand for civilian clothing was met under Minister of Labour Ernest Bevin's Code 11, which led to the free issue of staple items of dress to approximately five million servicemen who were demobilized in the eighteen-month period after June 1945. (Release dates were staggered according to age, length of service and time spent overseas.) Demobilization, or demob, clothing comprised a suit—or jacket and trousers, shirt, hat, overcoat, underclothes, two pairs of socks and one pair of shoes—and servicemen were also issued with an extra ninety clothing coupons with which to supplement this basic wardrobe. Although some men remarked ironically that the conspicuous universality of the demob suit was more a matter of 'one uniform received in exchange for another', thanks to the intervention of Major-General W. W. Richards, the War Office's director of clothing and stores, all garments were non-Utility and made from the best quality materials that were still available.[6] To meet demand, some 75,000 demob suits were being produced every week by October 1945, with many items of clothing manufactured by the likes of the Fifty Shilling Tailors and Burton's, the latter providing about a quarter of all demobilization suits.[7] But the Ministry of Supply even commissioned upmarket retailers such as Simpson to produce demob clothes for distribution.[8] Arthur Egerton-Savory was photographed by *Picture Post* on the day he went to pick up his demob suit in January 1946 from the clothing depot at Olympia, Kensington, although he was not invited then to comment how he felt about it.[9] In an interview with the BBC in 1984, however, he recalled the impersonal drabness of his experience in the following terms:

> The procedure was that you joined a great big long queue where first of all you were measured, your height taken, your chest size and so on, the size of your shoes, was all put down. Then you proceeded to the stores . . . There were three or four different types [of suit] as far as I remember and I chose a conventional pin-stripe which would serve me for office wear. They were made by the Fifty Shilling Tailors as they were then called . . . if one wanted to go out in the evening for something special it would hardly have been a very distinguished type of suit.[10]

A similar picture of the clothing depot at Olympia is painted by Nicholas Jenkins, the fictional narrator in Anthony Powell's *The Military Philosophers*, when he refers to the endless ranks of grey suits, drab mackintoshes (raincoats) and flannel trousers on display. But Jenkins also describes a sense of homosocial camaraderie, with assistants 'urbane and attentive', and the sense of oneiric closure that trying on demob clothing seemed to impart: 'If this were not a shop, what was it? Perhaps the last scene of the play in which one had been performing, set in an outfitter's, where you "acted" buying the clothes, put them on, then left the theatre to give up the stage and find something else to do.'[11]

By May 1944, expenditure on clothing had fallen by 60 per cent in comparison to 1938 largely as a result of rationing and, generally, winning the war had cost the British economy dearly.[12] The country became a debtor nation largely because the wartime government had borrowed too much—even Burton's had made an interest-free loan of £1 million to the British government—and reduced 70 per cent of the volume of exports.[13] This situation was exacerbated by President Truman's decision in 1945 to end the Lend-Lease system that had enabled Britain to pay for the war effort without having to produce exports to balance the cost of importing food and raw materials from America. In addition, although the population had increased to an estimated 49,207,000 by December 1946, there was a severe labour shortage of some four million workers to help with industrial reconstruction.[14] In particular, the textiles and clothing industries had witnessed an almost 25 per cent decline in the workforce, down from 1,803,000 employees in June 1939 to 1,405,000 by the close of 1946, and a concomitant dwindling stock of raw cotton.[15]

In order to balance the national budget and control the use and circulation of raw materials, therefore, Attlee's post-war Labour administration was initially forced to restrict domestic consumption and to divert resources to exports; as a result in 1950 the volume of exports was 50 per cent higher than in 1937.[16] Indeed, in comparison to his demobbed compatriot, the average post-war civilian male in Britain was shabbily dressed; as an exchange on 7 June 1945 between Mass Observation correspondent George Taylor from Sheffield and his tailor reveals, this meant that the culture of make-do-and-mend still persisted.[17] 'People had hard times after the last war', the tailor commented, 'and it will be just the same again.'[18] But so too did the black market persist, to the extent that all classes were prone to fall for the small talk and blandishments of the flashy spiv and street-smart barrow-boy, 'regarded with that blend of affection and mistrust which the English reserve for anyone who seems to symbolize the ways things are going'.[19] Another Mass Observation correspondent, for instance, recorded in his diary for 6 August 1946 that 'Alec said, quite as a matter of course, that he got his suit without giving any coupons . . . Of course, it is hardly to be wondered that people try to cheat such idiotic regulations.'[20] Similarly, Osbert Lancaster satirized this carnivalesque situation in a cartoon for the *Daily Express* on 26 June 1947, which represented a raffish, zoot-suited spiv soliciting a decorous and elderly city gent, as his wife exclaims, 'Don't be so stuffy, Henry!

I'm sure that if you asked him nicely the young man would be only too pleased to give you the name of a really GOOD tailor who doesn't worry about coupons!'[21]

In any case, between November 1948 and March 1949 Harold Wilson, president of the Board of Trade, relaxed controls on the purchase of many goods, and clothes rationing was finally abolished in March 1949. Thereafter, official statistics on the state of the economy portrayed a somewhat rosier picture. A 1950 government White Paper on National Income and Expenditure for the period 1946–50, for example, revealed sales figures for men's and boy's clothing of £157 million for 1946 and £271 million for 1949,[22] and the 1949 'Economic Survey' portrayed 1948 as a 'year of great and steady progress'.[23] Indeed, by summer 1948 rationing on footwear had ceased and men's suits could be bought with twenty clothing coupons.

But these changes masked the underlying volatile economic situation: from spring 1948 until August 1950 earnings had risen by a meagre 5 per cent due to a wage freeze, while retail prices rose by 8 per cent. (Anthony Head argued that clothes 'cost at least three times what they did before the war' and a ready-made suit could cost from £5 upwards.[24]) Most crucially, full convertibility between sterling and the dollar was reestablished in 1947 with the end result, announced by the Labour administration on 18 September 1949, the devaluation of sterling by 30.8 per cent, down from an exchange rate of $4.03 to the pound to $2.80.[25] A freeze on public expenditure swiftly followed, and dollar convertibility also led to a sharp increase in imports, which was compounded in turn by British involvement with the Korean War between July 1950 and July 1953. Thus in his first budget on 10 April 1951, Chancellor Hugh Gaitskell was forced to put 'guns before butter', committing £4,700 million to a three-year rearmament programme, raising income tax by sixpence in the pound, and levying charges on the provision of National Health spectacles and dentures to help pay for it.[26] In the face of this set of economic crises, growth in sales of clothing and apparel not surprisingly began to stall: by the early 1950s, the market constituted gross sales of £283 million[27], an increase of only 4 per cent from figures for 1949.[28] On 31 May 1950 price controls on men's bespoke, non-Utility suits and overcoats, which had been operative since 1 October 1947, were also rescinded. But in the difficult economic situation of the time retailers were only allowed to sell a non-Utility suit at limited profit, so that a suit that had cost 6 guineas in 1939 could only be sold for a few shillings more in 1950.[29] Combined with the drop in consumer demand this situation left Austin Reed, for instance, both overstocked and with dwindling profits in 1950 and 1951.[30]

Moreover, within this broad socio-economic context, class divisions still mattered. In his regular 'As I Please' feature for the *Tribune* on 4 February 1944, George Orwell crystallized the curious levelling in dress that clothes rationing had appeared to effect during the war, commenting, 'If the poor are not much better dressed, at least the rich are shabbier.'[31] In comparison to the interwar period, therefore, when in much of the south and the Midlands they had enjoyed relative prosperity, during and after the war it was the middle classes that struggled more than the working classes to come to terms with the material deprivation of clothes' rationing and austerity. In contrast, for working-class industrial communities the conditions of everyday life were even harsher in 1939 than during the war and its aftermath. Two articles in Picture Post, however, enable us to glean a more specific understanding of the situation and to realize that not only were there significant differences in the pattern of clothing expenditure within the same class structure but also still a considerable material gulf between one class and another.

The first article, which appeared on 4 June 1949, posed the eschatological question, 'Is the middle class doomed?' The piece investigated a range of middle-class household budgets for 1948 and in all cases revealed them struggling to make ends meet.[32] For example, Mr Walker, a hairdresser, his wife and two children from Paisley felt that 'the economic situation is worse for them now than before the war' and particularly found that the price of clothes was much higher. In regard to clothing, the mean expenditure for all eight families was just over 8 per cent of their annual budget. But at one end of the scale it constituted a mere 4 per cent of expenditure for scientist Dr Fremlin, his wife and three children, who lived in a nine-room Victorian property in Edgbaston, Birmingham, and at the other a more robust 13 per cent for psychologist George Ellidge, his wife and two children, who lived on a barge in Oxford. Even though the Ellidges were spending more than the other families on clothing, Mr Ellidge still relied on ex-army apparel (ironically, army surplus was one key way of compensating for the lack of civilian dress[33]), and his wife was making some of her daughter's clothes. By comparison, the clothing budget for costing clerk, Mr MacGrath, his wife and son, who lived in Peckham in southeast London, constituted nearly 9 per cent of spending, but Mrs MacGrath added that a new suit for both her and her husband came out of their savings. If the clothing budget of all eight middle-class families in the feature was restrictive, their financial situation was, however, a far cry from that of the typical working class household. For instance, a Picture Post article in 1950 dealing with the wage freeze's effects on the working classes, revealed that for Johnnie McGuirl, a railway worker from Darlington earning £5 5s. 6d. per week[34], his wife and three children, clothing was an 'extra' rather than an 'essential' that could only be purchased by his working for double-pay every alternate Sunday: 'Johnnie is always pleased when it comes . . . because it means something with which to pay for a new shirt or a pair of overalls for the twins.'[35]

Following the end of the Korean War in 1953, the British economy, aided by falling prices in world markets, began to stabilize. In 1954 not only did food rationing finally end and the Raw Cotton Commission was abolished but also international commodity markets were reopened. As historian Arthur Marwick described it, 'very much there was a sense that the British people now had entered into their just inheritance. The consumer market expanded and the pressure to fight for export markets lessened.'[36] At the same time clothes spending started to rally. Writing about women's clothing in the early 1950s Margaret Wray opined that the production and consumption of clothing had become more democratic, to the extent that 'class distinctions in clothing have tended to disappear. Clothing purchases for many consumers, particularly those in the 15–30 age groups who now earn good wages in offices and factories are no longer regulated by basic necessity.'[37] This general trend is borne out by the Household Expenditure Enquiry Report for 1953–54, prepared by the Cost of Living Advisory Committee for the Ministry of Labour, which put annual expenditure on clothing and footwear at 11 per cent of income in all households, whether the head earner was a manual or professional worker.[38] On a regional basis also there was parity—more or less—in household spending on men's outer clothing, underclothing and hosiery. Accordingly, in the North, Midlands, East Anglia, the South and Scotland, the weekly spending on outerwear averaged 4s. 3d., and underwear expenditure averaged 1s. 9d. In Wales the figures were higher at 7s. 2d. for outerwear and 3s. on underwear, but Northern Ireland revealed itself to be the most fertile area for sales of menswear: 9s. 6d. was spent there every week on outerwear and 4s. 2d. on underwear.[39] (*Men's Wear* speculated that the higher figures coincided with the higher incidence of bachelors living in the region.)

Yet in more specific terms, the household expenditure report revealed some variation in the purchasing patterns of different income groups for certain items of men's clothing. Thus households with a weekly wage between £10 and £13 spent 4s. 5d. on outerwear and 1s. 10d. on underwear, whereas those with an income of between £3 and £5 spent 1s. 2d. and 10d. respectively.[40] That the purchasing patterns of different class and income groups were prone to vary is also evident in the different prices charged for similar garments. In 1954, for example, a pair of sports trousers from Austin Reed, targeted primarily at groups A and B (see Table 1), sold for £5. 5s., whereas in 1958 a similar style of casual pants by Straddlers, targeted mainly at groups C1 and C2, cost £2. 15s.[41] And in the early 1950s, the cheapest two-piece made-to-measure suit at Austin Reed cost £14. 17s. 6d., whereas at Burton's it was £7. 15s.[42] Yet neither could compete with C&A, which had started to retail in the United Kingdom in 1922 and in September 1957 had opened menswear departments at its branches in Manchester, Birmingham, Leicester, Nottingham, Edinburgh and Aberdeen, selling ready-to-wear suits as cheaply as £4. 8s.[43] As we shall see in the discussion that follows, however, the way that many retailers and brands

Table 1 *IPA Social Groups, as defined in 1954.*

Table 1 Group	Social Status	Head of Household Occupation	Estimated Income
A	Upper middle class	Higher managerial, administrative or professional	£1,500 + p.a.
B	Middle class	Intermediate managerial, administrative or professional	£750-£1,500 p.a.
C1	Lower middle class	Supervisory or clerical; junior managerial, administrative or professional	Under £750 p.a.
C2	Skilled working class	Skilled manual workers	Over £10 per week
D	Working class	Semi- and unskilled workers	£5–£10 per week
E	Those at lowest levels of subsistence	State pensioners or widows, casual or lowest grade workers	Less than £5 per week

The respective 2000 equivalents were: £62,243 (£1,500); £31,121 (£750); £415 (£10) and £208 (£5).

Table compiled by author, based on 'First Report in IPA Continuity Survey', *Advertiser's Weekly* (7 December 1956), 10.

advertised in newspapers and magazines across the class spectrum and how the visual and verbal rhetoric of their publicity symbolized the needs or wants of actual or potential consumers both suggest (in keeping with Wray's argument) that a more fluid and dynamic market for menswear existed at this time.

Notes

1   Simon Garfield, *Our Hidden Lives: The Everyday Diaries of a Forgotten Britain 1945–1948* (London: Ebury Press, 2004), 515. In 2000, the equivalent of 2s. was £2.16. This and all subsequent monetary figures for 2000 have been calculated by using Lawrence H. Officer and Samuel H. Williamson, 'Purchasing Power of British Pounds from 1245 to Present', MeasuringWorth (2013). http://www.eh.net/hmit/ppowerbp, accessed 12 January 2013.

2   Paul Addison, *Now the War Is Over, A Social History of Britain 1945–51* (London: BBC, 1985), 20.

3   Henryk Frankel and Peter Ady, 'The Wartime Clothing Budget', *Advertiser's Weekly* (21 June 1945), 26.

4   Ibid., 27, 40.

5   'Wanted: 100 Families to Speak for Britain', *Sunday Pictorial* (7 July 1946), 4–5; Peter Hennessy, *Having It So Good: Britain in the Fifties* (London: Allen Lane, 2006), 121–2, 248.

6   Alan Allport, *Demobbed: Coming Home After the Second World War* (New Haven: Yale University Press, 2009), 119.

7   *Men's Wear* (4 March 1950), 20.

8   David Wainwright, *The British Tradition: Simpson, A World of Style* (London: Quiller Press, 1996), 56.

9   Sydney Jacobson, 'The Problem of the Demobbed Officer', *Picture Post* (26 January 1946), 26–7.

10 Addison, *Now the War Is Over*, 20.

11 Anthony Powell, *The Military Philosophers* (London: William Heinemann, 1968), 242.

12 Frankel and Ady, 'The Wartime Clothing Budget', 26.

13 *Men's Wear* (4 March 1950), 19. In 2000, the equivalent for £1 million was £32,284,004.

14 George Schuster, 'Are We TOO Few for the Job?', *Picture Post* (19 April 1947).

15 Ibid.

16 David Kynaston, *Austerity Britain 1945–51* (London: Bloomsbury, 2007), 432.

17 T.E.B. Howarth, *Prospect and Reality: Great Britain 1945–1955* (London: Collins, 1985), 45, reports how many men were repairing holes in their shoes with bits of cardboard and paper.

18 Garfield, *Our Hidden Lives*, 38.

19 David Hughes, 'The Spivs', in M. Sissons and P. French (eds), *Age of Austerity* (London: Hodder and Stoughton, 1963), 88–9.

20 Garfield, *Our Hidden Lives*, 261.

21 In London, Soho was the locus of the spiv and the black market. See Stanley Jackson, *The Indiscreet Guide to Soho* (London: Muse Arts Ltd, 1946), 11 and 'Meet the Spiv', *Tailor and Cutter* (15 August 1947), 561.

22 The 2000 equivalents were £3,847.5 million (£157 million) and £5,684.8 million (£271 million).

23 Alan Sked and Chris Cook, *Post-War Britain, A Political History* (Harmondsworth: Pelican, 1984), 36.

24 Cited by Hennessy, *Having It So Good: Britain in the Fifties*, 297. Edie Rutherford's diary for Mass Observation on 11 May 1948 states: 'Husband has decided to buy a two-piece suit. Asked me to have a look-see in town today. Can get any price from £5 and up and the look of them improves with price of them. He has decided to buy a ready-made for the first time ever, as he knows several men who've done this lately and successfully' (Garfield, *Our Hidden Lives*, 508). The 2000 equivalent for £5 was £108.

25 Sked and Cook, *Post-War Britain*, 37.

26 Ibid., 96. The 2000 equivalent of £4.7 million was £87,644,143.

27 The 2000 equivalent was £5,278.5 million.

28 Central Statistical Office, *The Treasury Blue Book* (London: HMSO, 1953).

29 The 2000 equivalent was £230.76.

30 B. Ritchie, *A Touch of Class: The Story of Austin Reed* (London: James and James, 1991), 107.

31 George Orwell, *The Collected Essays, Journalism and Letters, 1943–1945*, Vol. 3 (Harmondsworth: Penguin, 1978), 111.

32 The eight families and their 1948 budgets were as follows: (i) Mr Walker, hairdresser, his wife and two children, Paisley. Overall expenditure £379. 11s. 1d., clothing expenditure, £31 (6 per cent); (ii) Dr Fremlin, atomic scientist, his wife and three children, Edgbaston, Birmingham. Overall expenditure £1092. 0s. 2d., clothing expenditure £41. 8s. 4d. (4 per cent); (iii) Mr Ellidge, psychologist, his wife and two children, Oxford. Overall expenditure £603. 7s. 9d., clothing expenditure £79. 11s. 4d. (18 per cent); (iv) Mr Grath, clerk, his wife and son, Peckham. Overall expenditure £504. 9s., clothing expenditure £44 (8.7 per cent); (v) Mr. Scales, farmer, his wife and daughter, Peldon, Essex. Overall expenditure £456. 4s., clothing expenditure £21 (4.6 per cent); (vi) Mr. Brindley, schoolteacher, his wife and daughter, Rickmansworth. Overall expenditure £532. 13s., clothing expenditure £43. 7s. (8 per cent); (vii) Mr Norman, banker, his wife and two children, West Molesey, Surrey. Overall expenditure £565. 5s., clothing expenditure £63 (11 per cent); (viii), Mr Britton, lecturer, his wife and two children, Oxford. Overall expenditure £591, clothing expenditure £69 (11.7 per cent).

33 As Nik Cohn, *Today There Are No Gentlemen* (London: Weidenfield and Nicholson, 1971), 17, argues: 'It was cheap and it lasted and, if it wasn't elegant, it could at lest be tarted up and made bearable.'

34 The 2000 equivalent was £293.99.

35 Robert Kee, 'Can the Wage-freeze Hold for Them?', *Picture Post* (3 June 1950), 37–41.

36 Arthur Marwick, *British Society Since 1945* (Harmondsworth: Pelican, 1982), 107.

37 Margaret Wray, *The Women's Outerwear Industry* (London: Gerald Duckworth, 1957), 58.

38 *Men's Wear* (9 November 1957), 15; *Advertiser's Weekly* (7 February 1958), 18.

39 The 2000 equivalents were as follows: £9.40 (4s. 3d.), £3.87 (1s. 9d.), £15.85 (7s. 2d.), £6.64 (3s.), £21.01 (9s. 6d.) and £9.22 (4s. 2d.).

40 The respective 2000 equivalents were £442 (£10), £575 (£13), £9.77 (4s. 5d.), £4.05 (1s. 10d.), £132.71 (£3), £221.18 (£5), £2.58 (1s. 2d.) and £1.84 (10d.).

41 Advertisements for these garments appeared, respectively, in *Punch* (5 May 1954) and the *Daily Mirror* (16 September 1958). The respective 2000 equivalents were £85.43 (£5. 5s.) and £38.18 (£2. 15s.).

42 Advertisements for these garments appeared, respectively, in *Punch* (22 August 1951) and the *Daily Mirror* (March 1953). The respective 2000 equivalents were £277 (£14. 17s. 6d.) and £128.38 (£7. 15s.).

43 *Men's' Wear* (14 September 1957), 17; *Men's Wear* (26 October 1957),14. The 2000 equivalent of £4. 8s. was £62.94. An interesting potted overview of C&A as a global trader—taking into account the Brenninkmeyer dynasty's involvement with the Catholic church and its anti-Semitism in the 1930s—is Robert Lacey, 'The Richest Shopkeepers in the World', *Sunday Times Magazine* (17 December 1972).

2

MENSWEAR ADVERTISING

AGENTS, ACCOUNTS AND AUDIENCES: 'WILL IT BE SEEN? WILL IT BE REMEMBERED? WILL IT BE "ACCEPTED"?'

As in the interwar and war periods, the microeconomic dynamics of the fashion and advertising industries very much intersected with the broader economic situation after the war. A Board of Trade Survey revealed there were 16,905 menswear shops in Britain in 1950 but, by and large, it was the large retail chains such as Burton's (which, notwithstanding the loss of about 5 per cent of its establishments during the war, had more shops than any other tailor in 1950) that formed the mainstay of the early post-war market.[1] This enabled them economies of scale in producing both ready-to-wear and made-to-measure garments and thereby to have sufficient funds for widespread publicity campaigns, which on average accounted for 5 per cent of annual turnover.[2] The perennial issues for any menswear retailer, therefore, were where and how to advertise and to whom. In this scenario, menswear retailers relied on the expertise of the myriad advertising agencies to promote their wares through the most appropriate media. As advertising agent C. R. Casson (whose accounts in the 1950s included Peter England shirts) argued, the preparation of any advertising campaign involved three key questions: '1. Will it be seen? 2. What will be remembered? 3. Will it be "accepted"?'[3]

Eighty-three advertising agencies existed in Britain by 1896, including a handful of notable organizations that were to survive well into the next century (viz. the London Press Exchange, founded in 1892, and S. H. Benson in 1895),[4] and their offices were clustered in London around 'Printer's Land' in Strand, Fleet Street, High Holborn and Embankment.[5] The professionalization of the agency system in Britain had gained some impetus in 1904 with the founding of the Sphinx Club and the Association of Advertising Agents, the latter arguing at the outset, 'We are putting ourselves in the way of establishing precedents, principles and laws . . . for the encouragement of skilled advertising.'[6] Such early initiatives were consolidated by events such as the International Advertising Exhibition, held at White City in 1920; the series of British Advertising Conventions, the first of which was held in Harrogate in July 1925; and the establishment in 1927 of the Institute of Incorporated Practitioners in Advertisers (IIPA), later the Institute of Practitioners in Advertising (IPA). The IIPA supported the role of the advertising agency as a group of autonomous, professional experts, and it was largely through the activities of a new breed of agencies in the 1920s and 1930s, including W.S. Crawford (founded 1914), F.C. Pritchard Wood and Partners (1923), Stuart Advertising (1924) and C.D. Notley (1932), that advertising came of age as a respected profession in Britain. In 1954 the IPA held its first national conference in Birmingham and 10 years later had accrued a membership of 270 agencies, almost half of all those listed in the 1964 *Directory of Advertising Agents and Personnel*.[7]

During the interwar period many advertising agencies had attracted accounts for menswear publicity. Several of these were longstanding relationships, which survived into the post-war period (seventy-three menswear labels and retailers, alongside the advertising agents they employed between 1945 and 2000, are listed in Appendix I). Thus Pritchard and Wood continued the association it had formed with Austin Reed since 1932; W.S. Crawford its since 1936 with Daks Simpson and Barratt shoes; Rumble, Crowther and Nicholas Ltd its since 1937 with the Fifty Shilling Tailors; and Dorland its since 1932 with Hector Powe. At the same time, all four agencies held a portfolio of menswear accounts: Pritchard and Wood also looked after Saxone shoes and Tenova socks (1941), Mattamac (1942–48) and Lightning Zips (1955); Crawford also had Burton's (1954), Jaeger (1958), Tootal (1955–66) and Wolsey socks and underwear (1938–49); Dorland had the International Wool Secretariat (1947); and Rumble, Crowther & Nicholas also had Willerby Tailors (1954). Yet the longevity of any association between retailer and agent, no matter how fruitful, could not be taken for granted and accounts often changed hands (the average length that an agency held any advertising account was five years). After many years, for instance, the Meridian account was handed over from Willing's Press Service (which had executed it from 1939 until 1954) to S.H. Benson, and the Jaeger account went from Colman Prentis & Varley Ltd (which administered it from the 1930s to 1958) to Crawford's. Singularly, Pritchard Wood ceded the Austin Reed account to Clifford Bloxham and Partners Ltd in 1954 only to take it back again between 1962–67, due to a 'mutual divergence of opinion' between Reed and Bloxham's.[8]

It was the account planners in any agency who were responsible for choosing specific media in which to place advertisements; their preferences were in turn circumscribed by the circulation figures, class readerships and cost of advertising for respective daily newspapers and weekly magazines. To this end, they relied on the target group classifications that had been systematized in Britain during the 1930s by the likes of the Incorporated Society of British Advertisers (ISBA), which had argued, 'What is fundamental to a family's position in the social scale is its income, the income is decided by the occupation followed.'[9] The most influential and fundamental consumer category system that advertisers and retailers came to rely on was the A–E social group classification, formulated in the 1920s in the United States by Paul Cherington for J. Walter Thomson and modified by the ISBA in 1932. Later, it was espoused by the IPA and is still used today, with adjustments to occupation and estimated income, by the National Readership Survey (NRS). By the 1950s this system had apportioned the UK population according to six target groups, as described in Table 1.

But the limitations of the A–E system had been realized from the outset; in 1936, for instance, Will Davenport, the advertising manager of *Vogue*, found it hard to believe that 'all doctors, or directors, or widows have the same identical income'.[10] And with the rise of motivational research and the burgeoning interest in lifestyles. John Hobson argued in 1955 that, alongside social status categories, a more pluralist approach to the consumer that targeted 'the workings of the mind and the emotions' would be necessary.[11] As a general principle, however, he agreed with others in the advertising industry that the A–E groups furnished an initial working impression of the market and how to respond to it in relatively specific terms.

Notes

1 *Men's Wear* (14 June 1952), 12.

2 A. E. Lever, 'What Advertising Costs', *Advertiser's Weekly* (23 January 1947), 160.

3 'C. R. Casson Ltd.', *Art and Industry* (May 1953), 149.

4 T. R. Nevett, *Advertising in Britain* (London: Heinemann, 1982), 100.

5 Paul Jobling, *Man Appeal: Advertising, Modernism and Menswear* (Oxford: Berg, 2005), 12.

6 Ibid., 13.

7 Sean Nixon, 'In Pursuit of the Professional Ideal: Advertising and the Construction of Commercial Expertise in Britain 1953–1964', in P. Jackson et al. (eds), *Commercial Cultures: Economies, Practices, Spaces* (Oxford: Berg, 2000), 57.

8 'Current Advertising', *Advertiser's Weekly* (29 April 1954), 241; 'Current Advertising', *Advertiser's Weekly* (14 January 1961), 3.

9 'I.S.B.A. Research Converts "Circulation" into "Spending Power"', *Advertiser's Weekly* (27 August 1936), 276.

10 *Advertiser's Weekly* (17 December 1936), 387.

11 John Hobson, *The Selection of Advertising* (London: Business Publications, 1961), 12.

3

THE ECONOMICS OF PRESS ADVERTISING

A survey by the Advertising Association in 1952 demonstrated that advertising expenditure overall had grown exponentially from £100 million in 1946 to £160 million in 1950 and to £240 million in 1952, outstripping the growth in annual income tenfold in each instance.[1] More particularly, the survey revealed that the volume of press advertising in 1938, 1948 and 1952 remained consistently at just over half the annual expenditure on all publicity, standing at 54 per cent in 1952. Magazines and periodicals not only doubled their circulations between 1938 and 1952 but in the same period advertising in them also increased by about 40 per cent. Total expenditure on press ads for January–March 1950 was just under £2.3 million and just over £3 million in total for January–March 1951.[2] Between April and June 1953 £13.5 million was spent on press advertising,[3] while in 1955 the *Statistical Review of Advertising* stated the total sum spent was £85,600,100.[4] Direct mail and miscellaneous forms of advertising (such as flyers and theatrical film and lantern slide publicity) formed the next largest category, averaging 46 per cent of annual expenditure.

The major setbacks for press advertising at this time were the 10 per cent cut in newsprint production and the increase in the cost of buying paper levied in a government directive between July 1947 and July 1949.[5] Rather than raising their selling price, however, newspapers and periodicals decided to charge more for advertising space and, combined with paper shortages, this resulted in a drop in advertising revenue for most of them. In October 1947, the *Financial Times* estimated that such weekly losses for the Express and Mirror groups were about £1,300 and £5,200 respectively.[6] Notwithstanding these strictures and financial burdens, it is interesting to note that publicity for menswear still continued to appear in the pages of papers and magazines. In *Picture Post*, for example, the most consistent advertisers between 6 October 1945 and 23 December 1950 were Swallow and Baracuta raincoats, Radiac shirts, Barratt's and John White shoes, and various brands of underwear (Figures 4 and 9).[7] It also carried full-page colour promotions for Barratt's on 8 November 1947 and 28 February 1948, as did *Punch* for Austin Reed on 30 March and 1 June

1949. Moreover, as paper shortages abated so too did the volume of pages increase; thus from 15 July 1949 onwards the *Radio Times* was back to forty pages per issue and it printed the first full-page advertisement since 1939; more dramatically, in autumn 1949 *Vogue* was up to 152 pages, almost 99 of which were advertisements.[8]

With regard to expenditure on menswear publicity, E. A. Lever stated that the overall advertising budget for the average retailer in 1947 was almost 5 per cent of annual turnover, and the *Statistical Review of Advertising* (1950) recorded that £30.5 million was spent on advertising in 1949 in comparison to £28.5 million in 1939.[9] More specifically, with the end of price controls on men's bespoke, non-Utility suits and overcoats on 31 May 1950, the press and poster advertising budget for tailors was £35,923 and for men's underwear £35,458 between January and March 1951, while for the same period in 1952 it was £98,608 for tailors (a rise of 173 per cent) and £42,790 for underwear (a rise of 31.9 per cent).[10] One underwear brand alone, Wolsey, spent £11,035 on publicity for underwear and hosiery between April and May 1952, whereas in 1952 Burton's advertising budget accounted for 7 per cent of the total expenditure of all men's tailors on press publicity.[11]

In determining the most appropriate way to spend press advertising budgets, agencies had to take into consideration the circulation figures of respective newspapers and periodicals, which had been garnered by the Audit Bureau of Circulations (ABC) since 1931. By the time it celebrated its silver jubilee in 1956 with a supplement in *Advertiser's Weekly* (12 October 1956), the ABC had attracted 1,090 subscribers from both menswear retailing (including Austin Reed, Jackson the Tailor, Horne Brothers and Wolsey) and advertising agents with accounts for menswear (including W. S. Crawford, Charles Higham, McCann-Erickson, the London Press Exchange, Mather and Crowther, J. Walter Thompson and Young and Rubicam). The largest circulation national newspapers to attract menswear advertising at the time were the *Daily Mirror*, whose readership was predominantly groups C1, C2 and D, and the *Daily Express*, with a readership of groups B, C1 and C2. Daily circulation figures for the *Express* in 1944 stood at 3 million copies and rose in 1950 to over 4 million,[12] while those for the *Mirror* were in excess of 3 million copies in 1947 and over 4.5 million in 1950.[13] By contrast, a self-promotion for the *Daily Telegraph* on 22 September 1949 boasted that it had more class A readers (at the time, those earning £1,000 and upwards per annum[14]) than any other daily.

By extension, the size of a newspaper's circulation determined its advertising rates such that the best-selling titles could charge more on the grounds of having higher visibility among trade and public alike. According to Hulton's 'Men's Wear Trade Readership Survey' of 1947–48, for instance, not only did menswear retailers and advertisers consult professional titles such as *Men's Wear* or *Man and His Clothes* but they also favoured the *Daily Express* and *Radio Times* as a general guide to popular or public taste.[15] Advertising rates for the *Daily Mirror* in 1947 were £1,200 per full page and £200 per column (the first increase since 1941) and in 1950 were £1,500 per full page,[16] whereas in 1947 a full-page advertisement in the *Daily Telegraph* cost approximately £800.[17] Indeed, the Express Group (comprising the *Daily Express*, *Sunday Express*, *Evening Standard* and *Glasgow Evening Citizen*) made nearly £2 million—just over 20 per cent of their income—from advertising between June 1946 and June 1947.[18] Among the periodical press, the *Radio Times* (founded 1923), *Punch* (1841) and *Picture Post* (1938) continued to exert the hegemony in circulation they had accrued since their inception. The *Radio Times*, for example, had a weekly sale of over more than 6 million copies between January–June 1947 and over 7 million in 1948.[19]

During the 1950s a cluster of titles aimed exclusively at male readers was also launched and, as is to be expected, they became a focus for many menswear advertisers. On 14 May 1954 the first British edition of *Esquire* appeared with ad rates for a projected run of 85,000 copies of £234 per black-and-white page and £350 per colour full-page ad.[20] Two quarterlies were also published in 1954: *Sir*, launched in May with a print run of 10,000 copies, and *Man About Town* in December. The former was a short-lived affair but the latter was more successful, transmogrifying into *About Town* in 1960, when it was bought by Michael Heseltine and Carey Labovitch, and finally into *Town* in 1962. Almost one-third of the content of its first issue was advertising, and it also included a special twenty-seven-page supplement dedicated to promoting high-class tailors.

In keeping with pre-war precedent, there was a general correlation between the class markets for certain menswear labels and products and the periodicals in which publicity for them appeared. Thus the first British advertising campaign in spring 1952 for inexpensive Bata shoes appeared in class C1 and C2 titles *Picture Post* and *Men Only*, and publicity for Jackson the Tailor in *The Star* in January 1954, a London daily that was popular with class C2 and D readers. By contrast, Austin Reed advertisements, illustrated by Alexis Delmar, appeared largely in the *Times*, *Financial Times*, *Daily Telegraph*, *Evening Standard*, *Man About Town* and *Punch* throughout the 1950s. But, as in the interwar period, menswear advertising reflected class permeability. Thus publicity for Burton's could be seen in both the *Daily Mail* and the *Daily Mirror*, while promotions for Austin Reed were found in *Punch* and the *Sphere* (Figures 5 and 7), periodicals with predominantly upper middle and middle class readerships, and occasionally in the mass-circulation weeklies, *Picture Post* and *Radio Times*. Underwear and shirt advertising was probably the most democratic of all, appearing in national and local dailies across the class spectrum, and in *Picture Post*, *Punch* and *Radio Times* in the mid 1950s. Thus publicity for Lyle and Scott y-fronts appeared in *Picture Post*, *Daily Mirror* and *Daily Express* in 1955 (Figure 9), and that for Mekay shirts appeared between October and December 1957 in the *Daily Mirror*, *Daily Telegraph*, *Financial Times*, *Manchester Guardian* and *Evening Standard*.

More specific targeting could be achieved through regional advertising. In spring 1954, for instance, N.C. Lawton launched a combined advertising scheme for nineteen bespoke tailors in Manchester, including Pope and Bradley, which promoted their services in the *Guardian* and *Manchester Evening News* to men under 40 years old.[21] And from spring 1958 large-scale advertisements in local newspapers promoted Austin Reed's twenty-five provincial branches.[22] But it was not just local retailers that turned to regional advertising. Thus the Aertex brand advertised its underwear, vests and shirts on this basis in a special publicity campaign between 11 and 18 May 1953. Coordinated by its advertising manager, G.H. Platten, and the agency Osborne Peacock, the Aertex campaign took space in more than 800 local newspapers, organized a mannequin parade in the Savoy Hotel, London, and invited retailers to participate in a window display competition, as the 'Tie Week' campaign had done since its launch in June 1952.[23] Furthermore, because many menswear retailers did not allow the manufacturer's label to appear alongside the coats and suits they stocked, some brand names decided to promote themselves as widely and economically as possible by transferring their advertising budget from the national dailies exclusively to the provincial papers. Donald W. Allanach, the advertising manager of C & M Sumrie, a manufacturer of men's ready-to-wear woollen garments, decided to pursue this publicity tactic from autumn 1951, stating: 'As men's shops rarely make a forceful display of branded names, Sumrie believe that unless they can tell a man where he can buy his clothes, 80 per cent of the advertisement's value is lost.'[24] Hence, Sumrie's regional publicity, masterminded by agents Norman Davis Ltd and with artful illustrations by F. Whitby Cox, afforded the company more market control and fluidity because it was able to advise potential customers of stockists in any given area.

Notes

1   'What Is Spent on Advertising in Relation to Total Sales and National Income', *Advertiser's Weekly* (22 July 1954),156. The respective 2000 equivalents were £1,225.3 million (£100 million), £3,256.3 million (£160 million) and £4,099.6 million (£240 million).

2   'Magazines Take Lion's Share of Press Advertising Revenue', *Advertiser's Weekly* (31 May 1951), 371; 'Over £42 Million on Press Ads', *Advertiser's Weekly* (28 February 1952), 321–2. The respective 2000 equivalents were £2.3 million (£46.8 million) and £3 million (£56 million).

3   '£5 Million a Month Average on Press Ads', *Advertiser's Weekly* (27 August 1953), 350. The 2000 equivalent was £223.6 million.

4   The 2000 equivalent was £1,322.3 million.

5   *Advertiser's Weekly* (2 October 1947), 3.

6   'How Newsprint Cuts and Raised Costs Hit Press Advertising', *Advertiser's Weekly* (6 November 1947), 262. The 2000 equivalents were £30,095 (£1,300) and £120,380 (£5,200).

7   Advertising for Barratt and Swallow appeared in *Picture Post* at least once every four weeks between these dates and advertising for John White, Baracuta and Radiac on a cycle of once every six to eight weeks. Beginning on 2 February 1946, the following men's underwear labels were advertised intermittently: Harvester, Meridian, Y-front, Morley and Wolsey.

8   *Advertiser's Weekly* (1 September 1949), 357.

9   Lever, 'What Advertising Costs', *Advertiser's Weekly* (23 January 1947), 160. The respective 2000 equivalents were £639,802,166 (£30.5 million) and £1,043.9 million (£28.5 million).

10 The respective 2000 equivalents were £670,033 (£35,923), £661,360 (£35,458), £1,684,389 (£98,608) and £730,924 (£42,790).

11 'Press Ad Spending', *Advertiser's Weekly* (29 May 1952), 399; *Advertiser's Weekly* (27 August 1952), 369. The 2000 equivalent was £188,496.

12 *Advertiser's Weekly* (12 June 1947), 512–13; 'Candid Comment on Press Rate Rises', *Advertiser's Weekly* (4 January 1951), 31.

13 *Advertiser's Weekly* (6 March 1947), 377; 'Candid Comment on Press Rate Rises', 3.

14 The 2000 equivalent was £58,321.

15 'Men's Wear Trade Readership Survey', *Advertiser's Weekly* (17 June 1948), 526. The survey found that of readers in the trade 66 per cent favoured the *Radio Times*, 60 per cent *Men's Wear*, 38 per cent the *Daily Express* and 17 per cent *Man and His Clothes*.

16 Candid Comment on Press Rate Rises', 3. The respective 2000 equivalents were £27,780 (£1,200), £4,630 (£200) and £30,528 (£1,500).

17 'Newspaper Space', *Advertiser's Weekly* (21 March 1948), 504. The 2000 equivalent was £18,520. By contrast, in 1946 advertising rates for a more upmarket title such as *Vogue* were £150 (2000 equivalent, £10,899) for a full page in black and white and £220 (2000 equivalent, £15,985) for a four-colour full-page ad. *Advertiser's Weekly* (3 January 1946), 3.

18 'Express Group Publishes Its Accounts', *Advertiser's Weekly* (12 February 1948), 278.

19 *Advertiser's Weekly* (21 August 1947), 361 and *Advertiser's Weekly* (23 June 1949), 581.

20 *Advertiser's Weekly* (7 January 1954), 3. The respective 2000 equivalents were £3,807 (£234) and £5,695 (£350).

21 '19 Manchester Bespoke Tailors Launch Combined Advertising', *Men's Wear* (6 March 1954), 15–16.

22 *Advertiser's Weekly* (13 December 1957), 64.

23 'Press Plus Window Display Made Aertex Week a Success', *Advertiser's Weekly* (30 July 1953), 206. The scheme was a collaboration between the Tie Manufacturers Association and advertising agency Haig-McAlister Ltd in a deliberate attempt to circumvent the need for press or poster publicity (although they did take out space in the trade press to announce the scheme). In June 1955, a prize of £500 was awarded to the retailer with the best window display (*Advertiser's Weekly* (9 June 1955), 576 and 578.

24 'How Use of Provincials Solved Men's Clothes Maker's Branding Problem', *Advertiser's Weekly* (27 March 1952), 506.

4
THE DESIGN AND RHETORIC OF MENSWEAR PRESS ADVERTISEMENTS

Between 1945 and 1958 there were three main methods or styles of pictorialization in press advertising: hand-drawn illustration, scraperboard and photography. The first was by far the most prevalent in publicity for menswear at this time, with photography not beginning to make some impact until the mid 1950s in advertising for the likes of Austin Reed, Simpson and Burton's (Figures 4–6). The technique of scraperboard, which John Betjeman had impugned in the *Penrose Annual* of 1940 as 'a most hideous medium', was a kind of *juste milieu* between illustration and photography.[1] Often based on original photographs, scraperboard had the virtue of transcending the lack of definition of half-tone printing (the chief means of reproducing photographs in newspapers and magazines) by offering better contrast in form and an unlimited range of textural effects through line and cross-hatching. According to C. W. Bacon, it accounted for about one-quarter of all the illustrations in newspaper advertising in the early 1950s and was invaluable when it came to rendering the different qualities of material in advertising for clothing and fabrics.[2] However, using the menswear publicity in *Picture Post* and the *Radio Times* as a rule of thumb, the deployment of scraperboard was restricted to a handful of manufacturers at this time and can be found chiefly in small-scale advertisements for Old England and Radiac shirts (Figure 4), and to a lesser extent for Swallow rainwear (viz. *Picture Post*, 15 January 1949).

Of course, the style and content of menswear publicity were in large part due to the efforts of copywriters, typographers and commercial artists (the last known as graphic designers from the early 1960s onwards). During the interwar period, advertising had attracted a wide array of creative talent and the status of the advertising artist in Britain was forged in the crucible of modernism, with progressive agencies such as W. S. Crawford pioneering a new style of publicity that was based on the harmonious integration of illustration, type and copy.[3] In this regard, the example of German graphic modernism was the lodestar with its use of white space, austere geometric or abstracted forms and tendency towards sanserif type forms.[4] Moreover, many of the commercial artists who had come of age during the 1920s and 1930s proceeded to be active after the war and are listed in Appendix II. Andrew Johnson and Ashley Havinden continued their association with W. S. Crawford, the former producing figurative drawings for Barratt shoes, and the latter his signature-style typographic ads for Simpson of Piccadilly. Max Hoff also was illustrating ads for Daks Simpson into the early 1960s (Figure 11), while Fougasse (the alias of Cyril Bird) produced cartoon strips for Austin Reed until 1948. New talent also emerged during and directly after the war. Wartime designer F.H.K. Henrion produced a Christmas poster for Simpson in 1952; F. Whitby Cox designed posters for Baracuta (1947–48) and Sumrie (Figure 3); Alexis Delmar worked for Sumrie from 1952 and in 1957 went on to produce illustrations for Austin Reed,[5] whose most prolific interwar designer, Tom Purvis, had decided to continue his artistic collaboration only with the Blackpool Pleasure Beach after 1945. Philip Moysey, Brian Robb and Miles Harper also contributed to Austin Reed publicity after 1945,[6] and Francis Marshall worked on the Jaeger's menswear account in 1951–52.[7] Marshall was one of several producers affiliated to Carlton Artists Ltd, an agency that had been founded in 1900 to protect the interests of freelance commercial artists, while the Stuart Advertising Agency was the first agency to commission fine artists such as John Piper, Ben Nicholson, Barbara Hepworth and Paul Nash to illustrate advertisements and promotional brochures for the textiles manufacturer Courtaulds.[8]

W. S. Crawford, in conjunction with the Ministry of Education, had also taken the enterprising step of allowing art students into its creative department during slack periods.[9] This led it to employ photographer Hans Wilde for their Dannimac account (1950–52) and illustrator Brian Robb for Simpson and Tootal publicity from the mid 1950s. Similarly, Harry Ballam, creative director and copywriter for Osborne-Peacock, not only built up a strong portfolio of fashion accounts in the 1950s, including Littlewoods, Harvey Nichols and British Cotton, but as at Crawford's he also employed a rich seam of talent to produce them.[10] In the hands of Elva Carey, who had worked as a writer for *Vogue*, and designers K. Friedeberger and Allan Lofts, text and image in their poster advertising were closely integrated as a balanced entity through the use of various devices: the three-column grid in the case of Littlewoods; the 'package', which enclosed the merchandise in a particular shape or space such as a house, for the cotton campaign; and the border as a means of embodying quintessential 'character in a rectangle' for Harvey Nichols.

Several illustrators, namely F. Whitby Cox, Alexis Delmar and Poul Sprøgøe, had portrayed a common heroic masculine stereotype in their advertisements

(Figures 3 and 9), and certain agencies carved out an identifiable signature style for their clients through the use of a particular typeface, as in Pritchard Wood's advertising for Austin Reed and Crawford's for Barratt's, Simpson and Burton's (Figures 5–7). But, apart from this and, given the different media used in the production of advertisements, it would be difficult (if not impossible) to identify a uniform formal style in menswear publicity between 1945 and 1958. In regard to content, however, there were two chief themes evident across the spectrum of advertisements for different items of clothing. In the first place, the creative impulse of designers and copywriters was checked somewhat by the need for advertisers to underscore the message of post-war clothes rationing and austerity until 1950. Consequently, the 'Walk the *Barratt* way' campaign (emphasis in the original) more or less mined the same rhetorical seam as it had since 1933, although it was singular among post-war shoe advertisers such as John White or Delta for not merely depicting the product alongside some narrative copy but instead putting the product into a situational context.[11] Consisting of Andrew Johnson's illustrations of William Barratt in the guise of the expert salesman and lapidary copy by G. H. Saxon Mills that set up a fictive conversation between Barratt and his male customers, the advertisements elaborated the patriotic stoicism of the British people in adverse times. One advertisement in 1946, for instance, linked the shortage of materials with the need for demobilized military to recycle the shoes they had bought before their call-up; the tag line exclaims, 'Two old friends welcomed me home, Mr, Barratt!' and the copy picks up the thread: 'I remembered a pair of Barratts in the cupboard, which I hadn't seen for two years. A bit of polish and they came up wonderfully' (*Picture Post*, 9 February 1946). Almost two years later, the role of Barratt shoes in post-war reconstruction was still evident in advertisements such as 'It's an Englishman's privilege, Mr. Barratt!' (*Picture Post*, 13 December 1947), where the jingoistic copy portrays the product as the 'world's best' and as a universal compensation for the British weather (be it hot or cold).

By contrast, the advertising rhetoric of two other well-known middle-class retailers, Simpson and Austin Reed, elaborated the second key motif of post-war menswear publicity—delayed gratification—apologizing in *Picture Post* for the lack of sufficient merchandise such as Daks trousers (8 February 1947) and Summit shirts (23 August 1947), while portending the promise of better times to come. Austin Reed also took the opportunity to capitalize on austerity measures by introducing a 'new look' in men's suits that involved a longer but more tapered jacket with narrow lapels and sleeves and two buttons, under the populist advertising banner 'Ways in Which We Serve' (*Picture Post*, 20 March and 21 August 1948), which paraphrases the naval prayer that David Lean and Noel Coward had also used in 1942 as the title of their patriotic war film. More particularly, their austerity campaign emphasized human interest in dressing well and mobilized eloquent and measured copy by Donald McCullough, which embodied Godfrey Hope Saxon Mills's maxim that successful publicity was a case of 'short words, short sentences, short paragraphs'.[12] Thus, 'Getting back to it all', a quarter-page advertisement in *Punch* (6 February 1946), depicted a thronging scene of Piccadilly in London alongside copy that crystallized the bittersweet pleasure of delayed gratification:

> When man has been reconstructed and becomes a citizen at peace, we will once again be able to supply him with the good things he used to enjoy. In the meantime, a man will always find something at Austin Reed's to help fortify him against the weather. The necessities are there even if abundance is absent.

Such a sense of contented resignation is connoted more poetically still in a set of advertisements that appeared during the summer of 1946 in *Punch*, *Picture Post* and the *Sphere*. In them, people are represented at repose—a man sits smoking a pipe with his dog at his side (*Punch*, 24 July and *Picture Post*, 17 August); a family watches a cricket match from a secluded glade at the perimeter of the pitch (*Sphere*, 29 June). The archetypal lifestyle of both the middle-class market for Austin Reed clothing and readership of the *Sphere* is also much in evidence in the latter advertisement, as the cricket match appears to be a public school affair and the sports equipment illustrated at the bottom of the page includes a rugby ball, hockey stick and lacrosse net, cricket bat and stumps, as well as a football. And yet, McCullough's epigrammatic terzain transcends such a one-sided reading by connoting the scene as an aspirational idyll, an allusive moment in time that could have universal appeal not only to all classes but also to all ages and both sexes. It reads: 'For those days when life has come to a sunny standstill/ and the mind is quiet, Austin Reed's provide clothes/ that are casual and comfortable' (Figure 5).

Following the end of clothes rationing in March 1949 it is possible to discern a shift from the self-effacing discourse of austerity advertising for menswear towards one that connoted more confident and playful lifestyles. Thus more full-page colour advertisements began to appear in *Punch* and *Picture Post*. A promotion for Austin Reed summer clothing in *Punch* (1 June 1949), for example, actually reproduced the items on sale and their price (32s. 6d.), unequivocally declaring, 'You could probably do with a sports shirt or two.'[13] And the depiction of a young couple water-skiing alongside the promise, 'You'll be sensational in your new Jantzen', in an advertisement for swimsuits in *Picture Post* (10 June 1949) mimicked the narcissism and unbridled freedom in Pete Hawley's iconic drawings for Jantzen's American publicity. (In fact, a small-scale monochrome version of one of Hawley's advertisements had already appeared in *Picture Post* on 5 April 1947.[14]) As the Jantzen ad also revealed, another significant challenge to advertisers from the early 1950s onward was the impact of synthetic materials—in this case the use of rayon (patented since 1925) for men's swimwear. As Susannah Handley has argued, 'If nature could not provide it, then the chemist would,'[15] and man-made materials were a strategic way of circumventing the post-war shortage of natural materials and meeting the demands of a mass market for clothing and textiles.

The majority of synthetics were pioneered by Du Pont in America, but the polyester Terylene was developed in Britain in 1946 by Imperial Chemical Industries (ICI) and provided a contemporary challenge to manufacturers and advertisers alike. Thus Mather and Crowther employed the German graphic designer Zéró (Hans Schleger), to conceive press publicity that would combine art and science and thus symbolize 'the beautiful qualities of the material and its origin as a man-made fibre'.[16] By this time Zéró had accrued considerable experience in the world of advertising, working as art director at Crawford's Berlin office and, after he emigrated to England in 1932, producing a series of imaginative posters for Shell-Mex and BP Ltd and press ads for Charnaux corsets. For the Terylene campaign between 1954 and 1956 he mobilized physio-harmonic photographs by Swiss scientist Professor Gysi, which traced the gravitational to and fro of a tuned pendulum, to evolve a series of abstract graphic forms and express the idea that Terylene was a dynamic filament yarn that offered 'endless' physical possibilities and haptic experiences. *Art and Industry* commended Zéró's work, therefore, for the way it managed to harness science to art in the campaign as 'an outstanding contribution to . . . imaginative advertising'.[17]

Notes

1   John Betjeman, 'Current Advertising—A Commentary', *Penrose Annual* (1940), 20.

2   C. W. Bacon, 'Scraperboard in Advertising', *Art and Industry* (November 1951), 168.

3   G.H.S. Mills, 'The New Idea in Advertising', *Commercial Art* (November 1923), 298.

4   Paul Jobling, *Man Appeal: Advertising, Modernism and Menswear* (Oxford: Berg, 2005), 62–66.

5   B. Ritchie, *A Touch of Class: The Story of Austin Reed* (London: James and James, 1991), 112.

6   J. K. Goldthorpe, 'Fifty Years of Advertising', *Art and Industry* (January 1951), 20.

7   'Colman Prentis & Varley Ltd', *Art and Industry* (May 1952), 148.

8   'Stuart Advertising Agency Ltd', *Art and Industry* (November 1952), 157.

9   Alison Settle, 'The Fashion Artist in Advertising', *Art and Industry* (December 1948), 212.

10   Mary Gowing, 'Harry Ballam', *Art and Industry* (April 1957), 119–25.

11   Jobling, *Man Appeal*, 71–4 and 117–19.

12   G.H.S. Mills, 'Advertising is Largely a Matter of Words', *Art and Industry* (December 1948), 211.

13 The 2000 equivalent was £34.09.

14 Hawley began to work as an advertising illustrator for Jantzen in 1942, a collaboration that lasted for 19 years. See Archives of Advertising, *Pete Hawley The Jantzen Ads: A Survey, 1942–1960* (Hartford: McBride, 2005).

15 Susannah Handley, *Nylon: The Story of a Fashion Revolution* (Baltimore: John Hopkins University Press, 1999), 54.

16 *Art and Industry* (March 1954), 99.

17 Ibid.

5

THE ART VERSUS COMMERCE DEBATE

Indeed, the relationship of art to advertising was a key debate of the period and had been addressed by critic Eric Newton in a speech delivered to the Women's Advertising Club of London in 1947. Its president at the time was Mary Gowing, one of a handful of female creatives who had managed to make a breakthrough in a male-dominated profession by the 1950s. She had entered advertising as an account executive in the 1930s and eventually became a copywriter for the agencies S. H. Benson and Mather and Crowther.[1] Other notable members of the organization included Florence Sangster, who had joined Crawford's in 1915 and became its vice-chairman in 1950,[2] and Ruth Gill, a graduate from Chelsea School of Art who worked for the agency John Tait and Partners during the war and became its art director between 1945 and 1954, running the account for Pringle's knitwear among others.[3] In his talk to the members (published in *Art and Industry*), Newton expressed a general resistance to advertising, although he did give general approval to the collaborative efforts between artists and agencies, such as the commission given to Feliks Topolski by Stewart Alexander Advertising to produce a set of posters promoting Lotus shoes in spring 1947.[4] More contentiously, however, he also observed that artistic advertising was class based, affirming that 'the lower you go in the social scale the worse the drawing must be . . . taste goes down as you go down the strata of society'.[5]

To a certain extent he was right to press the point, as much publicity for small-scale menswear retailers was prone to representing the lifeless 'tailor's dummy' that critics John Herrick and A. H. Williams had impugned in the early twentieth century.[6] But, as Gowing insisted in her response to Newton's article in *Art and Industry*, 'it *is* often the manufacturer who puts the brake not only on the artist, but on the advertising agent.'[7] This conservative approach was a consequence of failing to dedicate sufficient wherewithal to pay for decent publicity, as well as a lack in advertising expertise, which the trade monthly *Style for Men* tried to rectify in its merchandising scheme in 1954, arguing, 'Good artwork is essential to attract favourable attention . . . A simple, even severe arrangement is best.'[8] To meet this aim the magazine commissioned F. John Roe Ltd to create a prototypical advertisement that small-town retailers could adapt for use in their local newspaper and, despite a slow start, interest in the scheme eventually mushroomed. Moreover, Gowing soundly countered Newton's elitism by arguing that good art in advertising was more a question of attaining an appropriate balance between artistic expression and public expectation rather than simply a matter of being '*bewilderingly* abstract'.[9] Consequently, she reproduced key examples of well-wrought press publicity for brands that had proved popular across class barriers. They included the Mr. Therm campaign for the Gas Light & Coke Company by the London Press Exchange, and advertising by Pritchard Wood for cheaper brands such as Saxone, which had used copy and cartoons by the illustrator Anton to reinforce the idea that buying inexpensive shoes did not have to exclude quality and comfort of fit.

But in any case, Newton's one-dimensional argument conveniently overlooked both the fact that in the interwar period good taste in advertising had been much in evidence in publicity for cheap (Fifty Shilling Tailors) as well as middle-market (Hector Powe) tailors, and that, even if they were not going to buy a Baracuta raincoat or shop at Austin Reed, at least the general public would have seen posters for them in a 'people's picture gallery' on railway and Underground stations.[10] As Milner Gray concluded in *Penrose Annual*, therefore, 'The art *of* advertising . . . is clearly an elusive commodity . . . Nonetheless, *all* advertising should be and must be prestige advertising.'[11]

Pritchard Wood was certainly one agency dedicated to producing the kind of 'prestige advertising' to which Gray alludes, and its publicity for Austin Reed was singled out for as much praise after the war as it had been during the 1930s. In particular, Pritchard Wood was commended for its persistent use of the Bodoni typeface, widely regarded as the most versatile and legible of fonts on coarse newsprint and glossy paper alike because both its thin hairline and main strokes reproduced equally well in the printing process (Figure 5).[12]

In general terms, the different type forms used in advertisements were not as intensively scrutinized after 1945 as they had been in the interwar period. But Harold Butler, technical production manager at Saward, Baker and Co, Ltd, did continue to investigate the typography used in press display advertising, an exercise he had conducted since 1928. In both 1947 and 1949, for example, he found the modern sanserif family of typefaces predominated for titles and headlines in advertisements in the *Times*, the *Daily Telegraph*, the *Daily Herald*, the *Daily Mail*, the *Daily Mirror*, *Picture Post*, *Punch*, the *Radio Times* and *Vogue*.[13] Such typefaces were used in publicity for Barratt shoes and Kangol caps (Gill Sans) and Daks trousers (Condensed Gothic and Gill Sans), and their popularity was unabated in 1951 and 1953, when Butler calculated that sanserif accounted, respectively, for 62 per cent and 75 per cent of all display advertisement settings.[14] But, in terms of legibility, Bodoni, Mono Plantin (110 Series) and Times Roman were the most popular individual fonts for reproducing copy as well as headings and captions. In particular, the Walbaum mono typeface, a German font that originated about 1800 and was introduced into England by the Curwen Press in 1925, was favoured by Burton's (Figure 7), which won a Layton Award in 1955 for its use in its press advertisements.[15] At the same time, some designers took a more calligraphic approach to type, something that Ashley Havinden referred to as 'company handwriting', because it would be 'recognizable at once and associate itself, in the mind of the casual reader or passer-by, with the product or service to be advertised'.[16] To achieve this, Havinden coined his own Ashley monotone brush script in the mid 1930s that appeared in publicity for Simpson and Wolsey (Figures 11 and 14), and Arpad Elfer, a graduate from Crawford's Berlin studio and creative director for the agency Colman, Prentis & Varley Ltd in the 1950s, devised the distinctive name block for Jaeger that was widely used alongside illustrations by Gruau in their press and poster publicity.[17]

As we have already seen in the case of publicity for Austin Reed and Barratt, however, text and image needed to be successfully harnessed to form a sympathetic entity, and many designers and professionals in the post-war British advertising industry echoed Godfrey Hope Saxon Mills's earlier concern for the harmonious balance of illustration, typography and copy in advertising.[18] Thus Milner Gray argued that 'the art in advertising is the whole advertisement—not just the picture, not just the type, and not just the text, but all three together',[19] and Mary Gowing likewise affirmed, 'Too many so-called advertising artists are nothing more than the "hands" of the copy-writer or administrator . . . That a good advertisement is a synthesis of word, picture and idea, that it must make a total (not a piecemeal) impact, is still very little understood.'[20]

Such a holistic attitude to publicity informed two influential award schemes of the post-war period in Britain. The first was initiated by *Vogue* in 1947 and dedicated exclusively to fashion promotion. Its panel of judges included designer Misha Black, painter Graham Sutherland and Sir Leigh Ashton, then director of the Victoria and Albert Museum.[21] In comparison, the Layton Annual Awards started in 1954 with the formative objective to 'promote and encourage the growth of improved press advertising techniques' across the board, and were eventually replaced by the Design and Art Directors Association (D&AD) Awards in 1963.[22] In regard to menswear publicity, W. S. Crawford—for whom Saxon Mills was copywriter—was the chief beneficiary of both schemes in their early days, winning *Vogue*'s second annual advertising award (October 1948–September 1949) for colour press ads for Wolsey hosiery in July 1949 and the first Layton Trophy in 1955 for its Daks sports trousers campaign in the *Times*, 4 July 1954[23], as well as sharing third place with Mather and Crowther's Terylene account in the textiles and clothing category for the 'You can't beat Burton tailoring!' campaign (Figures 6 and 11). In fact, Ashley Havinden initially conceived the format of the Daks campaign in 1935 with a New Objectivity styled photograph by Geoffrey Morris of truncated legs that was in use from 1937.[24] This trope mimics publicity for '232' flannels in the *Daily Mail* in 1930 by Stephens Advertising Service and, in turn, was highly influential in advertisements for other brands such as Austin Reed's sports trousers—with copy set in Perpetua type, in *Punch* on 5 May 1954 and 4 May 1955—and for Straddlers pants in the 1960s.[25] The cut-off body in such advertising can be seen, therefore, to replicate the shop-window dummy. But it also inverts the spectatorial dynamic between what Jacques Lacan calls the *je*, that is, the incomplete real subject whom he argues is headless and 'devoid of the self', and the *moi*, whom he contends is the complete ego represented in images.[26] Thus publicity for all these brands of trousers symbolized instead the idea that it is the imaginary ego that is 'devoid of the self' and that consequently awaits fulfilment through the gaze of the spectator, who is able to envisage his own body on top of the legs represented.

Notes

1 Mary Gowing, 'Harry Ballam', *Art and Industry* (April 1957).

2 'W. S. Crawford Ltd', *Art and Industry* (July 1952), 4.

3 Mary Gowing, 'Ruth Gill', *Art and Industry* (September 1957), 84.

4 *Art and Industry* (March 1947), 89.

5 Mary Gowing, 'Can Good Art Be Bad Propaganda?', *Art and Industry* (July 1947), 9.

6 Paul Jobling, *Man Appeal: Advertising, Modernism and Menswear* (Oxford: Berg, 2005), 27.

7 Gowing, 'Can Good Art Be Bad Propaganda?', 12, italics in the original.

8 As quoted in 'Advertising Aid for Small-town Men's Wear Retailers', *Advertiser's Weekly* (14 January 1954), 74.

9 Gowing, 'Can Good Art Be Bad Propaganda?', 12, italics in the original.

10 As John Hewitt points out, the phrase was common parlance in the 1920s and 1930s 'in journals from *Advertising Display* and *Commercial Art* to *Posters and Publicity* and its successor *Modern Publicity*'. J. Hewitt, *The Commercial Art of Tom Purvis* (Manchester: Manchester Metropolitan University, 1996), 24.

11 J. de Holden Stone and Milner Gray, 'In the Case of Art v. Advertising: A Summing Up', *Penrose Annual* (1953), 63 and 61.

12 R. Darcy, 'Bodoni Would Be Amazed', *Advertiser's Weekly* (3 September 1953), 398.

13 Harold Butler, 'The Types We Use', series of articles in *Advertiser's Weekly* (9 October 1947), 59 and 60; *Advertiser's Weekly* (23 October 1947), 170 and 171; and *Advertiser's Weekly* (6 October 1949), 10.

14 Butler, 'The Types We Use', *Advertiser's Weekly* (12 December 1958), 40.

15 *Art and Industry* (July 1955), 33.

16 Ashley Havinden, 'The Importance of "Company Handwriting"', *Penrose Annual* (1955), 58.

17 Mary Gowing, 'Arpad Elfer', *Art and Industry* (March 1957).

18 G.H.S. Mills, 'The New Idea in Advertising', *Commercial Art* (November 1923), 298.

19   de Holden Stone and Milner Gray, 'In the Case of Art v. Advertising', 62.

20   Mary Gowing, 'Tom Eckersley', *Art and Industry* (November 1957).

21   *Advertiser's Weekly* (24 November 1949), 345.

22   'The Layton Annual Awards', *Advertiser's Weekly* (17 March 1955), 649. On the D&AD see Jeremy Myerson and Graham Vickers, *Rewind: Forty Years of Design and Advertising* (London: Phaidon, 2002).

23   Other notable winners of the Layton Prize in the early 1960s included Austin Reed, who won first prize for a colour advertisement in the press (*Men's Wear,* 24 November 1962: 10), and Jaeger, who won the prize for best colour advertisement for clothing and fashion in 1963 (*Advertiser's Weekly,* 29 November 1963: 26). Vernon Stratton was director of advertising at Jaeger, eventually forming Stratton Wolsey Advertising Ltd in 1964 with Tom Wolsey and taking the Jaeger account with him (*Advertiser's Weekly* (17 July 1964), 5).

24   Jobling, *Man Appeal*, 103–4.

25   H.L. Selby, 'In Eight Years—', *Advertiser's Weekly* (12 December 1930), 416.

26   Jacques Lacan, *The Seminar of Jacques Lacan, Book 1* (Cambridge: Cambridge University Press, 1988), 170.

6

POSTER PUBLICITY
AND MENSWEAR

Of all the types of advertising addressed in the 1952 Advertising Association Survey, poster publicity constituted the smallest category in regard to annual expenditure, accounting for 6.5 per cent of the total budget in 1938 and 9 per cent in 1952.[1] However, it was also widely regarded to be the form of advertising that facilitated more creative or artistic freedom than press advertising. To a certain extent the display of posters was constrained by the terms of the Town and Country Act of 1947, which made it imperative for any advertiser to seek consent from the local planning authority concerning the placement of posters in outdoor spaces. In economic terms, however, a poster promotion could work out cheaper than press publicity; weekly rates for the London Poster Advertising Association (LPAA) in 1951, for instance, were 7s. 6d. per single sheet for a display period of 13 to 52 weeks.[2] And when newsprint was rationed in the late 1940s and retailers forced to queue for an allocation of periodical advertising space, C. W. Stokes aptly argued that 'the "whither" of advertising might quite understandably be out of newspaper advertising and into something easier'.[3] Hence, in 1951 Rego Clothiers overcame the difficulty of finding scarce space in the press by resorting to a sixteen-sheet poster promotion, which on the LPAA's weekly basis would have set them back £120 per site.[4] As a highly visible form of graphic communication, poster promotions also transcended the IPA class typologies that circumscribed advertising in newspapers and magazines and, depending on the site used, would have been seen by millions of people—railway stations and the London Underground, for instance, were extremely popular with many menswear advertisers.

This point was underscored by the graphic designer Austin Cooper, who had worked on publicity for Austin Reed and I. R. Morley in the 1930s, in his book *Making a Poster*, where he argued that poster promotions had a dual function: 'to arrest the attention and then, having caught the eye of the passer-by, to deliver a message swiftly, convincingly, effectively'.[5] Certainly, in comparison to the majority of monochrome small-scale advertisements that appeared between 1945 and 1948 in newspapers and magazines, poster publicity was more eye-catching on two counts: it was larger in scale and designed in full-colour. One of the most lavish and artistic posters of this kind was a sixteen-sheet campaign devised by the agents W. H. Emmett and Co Ltd for Baracuta rainwear in 1947 (Figure 3), which reproduced a painting by F. Whitby Cox and was exhibited in main railway stations across the country as well as in 135 sites on the London Underground.[6] The poster campaign was also backed up by press advertising (viz. *Picture Post*, 10 January 1948), and the way that Cox depicted the garments being worn in the wind and rain reflects the aesthetic of the *actualité*, or drawing from life, that Alison Settle argued set apart the 'clever, flexible mind' from the mediocre fashion illustrator.[7] Advertising on the Underground also enabled men's outfitters and brands to buy a sequential allocation of space, such as the five-panel display organized by T. B. Browne for Moss Bros at Waterloo Underground station in spring 1951 that portrayed different aspects of temporal clothing from the morning suit to the work suit and dinner jacket. The campaign was designed to fit in with the theme 'Dressing for the Occasion', which had been launched in January 1951 by *Style for Men* in an attempt to encourage males not only to spend more on clothes but also to dress appropriately. Accordingly, it won wide support from retailers as diverse as Moss Bros, Hector Powe and Rego Clothiers, who set up a temporary shop in the Festival of Britain Gardens at Battersea Park.[8]

Although eminent designers such as Tom Eckersley and Tom Píesakowski had also produced striking Underground posters for Tootal ties and socks in summer 1955 and spring 1956 respectively, Abram Games lamented what he saw as a general decline in the standard of work since the war.[9] Games had been appointed Official War Poster Designer by the War Office between 1942 and 1946, producing over 100 designs. At this time he had also developed a signature style that centred on the metaphorical use of images and messages. In one of his seminal posters for the 'Grow Your Own Food' campaign (1942), for instance, he draws together the interior space of the dining room and exterior space of the garden by transforming a knife and fork on a table top into a fork and spade for cultivating soil. Accordingly, for Games, effective poster publicity invited the designer 'not only to create a pictorial idea but to construct an *operational form*' to the extent that 'the originality and freshness of a poster should lie in its mental, rather than visual substance'.[10] Here, he invokes the psychological potential of advertising and the way that the designer can use form to connote a symbolic response from the spectator, a point to which I return in more detail in later chapters.

Notes

1   'What Is Spent on Advertising in Relation to Total Sales and National Income', *Advertiser's Weekly* (22 July 1954),157.

2   'Magazines Take Lion's Share of Press Advertising Revenue', *Advertiser's Weekly* (31 May 1951), 407. The 2000 equivalent was £7.

3 C. W. Stokes, 'Modern Publicity', *Art and Industry* (January 1949), 30.

4 The 2000 equivalent was £2,238.

5 Austin Cooper, *Making a Poster* (London and New York: Studio Publications, 1945).

6 'Current Advertising', *Advertiser's Weekly* (4 December 1947), 510; *Advertiser's Weekly* (15 January 1948), 128.

7 Alison Settle, 'The Fashion Artist in Advertising', *Art and Industry* (December 1948), 270.

8 *Men's Wear* (21 July 1951), 12.

9 Tom Eckersley trained at Salford School of Art and in 1935 collaborated with Eric Lombers in the design of posters for Austin Reed Summit shirts. He was awarded the OBE for his services as poster artist during the war; his work was described by one writer as making 'the walls of our cities and the pages of our journals smile' (Mary Gowing, 'Tom Eckersley', *Art and Industry* (November 1957), 159). He taught poster design at the Westminster School of Art and the London School of Printing and Graphic Arts (latterly the London College of Printing and currently the London College of Communications).

10 Abram Games, 'Approach to the Poster', *Art and Industry* (July 1948), 24 and 26.

7

EARLY COMMERCIAL TELEVISION AND MENSWEAR, 1955–60

And yet, by the mid 1950s both poster and print advertising had to face up to the challenge of commercial television and to compete for attention, therefore, with a new form of publicity. On 2 November 1936 the BBC made its first transmission from Alexandra Palace to 400 homes in the London area and by 1 September 1939 an estimated 20,000 to 25,000 homes had television sets.[1] With the outbreak of the Second World War, however, broadcasting was suspended for nearly seven years and was not resumed until 7 June 1946, at which time a joint radio/television licence costing £2 was introduced.[2] To promulgate and subsidize the spread of television, the Beveridge Committee mooted a commercial channel in 1949, but it was not until 1952 that the Conservative government took the first steps to introduce competition in broadcasting. Its Television Bill was published on 4 March 1954, though widely contested. Lord Reith compared the advent of commercial television to smallpox, the Black Death and bubonic plague, and Ashley Havinden was 'appalled and sickened by it 'from a creative point of view.[3] In line with Fabian opposition to the insidious Americanization of British culture and the need to counter what J. B. Priestley described as the 'Admass' society, Attlee also promised that if Labour were returned to power in the 1956 election it would abandon the idea of independent television.[4] Nevertheless, the Television Bill received Royal Assent on 30 July 1954, after which it became the Television Act 1954.

Independent Television (ITV) celebrated its opening night uncontroversially in the central London area (Associated Rediffusion on weekdays and Associated Television (ATV) at weekends) on 22 September 1955, and the first 60-second commercial breaks for Gibbs SR toothpaste, Cadbury's Drinking Chocolate and Ford Motors respectively were screened at 8.12 p.m., the last directed by Karel Reisz and designed by Terence Conran. Indeed, James Garrett, who had joined British Transport Films in 1948 and went on to form one of the first television commercial production companies in June 1955, relates how in the early days of television publicity ad agencies were forced to glean relevant expertise 'from any area of activity concerned with entertainment and the making of messages'. This meant that the television advertising industry of the 1950s was populated by technicians and directors from documentary and feature film, as well as those with a background in theatre, design and radio.[5] In 1955 also, the average cost of making a 30-second monochrome advertisement was £500.[6] Acetate film was the usual and preferred medium for recording advertisements but was gradually replaced by videotape recording systems. Ampex, the first of these systems, was introduced in 1958 at a cost of £25,000 per machine and was deployed by both the BBC and ITV. In comparison to film, however, the optical effects of early videotape were crude and it was not until the late 1960s that improved methods became available.

Only 10 per cent of hourly airtime could be dedicated to advertising, but themed 'Admags' lasting 10 minutes were allowed outside this quota and became popular with the public. Yet the early days of ITV were shaky. In December 1955 transmissions were discontinued due to low viewing figures and the lack of sufficient advertising revenue. Media Records, a monitoring organization, estimated advertising revenue for 1956 as £13 million, but in July 1956 Associated Rediffusion alone had suffered losses of £2.7 million.[7] It was not until early 1957 that ITV financially turned a corner and by the end of the year the network extended to Greater London, the Midlands (ATV), Northwest (Granada) and Central Scotland. South Wales and the West of England (Harlech and Television Wales and the West (TWW) followed suit in January 1958, Tyne Tees Television in January 1959 and Anglia and Ulster Television in October 1959, swelling the national audience for ITV to some 8 million viewers. As a result, advertising revenue for 1958 stood at £46,671,000 and began to rise incrementally as ITV expanded its coverage to most regions in the United Kingdom by autumn 1962.[8] Like press and poster advertising, therefore, television publicity enabled advertisers to promote their goods and services either regionally or nationally. Hence, each independent television company was allowed to set its own advertising rates, with peak time spots between 7.30 p.m. and 10.30 p.m. being the most sought after by advertisers, though also the most expensive to buy. In London, for instance, Associated Rediffusion and ATV set respective rates of £975 per minute and £950 per minute for a peak time spot in 1955.[9]

Household products dominated advertising slots in the first five years of ITV; indeed, the majority of ads between 1955 and 1985 were for Unilever cleaning products, underscoring the ideology of what the advertising industry in America referred to as the 'creativity of housework'.[10] In the early days of independent television, clothing and menswear promotions were intermittent and, in any case, as discussed in Part 3, it was mainly Brutus, Levi's and Wrangler jeans that resorted to television publicity on a more consistent basis from 1972 onwards (a representative list of television and cinema campaigns for menswear from 1956 until 2000 is collated in Appendix III). However, on 22 September 1955, a one-minute promotion for Burton's was aired, depicting a sharp-suited man driving his sports car to rendezvous with his girlfriend, and as early as autumn 1955 the first ads for Swallow zipper raincoats for men and Morley socks had appeared on Rediffusion in London. As more television networks came into existence, campaigns for the following began to trickle through for the remainder of the decade: McGregor dressing gowns (promoted in London and Manchester as the ideal Christmas gift by comedian Bob Monkhouse in winter 1956); Wescot jeans (summer 1957); Radiac, Mekay and Mentor shirts (autumn 1957); Fingerflex shoes and Rael Brook shirts (1957 and 1958); y-fronts by Lyle & Scott and Weatherlux's washable Dhobi men's raincoat (spring 1958); Burton's slacks (spring and autumn 1958); and Peter England shirts (spring and summer 1959). Archival footage for the majority of these early ads unfortunately does not exist but, in common with promotions for other products, television and press campaigns for men's clothing bore a complementary relationship to each other.[11] The narrative form of many early television ads also mimicked the combination of symbolism and testimonial realism that had been established in press advertising during the 1930s and 1940s, to the extent that, as Helen Wilkinson has argued, they seemed to be 'essentially a moving 1930s press advertisement'.[12] Thus it is possible to glean an indicative impression of the form and content of such early television ads from their counterparts in the press, a representative case in point being a campaign for Rael Brook shirts in 1957 and 1958.

Harry and Graham Rael Brook had launched the brand in 1947 with less than £1,000 in capital and 12 years later their company had grown exponentially, manufacturing 40,000 shirts per week in five factories.[13] Rael Brook's most popular product became the Toplin, a non-iron cotton poplin shirt, which it began to promote in national and provincial newspapers in autumn 1955. The firm was also one of the first to realize the potential of television publicity and by 1959 dedicated a budget of £50,000 to it as well as a supplementary £7,000 for cinema advertising in those areas not yet served by ITV.[14] In 1957 Lucien Advertising produced a series of television advertisements for the Rael Brook Toplin shirt, and in one of their 1958 campaigns, which also appeared on television, in the *Daily Mirror* and in colour in magazines such as *Woman's Own*, the product was represented in a cartoon as six anthropomorphic trumpeters, heralding the arrival of 'The London Look', symbolized by another shirt that takes the place of Eros atop his fountain in Piccadilly Circus. The copy beneath the cartoon enunciates a fictive conversation between Harry Rael Brook and a young woman, extolling the benefits of the first collection of exclusively designed Toplin shirts, available in different styles, colours and patterns that 'are a tonic to wear' and reasonably priced between 32s. 6d. and 49s. 6d. (Figure 8).[15] Thereby, the visual and verbal rhetoric of the campaign simultaneously portrayed the practical, critical, ludic and utopian valorizations of the shirt as well as making an indirect appeal to the new youth market's desire for more colourful clothing, to which I return later. Although the television campaign could not take advantage of colour at this time as the ads in *Woman's Own* had, it did, of course, have the added benefit of movement and sound. Thus in each of the three 30-second advertisements, testimonial footage was interlarded with a cartoon sequence in which the shirts came to life, dancing, respectively. to a jingle composed by Johnny Johnston that was orchestrated in skiffle, mambo and Russian music styles. Horace Schwerin regarded this type of aesthetic admixture as one of the hallmarks of successful television publicity, arguing: 'Cartoon commercials that include a short live-action sequence have tended to be more effective than wholly animated ones.'[16]

Notes

1   I am indebted to Brian Henry (ed.), *British Television Advertising: The First Thirty Years* (London: Century Benham, 1986), 26–71, for the factual information on commercial television cited throughout this chapter.

2   The equivalent of £2 in 2000 was £49, although in actuality the Television Licence itself cost double the amount by then.

3   H. Jones, 'Crawford's Genius of Good Taste', *Adweek* (15 June 1973), 28.

4   J. B. Priestley and J. Hawkes, *Journey Down a Rainbow* (London: Heinemann Cresset, 1955), ix.

5   James Garrett, 'Commercial Production', in B. Henry (ed.), *British Television Advertising,* 389–90. Henry also argues, 'It came as something of a surprise to discover on opening night that many of the commercials adopted the polite and informative tone of a Crown Film Unit documentary' (*British Television*, 38).

6   Garrett, 'Commercial Production', 396. The 2000 equivalent was £7,782.

7   The respective 2000 equivalents were £192,891.1 million (£13 million) and £40,062 million (£2.7 million).

8   The 2000 equivalent was £648,021.8 million.

9   The respective 2000 equivalents were £15,175 (£975) and £14,786 (£950).

10   Betty Friedan, *The Feminine Mystique* (London: Victor Gollancz, 1971), 214.

11   Thus the television ads for Burton's screened on Rediffusion in autumn 1955 echoed the lifestyle of the debonair bachelor already represented in its national 1954 press campaign by Crawford's. And advertising for Mekay shirts appeared on television between October and December 1957 in London, Midlands and the North and was backed up by a national press campaign in the *Daily Mirror*, *Daily Telegraph*, *Financial Times*, *Manchester Guardian* and *Evening Standard*.

12   Helen Wilkinson, 'The "New Heraldry": Stock Photography, Visual Literacy and Advertising in 1930s Britain', *Journal of Design History* 10:1 (1997), 35.

13   The 2000 equivalent was £23,150.

14 'All the Profits Went Into Ads—and He's Made a Million', *Advertiser's Weekly* (3 April 1959), 26 and 28. The respective 2000 equivalents were £690,444 (£50,000) and £96,622 (£7000).

15 The respective 2000 equivalents were £22.60 and £34.40.

16 'All the Profits Went into Ads', 4.

8

THE IMPACT OF CONSUMER PSYCHOLOGY AND MOTIVATION RESEARCH

Probably the thorniest issue that both retailers and advertisers had to face was the extent to which newspaper readers and television viewers actually took notice of their publicity and what the subconscious impact of it might be. The psychology of advertising had been probed in the United States from the start of the twentieth century by the likes of Walter Dill Scott, a professor of psychology at Northwestern University, Illinois, who espousing the principle of apperception had advised advertisers to 'awaken in the reader as many different kinds of images as the object itself can excite', and by Henry Forster Adams, a professor of psychology at the University of Michigan, who in *Advertising and its Mental Laws* (1916) spoke of the need for advertisers to make an appeal to the senses in their publicity 'so that it will secure better attention, be remembered longer'.[1] To put his ideas to the test, Scott had also observed the reading habits of 600 men who attended the reading room of the Chicago Public Library to see what materials they concentrated on most. Although his research revealed that the majority of readers paid only scant attention to press advertisements he used this evidence to conclude that, even if glanced at cursorily, advertising could have an insidious effect on people and work on the unconscious mind when it came to making a purchase. In other words, he contended that while the public denied that they had been influenced by advertising, 'they had simply forgotten they had originally encountered the product through publicity.'[2] By association, Scott admonished advertisers that if they really wanted their publicity to make any mental impact it should be carefully designed and resort to symbolic language.

Early research methods concerning the relationship between the design of publicity and whether the public remembered any of the advertising messages they saw were clearly inconclusive, if not without some application, and this unverified relationship was an issue that still exercised advertisers after the Second World War. Thus in 1949, the Advertising Service Guild, comprising Cecil D. Notley, C.R. Casson, Stuart Advertising Agency, Everetts Advertising and Basil Butler, sponsored Mass Observation to undertake a qualitative survey into the habits of newspaper readers both in their homes and in public libraries.[3] The survey examined reader remembrance of advertisements for cigarettes, alcohol, skirts and air travel in the *Times*, *Daily Express*, *Daily Mail*, *Daily Mirror*, *Daily Telegraph*, *Daily Graphic* and *News Chronicle* with some interesting results. For example, when they were initially asked in the questionnaire what they had consciously read in these newspapers only 4 per cent of all consultants mentioned the advertisements, whereas when they were prompted to comment on the kind of advertisements that appealed to them, 46 per cent of *Express* and *Telegraph* readers and 40 per cent of *Mirror* readers remembered between three and six campaigns. In particular, the survey revealed that people tended to remember publicity for a product in which they had a special interest; hence twice as many women than men recalled campaigns for skirts. Much like Scott's research, therefore, the Mass Observation survey attested that even if conscious interest in advertising appeared low, the subconscious impact of advertising was considerably higher. On this basis it is illuminating to hear how art critic Eric Newton, notwithstanding his general antipathy for advertising, was forced to concede that 'because my unconscious mind has read the words Austin Reed in so many tubes' he ended up shopping there for socks without even thinking about it.[4]

In comparison to the newspaper survey conducted by Mass Observation, the findings of a survey by the Screen and Radio Department of the London Press Exchange revealed that filmgoers had a much higher conscious recall of the advertisements they saw. The research took place between October and November 1953 in eleven cinemas in London, Leeds and Manchester, and in-volved 456 interviews with men and women across the age and class spectrum.[5] To ensure parity with press surveys, the correspondents were interviewed 24 hours after they had seen an advertising filmlet, a five-minute cinema ad, for a national brand such as Bisto gravy or Sunlight soap that had been screened as part of the programme they viewed. The popularity of the feature film itself had a direct effect on the ability of the spectators to recall the advertising but, on average, 69.5 per cent remembered what the filmlet was advertising. In fact, both men and women—in particular, those under 35 years old (55 per cent of the survey) and social grades A, B and C (39 per cent)—recalled the advertisements to a similar degree, suggesting that recall did not vary strongly across gender, age and class. And, in common with the Mass Observation press survey, more people tended to remember cinema advertising for products they already used, with advertisements for Persil detergent, Seager's Egg Flip and Gloria shampoo scoring a recall over 80 per cent.

While neither of these qualitative surveys was conducted to infer that the psychological impact of advertising could act as an enticement to purchase a particular product, the correlation between the emotional—rather than factual— messages of publicity and purchasing patterns was precisely the objective of motivation research. It was initially popularized in post-war America by psychologist Ernest Dichter, a Viennese émigré who had arrived with his wife Hedy in New York in September 1938 and set up the Institute for Motivational Research in 1946. Intensely influenced by the psychological theories of Sigmund Freud and Alfred Adler, which he had studied in Vienna, Dichter aimed to probe the role of the subconscious mind in forming preferences about different goods, allying the precepts of free association, wordplay, and Freud's pleasure principle, with its emphasis on the libido and sexual desire, to consumer culture.[6] Lawrence Samuel sums up his approach as, 'swapping marketing's "four essential p's"— product, price, promotion, and packaging—with four s's—sustenance, sex, security and status'.[7] Thus Dichter gave emphasis to what Floch later termed the ludic and utopian valorizations of the ad's messages rather than its practical and critical ones. In 1951 he exhorted advertising agencies to realize they were 'one of the most advanced laboratories in psychology', and in 1952 motivation research became centre stage at the annual convention of the American Marketing Association. Both Ernest van der Haag and Ralph Ross's *The Fabric of Society* and Vance Packard's best-selling book *The Hidden Persuaders* exposed Dichter's intervention into marketing as blatant brainwashing in 1957. But it was endorsed in academic texts such as George Horseley Smith's *Motivation Research in Advertising and Marketing* (1954) and Joseph N. Newman's *Motivation Research and Marketing Management* (1957). And its concern with the consumer's inner psyche or id survives to this day in the account planning departments of advertising agencies, audience testing and focus groups, and lifestyle classifications such as VALS (which I address in Part 3), where 'Dichter is "there" by proxy'.[8]

Packard informs us that, for a standard daily fee of $500, Dichter's clients were 'apt to get an outpouring of impressive suggestions'.[9] But the motivation research that Dichter propounded in *Strategy of Desire* (1960) may be distilled to two interconnecting precepts: first, to probe the subconscious mind to find out why people behave as they do (to this end, he was an advocate of the depth interview, which lasted for two or three hours); second, to find a way of giving human behaviour symbolic form. Louis Cheskin, who was director of the Color Research Institute of America and the author of *How to Predict What People Will Buy* (1957), was one of the first to apply these ideas to package design, rebranding Marlboro, for instance, with its red-and-white label, while the advertising agencies Young and Rubicam and McCann-Erickson also began to take advantage of motivation research (the latter employing five psychologists— including Herta Herzog—in its New York office in 1955).[10] From the mid 1950s these ideas were likewise beginning to gain a foothold in the practice of some agencies in Britain as part of a broader 'Americanization' of the advertising profession, whereby Ted Bates took over Hobson's and approximately 50 per cent of the top British agencies came to be controlled by their US counterparts.[11] Greenlys Ltd. (founded 1914) argued, for instance, 'The mental attitude of the reader is a point of great importance.'[12] But Harry Henry, research director in the London office of McCann-Erickson, was more specific, defining motivation research as 'the relationship between the personality of the product . . . and the personality of the consumer, actual or potential' and stressing its purpose to realize the difference between the question of 'who *uses* what' and 'who *wants* what'.[13] At the same time, he echoed Herzog's belief that motivation research should complement—not cancel out—the quantitative analysis of markets and pointed out the danger that, if not conducted with due rigour, it would simply be pseudoscientific and lead to loose generalization, 'whether what is being studied is the actual pattern of consumer behaviour or the personality differences which have helped to form that pattern'.[14]

Notes

1   Paul Jobling, *Man Appeal: Advertising, Modernism and Menswear* (Oxford: Berg, 2005), 24.

2   Ibid., 25.

3   Eventually published in November 1949 as *The Press and its Readers* by *Art and Technics* Ltd and costing 7s. 6d.

4   Mary Gowing, 'Can Good Art Be Bad Propaganda?', *Art and Industry* (July 1947), 9.

5   J. S. Beard, 'Filmlet Survey Measures Impact of Screen Advertising in Three Cities', *Advertiser's Weekly* (6 May 1954): 268. The cinemas in the survey were as follows: Leeds (Gaumont, Palace, Ritz, Queen's); Manchester (Odeon, Regal, Capitol, Apollo); and London (Odeon Dalston, Savoy Wandsworth and Savoy Edgware).

6   In the 'Formulations of Two Principles of Mental Functioning' (1911), Freud addressed the ego's quest for pleasure, positing an ongoing tension between 'the reality principle' and the 'pleasure principle'. In 'Beyond the Pleasure Principle' (1920), Freud built on these ideas, postulating a theory of binary opposites based upon the 'ego instincts' (his quotation marks) and the sexual instincts. However, he also stressed that sexual instincts can be part of the ego insofar as they concern libido or the compulsion to fulfil desire. Sigmund Freud, *On Metapsychology*, J. Strachey (ed.) (Harmondsworth: Penguin, 1991), 329–36.

7   Lawrence R. Samuel, *Freud on Madison Avenue: Motivation Research and Subliminal Advertising in America* (Philadelphia: University of Pennsylvania Press, 2010).

8   B. B. Stern, 'The Importance of Being Ernest: Commemorating Dichter's Contribution to Advertising Research', *Journal of Advertising Research* (June 2004), 165.

9   Ibid., 29 and 33.

10 Vance Packard, *The Hidden Persuaders* (Harmondsworth: Penguin, 1991), 47.

11 Nixon, 'In Pursuit of the Professional Ideal: Advertising and the Construction of Commercial Expertise in Britain 1953–1964', and P. Jackson et al. (eds), *Commercial Cultures: Economies, Practices, Spaces* (Oxford: Berg, 2000), 59.

12 'Greenlys Limited', *Art and Industry* (January 1953), 5.

13 H. Henry, 'Motivation Research?—It's out of the Swaddling Clothes', *Advertiser's Weekly* (5 July 1957), 24 and 26, italics in the original.

14 Ibid.

9

'FEELING WITH' AND 'FEELING INTO'

APPEALING TO MEN AND WOMEN

In the first instance, motivation research was mobilized somewhat stereotypically to probe what made the female consumer tick, even though a Home Office Social Survey on shopping hours for 1946 had stated that 62 per cent of men undertook some kind of personal shopping.[1] Yet, as a 'woman correspondent' wrote in *Men's Wear* on 12 May 1956: 'The most obvious difference between the approach of the two sexes is that whereas men are inclined to view shopping as a chore, women look on it as a pleasure and a pastime.' It is not for nothing, therefore, that ad agencies in their human-centred approach began to resort to the in-depth interview, whereby 'the difference between an adman and a behavioural scientist became only a matter of degree', according to Edith Witt.[2] The conflation of professional categories to which Witt refers and the intense probing of the consumer's subconscious that motivation research entailed are evident in a piece of self-publicity in 1958 by the London PR company, Robert Sharp and Partners, which represented a female shopper supine on a couch, with a basket of purchases on her lap and surrounded by three bowler-hatted (psycho-) analysts. Likewise, the involvement of women in the purchase of male clothing was one of the main issues that menswear advertisers had to face when finding a symbolic fit between product and purchaser (actual or potential): 'So much menswear shopping is repetitive that a woman finds it convenient to ask for something by name. Psychologically, it gives her confidence to do so.'[3]

Forty-two per cent of the females in a 1953 survey by Odhams for *Woman*, a magazine that at that time had an average weekly circulation of 2,370,685 readers across the class spectrum, had stated they accompanied their partners to the tailor, but only 6 per cent admitted to buying a suit for them outright.[4] Men's underwear, hosiery and shirts were the staple garments that many women actually bought. Research by George Smith and Co Ltd into subscribers of *Men's Wear* and the *Outfitter* drawn from the professional class revealed, for instance, that 85 per cent of men's socks and underwear were bought by women on behalf of their partners.[5] And the *Woman* survey stated that 64 per cent of its readers bought their men's socks, 60 per cent their underwear and 54 per cent their shirts.[6] Certainly, some shirt, hosiery and underwear manufacturers made a deliberate address to the housewife in their publicity on the grounds of hygiene and/or their products' labour-saving properties. In mid July 1956, for example, an ad for Rael Brook's no-need-to-iron Toplin shirt, retailing at 39s. 6d., was screened in one thousand cinemas across the United Kingdom with the tag line, 'From Hanger to Husband'.[7] And while the rhetoric of a promotion for Harvester underwear in *Man and His Clothes* (December 1947), comprising the banner 'Made for Men . . . Who Think A Lot of Their Wives' and an illustration of a man in long johns smiling admiringly at a portrait of his spouse on the mantelpiece, avowed that 'the ideal husband' actually bought his own underwear, it concluded in a patriarchal vein that he did so thinking of ' "the little woman" who has to wash and mend it and juggle the family coupons'. By contrast, market research conducted by the manufacturer Lyle and Scott in 1954 revealed that men were becoming less self-conscious about purchasing their own underwear and also more brand-led: for example, 56 per cent admitted they had bought their own and 46 per cent recalled the brand they had most recently bought.[8] In fact, by the late 1950s, y-front briefs (sold in Britain from 1938) were the favoured form of underwear with the majority of men on the grounds of style and comfort.[9] At this time also, gay men began to speak about the erotic charge of y-fronts. One of the correspondents in the Brighton Ourstory project, for example, related how exciting and outrageous y-fronts seemed in comparison to all the other 'horrible flannel things' that were retailing after the Second World War.[10]

Along with promotions in the 1920s and 1930s for brands such as Celanese and Irmo, publicity for Lyle and Scott y-fronts made an overt association with sporting paradigms and masculinity. (Y-fronts were issued as support garments to the British men's team for the Olympic Games in London in 1948, Helsinki in 1952, and Melbourne in 1956.[11]) This athleticism is evident in a ludic campaign by Legget Nicholson and Partners (Figure 9), based on a drawing of an ebullient male gymnast by Danish artist Poul Sprøgøe, a specialist in menswear illustration since 1932, and appearing as a half-page advertisement in national dailies and as a full-page ad in *Picture Post* throughout 1954 and 1955. Moreover, the rhetoric of such publicity can be seen to fulfil the motivational ideal that 'advertising is seldom purely a problem of advertising only. It is a matter of "feeling with" and "feeling into" — sympathy and empathy.'[12]

The y-front campaign, then, still harped on the practical values of hygiene and ease of laundering, but it was also singular in the way its deictic mode of address to the potential male customer connoted the psychological and physical momentum to be had from purchasing and wearing underwear entirely from a masculine perspective. Thus the advertising copy made no mention of the housewife and foregrounded instead the haptic and visual pleasure that men would get from wearing y-fronts; to coin a phrase, of not only looking good but feeling good (a similar message was codified in Coopers' 'Feel like a million!' early 1950s campaign in the United States).[13] Rather than being something that should be kept out of sight or regarded as merely utilitarian garments, the vest and pants are depicted as actively worn in an act of conspicuous consumption, and the way that the advertisement represents pleasure as an embodied experience, therefore, elicits a key idea of Maurice Merleau-Ponty concerning 'the two "sides" of our body, the body as sensible and the body as sentient (what in the past we called objective body and phenomenal body)'.[14] He argues in his essay, 'The Visible and the Invisible', that the body that touches is inextricably intermeshed with the body that is touched, and the body that sees is imbricated with the body that is seen: 'There is a circle of the touched and the touching, the touched takes hold of the touching; there is a circle of the visible and the seeing, the seeing is not without visible existence.'[15] Hence, the verbal rhetoric of the y-front promotion epitomizes 'a circle of the touched and the touching' in the way it connotes the sensory veiling of skin by fabric, referring to the product as 'the modern conception of underwear comfort . . . trim, snug', indeed, 'sized to fit YOU'. While Sprøgøe's illustration connotes 'a circle of the visible and the seeing', it depicts the male athlete not only as a solipsistic narcissist, who appears comfortable in his own clothed skin, but, as he looks and smiles directly at us, also as a (some)body for the spectatorial pleasure of others—whether women or men (much as underwear publicity for Irmo, Morley and Meridian had done in the interwar period).[16] In addition, the enticement to 'Look good . . . feel good' instantiates for the spectator the doubling of sensations that Merleau-Ponty crystallizes as the dialectic of haptic visuality and the criss-crossing between the pleasure experienced in touching and seeing it entails: 'Since the same body sees and touches, visible and tangible belong to the same world . . . there is even an inscription of the touching in the visible, of the seeing in the tangible—and the converse.'[17]

The nexus of touching to looking is something that Freud also briefly illuminated in the *Three Essays on the Theory of Sexuality* (1905), where he posits that 'tactile sensations of the skin' pave the way to 'visual impressions . . . along which libidinal excitation is aroused'.[18] In turn, the doubling of physical and psychological pleasure to which Freud refers aligns with the scopophilic drive, which involves an interplay of concealing and revealing and which is connoted in the y-front promotion by the pun 'Y's men wear Y-front' and the deliberative exhortation to be 'twice the man'. Thus Freud maintains: 'The progressive concealment of the body which goes along with civilization keeps sexual curiosity awake. This curiosity seeks to complete the sexual object by revealing its hidden parts.'[19] More particularly, in Freud's telling underclothing has a fetishistic part to play in such a scopophilic regime because it pinpoints 'the moment of undressing, the last moment in which the woman could still be regarded as phallic'.[20] If, as he argues, for the male subject the fetish becomes a symbolic way of warding off the threat of castration then, by extension, men's underwear could be regarded both as a way of concealing the phallic power of the male subject and as a form of protection from his own (potential) unveiling and castration. It is on this level, therefore, that the advertisement for y-front enacts what Stefan Zweig called the creative process of psycho-synthesis through which the Freudian 'Hemmung', or deep-seated repression, is transformed from a negative into a positive feeling.[21] Hence, it symbolizes the idea that the briefs will keep you one step ahead in the phallic game by simultaneously underscoring your savvy ('Y's men wear Y-front') and doubling your sexual prowess ('Be twice the man').[22] Lyle and Scott emphasized a similar psycho-synthetic message with its window display contest in spring 1955, which was organized around the conciliatory theme, 'Size won't matter. Little men will have an equal chance with the big ones in this competition.' The first prize was awarded to Owen Owen Ltd of Liverpool, who customized a miniature cardboard cut-out of the gymnast to represent a trapeze artist flying through the air in his vest and pants alongside the actual merchandise.[23]

Notes

1   *Advertiser's Weekly* (19 June 1947), ii.

2   E. Witt, 'The Personal Adman', *Reporter* (14 May 1959), 36–7. As cited by Lawrence R. Samuel, *Freud on Madison Avenue: Motivation Research and Subliminal Advertising in America* (Philadelphia: University of Pennsylvania Press, 2010), 10.

3   'The Influence of the Woman Shopper', *Men's Wear* (12 May 1956), 19.

4   *'Woman' Readers Buy for Men* (London: Odhams Press, 1953).

5   'Over £42 Million on Press Ads', *Advertiser's Weekly* (28 February 1952), 325.

6   *'Woman' Readers*. Similar figures are cited in a survey by the hosiery manufacturer, I and R Morley, of 1,240 men, 60 per cent of whom attested that their wives always bought socks for them. *Men's Wear* (25 March 1950), 25.

7   *Advertiser's Weekly* (20 July 1956), 24 and 28. The 2000 equivalent was £69.49.

8   'Mr. Average Now Buys More Underwear', *Men's Wear* (21 April 1956), 34.

9   *Man and His Clothes* (November 1957), 27.

10 P. Dennis, *Daring Hearts: Lesbian and Gay Lives of 50s and 60s Brighton* (Brighton: Queenspark, 1992), 52.

11 In 1948, to coincide with the London Olympics, Austin Reed also elaborated a sports theme in its publicity. Pritchard Wood produced a series of cards for display

on the London Underground, one such representing a marathon runner carrying a torch with the slogan, 'When a man needs clothes it's quicker by tube . . . to Austin Reed of Regent Street', *Advertiser's Weekly* (29 July 1948), 234.

12   'The London Press Exchange', *Art and Industry* (March 1953), 76.

13   See Richard Martin, ' "Feel Like A Million!": The Propitious Epoch in Men's Underwear Imagery, 1939–1952', *Journal of American Culture* 18:2 (1995), 51–8, for an assessment of men's underwear advertising in America between 1939 and 1952.

14   Maurice Merleau-Ponty, *The Visible and the Invisible*, trans. A. Lingis (Evanston, IL: Northwestern University Press, 1968), 136.

15   Ibid., 143.

16   Paul Jobling, *Man Appeal: Advertising, Modernism and Menswear* (Oxford: Berg, 2005), 129–32.

17   Merleau-Ponty, *The Visible and the Invisible*, 134 and 143.

18   Sigmund Freud, 'Three Essays on the Theory of Sexuality' [1905], *On Sexuality*, J. Strachey (ed.), Penguin Freud Library, Vol. 7 (Harmondsworth: Penguin, 1977), 69.

19   Ibid.

20   Sigmund Freud, 'Fetishism' [1928], *On Sexuality*, J. Strachey (ed.), Penguin Freud Library, Vol. 7 (Harmondsworth: Penguin, 1977), 354–5.

21   Stefan Zweig, *Mental Healers: Hans Mesmer, Mary Baker Eddy, Sigmund Freud*, trans. E. and C. Paul (London: Cassell and Co, 1933), 358. Zweig argues: 'Analysis can give knowledge and nothing more . . . If it is to be supplemented until it becomes truly creative, the analysis and enlightenment effects must have superadded to them a conjoining and fusing technique: psychoanalysis must be supplemented by psychosynthesis.'

22   A psycho-synthetic message is also evident in a y-front campaign that appeared in *Man and His Clothes* (December 1945), 35, in the scene of a bespectacled nerd standing nervously looking at men and women dancing and the caption, 'He should wear Y-front my friend.'

23   *Man and His Clothes*, April and July 1955. The first prize was £100 (2000 equivalent was £3,795), with the runner up, Brown Muff & Co Ltd, of Bradford, winning £50 (£1,898) and third place, Sutterby & Gay, of March, Cambridge, receiving £25 (£949).

10
THE TURN TO NEW CONSUMERS AND YOUTH CULTURE

The survey Lyle and Scott had conducted in 1954 revealed that it was young men who preferred to wear y-fronts, but the generation gap in the taste for different styles of underwear had been adumbrated in the visual and verbal rhetoric of publicity for several retailers since 1946. Crawford's, for instance, had portrayed this contrast in its 'Underwear Types' campaign for Wolsey, where older men and styles of garments are not only unfavourably compared with younger ones but the former are also ridiculed by the latter. Accordingly, Havinden's illustrations and Saxon Mills's copy satirized the older generation as corpulent and outmoded, whereas the youthful males were objectified as more athletic (even when smoking a pipe) and aesthetic in their light woollen vests and shorts.

It comes as some surprise, therefore, that one of the first signs of sartorial revolt against the drab uniformity of Utility and rationed dress was manifested about 1948 in the revival and modification of a sober, 'older' way of dressing, popularized first of all by well-heeled young males in London's West End. The new style that incorporated a bowler hat, dark suit with narrow trousers and jacket with cuffs, and a velvet-collared topcoat, as Geoffrey Gilbert aptly framed it, 'made more conservative men move forward' in the way it adapted the dress codes of the early-twentieth-century gentleman to the urban milieu of the 1950s.[1] According to Gilbert this dress code, which he referred to as the hallmark of 'a twentieth century Elizabethan', also became gradually more casual and widespread with all classes of young men, who could visit their local tailor to have trousers tapered in keeping with the latest silhouette. However, rather than being called neo-Elizabethan, the style eventually became known as neo-Edwardian and was most notoriously associated with the working-class subculture of Teddy boys, following newspaper reports of a fatal stabbing on Clapham Common in July 1953.[2] Furthermore, the 'Teds' had customized the look, wearing draped jackets with an elongated body and wide shoulders, stovepipe trousers and brocaded waistcoat—often buttoned with glass beads.

While such *bricolage* fashion did not find its way into the menswear advertising of the period, the Teddy boy style nonetheless introduced a more subversive form of youth dress and several critics remarked on the fact that the postwar 'new man' (as Gilbert had referred to him) was also prone to adding a splash of colour through certain items of dress—decorated brocade waistcoats, picture and paisley ties, and boldly dotted socks.[3] In a letter to *Men's Wear* (1 July 1950) an anonymous reader also lamented the fact that men's underwear in Britain was only available in white, and an article titled 'Today's Teenage Male' in *Men's Wear* (7 April 1951) had commented, 'Its taste is flamboyant, with an eye on colour. Grey flannels are, for instance, "out" in this huge market. Toned and even violent hues are "in." ' At the same time, the predilection for check shirts as leisurewear became popular after the Duke of Edinburgh had worn one while square-dancing with Princess Elizabeth on a royal visit to Canada in autumn 1951. Hence, Rael Brook promoted its version in an advertisement in *Men's Wear* in December 1951 and, as discussed above, in 1958 the company also began to advertise its London Look patterned shirts on television and in print. Some remnants of a wartime dress code, however, did survive into the 1950s. In January 1950 a young-man's shop, catering for 16- to 20-year-olds, was opened at Bentall's, a department store in Kingston-on-Thames, but was closed by August of the same year because of its restrictive stocking policy and difficulties in getting to grips with the diversity of taste and expenditure within its own market—all the garments it sold, for instance, were Utility.[4] And the duffle coat, which had originally been worn by naval officers during the war, by the mid 1950s was being restyled and rehabilitated as a fashion item by male undergraduates, with fawn as the most popular shade.[5]

Several mainstream tailors also began to wake up to the fads and fancies of the fashionable young male in the mid 1950s. Thus the new managing directors of Burton's, Lionel and Sydney Jacobson, aimed to orient the company towards a more youthful market and to appeal to their more casual approach to dress, contending: 'The wearer wants to project an image of himself of being slightly careless but somehow just right.'[6] To this end, W. S. Crawford masterminded the national press campaign, 'You can't beat Burton tailoring!', which began early in 1954 and was complemented by advertising on television in autumn 1955. Burton's interwar publicity had been somewhat staid and unimaginative, centring on the ideal of the English gentleman (often depicted as the proverbial 'tailor's dummy') and orchestrated on a regional basis. Indeed, Burton's management at that time regarded the branch shop window rather than advertising as paramount in affording the local clientele a more personal relationship to the in-store merchandise:

A well-dressed window is a greater selling force than a newspaper and other forms of publicity combined . . . the shop window is better than a picture, for the prospective customer sees the original. Ten thousand words could not convey the same description that a good window does.[7]

By contrast, Crawford's promotional approach exploited the new market by taking a leaf out of the book of one of Burton's chief competitors in the 1930s—the Fifty Shilling Tailors—which, like Austin Reed, had been altogether a more visible advertising presence. In the Fifty Shilling Tailors's interwar press advertisements, the trope of the male peacock loomed large and he was represented in situational contexts, taking pleasure both in the wearing of fashionable clothes and the admiring looks of women he received in the process.[8] Just as in these promotions, therefore, the copy of Burton's advertisements from 1954 until spring 1962 acknowledged the idea that, even if men were keen shoppers, women's approval of what they purchased still mattered.

But Crawford's had also given a new twist to how male desire could be objectified in the photographs and text of their campaign for Burton's by emphasizing the role of play and leisure. Accordingly, the advertising scenario was shifted from the homosocial space of the shop floor to one of flirtation and romance, with the young man and his partner seen out on a date or at work and clothing represented as actively worn, while the copy was purposively crafted to portray how both the man who wore the garment and his female admirer appreciated the quality, social benefits and look of Burton's tailoring. Thus 'At times like this . . .' (Figure 7) represented a man and his female companion on a picnic in the countryside alongside copy proclaiming:

Right spot, bright weather . . . Looks like one of those moments when everything turns out the way you want! But our friend is super-lucky. Cocking an eye in the mirror before starting out on this expedition, he was pleasantly aware of something which (thanks to Burton's) had turned out absolutely right—the clothes he's wearing. And if you don't think this has made a big difference to his day, then you don't know how much man's happiness depends on woman's admiration.

Indeed, in his lecture to the Leeds branch of the Clothing Institute on 13 October 1954, Sydney Jacobson echoed one of the key psychological precepts of motivational research, arguing that dressing well was a matter not just of wherewithal but of mental outlook as well: 'The present advertising is designed by subtle methods . . . and it impinges on the subconscious and raises doubts and questions in people's minds as to whether they are correctly dressed.'[9] And yet, for all its alignment (sartorial or psychological) with young men, as Frank Mort aptly argues, 'Burton's new man was decidedly not a teenager . . . he did not present a wholly coherent identity at all.'[10] In the next part, therefore, I want to deal in closer detail with what may be regarded more properly as a youth culture market, which embraced men in their teens and twenties, and how it made an impact on menswear advertising generally between 1958 and 1978.

Notes

1   G. M. Gilbert, 'Meet the New Man', *Man and His Clothes* (August 1953), 26.

2   *Men's Wear* (3 October 1953), 34; Hilde Marchant, 'The Making of Boy Gangsters', *Picture Post* (10 October 1953).

3   Marchant, 'The Making of Boy Gangsters', 17; Hardy Amies, *Just So Far* (London: Collins, 1954), 245; Richard Hoggart, *The Uses of Literacy* (Harmondsworth: Penguin, 1957), 248.

4   *Men's Wear* (4 February 1950), 10; *Men's Wear* (19 August 1950), 13.

5   *Men's Wear* (14 January 1956), 9.

6   Frank Mort, *Cultures of Consumption—Masculinities and Social Space in Late Twentieth-Century Britain* (London: Routledge, 1997), 139.

7   Frank Mort, 'The Commercial Domain: Advertising and the Cultural Management of Demand', in B. Conekin, F. Mort and C. Waters (eds), *Moments of Modernity: Reconstructing Britain 1945–1964* (New York: Rivers Oram, 1999), 60.

8   Paul Jobling, *Man Appeal: Advertising, Modernism and Menswear* (Oxford: Berg, 2005), 98–9.

9   'Clothes Advertising Campaigns Are Educating Public', *Men's Wear* (16 October 1954), 17.

10 Mort, *Cultures of Consumption*, 142.

PART TWO

THINKING YOUNG

MENSWEAR ADVERTISING AND THE GENERATION GAME, 1958–78

The bachelor under twenty-six years allocates a larger proportion of his weekly wage to clothing than any other section of the community. (*Men's Wear*, 2 January 1960)

Clothes are an example of the trend . . . the added values here have become more important than the functional. (S. King, *Adweek*, 20 April 1973)

Introduction

In April 1959 British *Vogue*'s opening editorial noted that the word 'young' was appearing everywhere as 'the persuasive adjective for all fashions, hairstyles, ways of life', while in the same year Catherine Connor was appointed as fashion consultant in the London office of advertising agency McCann Erickson.[1] Both events signal how seriously were being taken the burgeoning youth culture and its interest in clothing, which had evolved during the first wave of post-war affluence, as well as the challenge it posed to the hegemony of conventional lifestyles and values. In 1955, 15- to 19-year-olds constituted 6.5 per cent of the population, rising to 8 per cent in 1963–64, and during this time, with unemployment and inflation almost non-existent in Britain, the wages of teenagers rose twice as fast as those of other employees.[2] As a corollary, this new youth cultural movement forged a distinctive social identity, having its own economic, political and aesthetic agenda that postulated more pluralist patterns of production and consumption. In terms of shopping for men's clothes this led to the rise of boutiques such as Vince Man's Shop and John Stephen's His Clothes, which originated around London's Carnaby Street.

But, as we shall also see in this part, there was considerable seepage from youth culture to the mainstream such that national retailers like Burton's, Austin Reed and Hector Powe began to latch onto the style and dress codes of the male peacock at a time when, as Mary Quant aptly put it, 'Everyone wanted to look as though they were young whether they were or weren't.'[3] In 1956, for instance, Powe opened its Younger Man's Shop in Regent Street, and in 1959 Austin Reed commissioned a mural by Robyn Denny, featuring a typographic collage in red, white and blue that 'celebrated London as "GREAT, BIG, WIDE, BIGGEST!"' to appeal to the new youth consumer.[4] These initiatives were consolidated when Reed opened its in-store boutique Cue Man in September 1965 and Moss Bros launched the One-Up shop at its Covent Garden branch to sell 'pace-setting clothes' in spring 1967 (advertised at the same time by the agency TB Browne in the *Evening Standard* and *Town*).[5]

It was not for nothing that Nick Tomalin could state on the eve of the 1970 General Election, 'All that was left for us to celebrate was each separate, beautiful young human body . . . Late Wilsonian male fashion is . . . still only suitable for the very young, and exhibitionistic.'[6] And yet, it would be too simplistic to argue that age differences no longer mattered, as Quant's comment implies, or that menswear advertising managed to appeal seamlessly to new and traditional markets alike. For, as the verbal and visual rhetoric of the press advertisements 'Tern shirts take a timid step towards Carnaby Street' (1967) and 'Is your father stopping you going to Hector Powe?' (*Sunday Times Magazine*, 27 September 1970) also demonstrate, the challenge for menswear manufacturers and multiples lay in pulling off a delicate balancing act: how to provide similar types of clothes for distinct age groups and how to build brand loyalty across the generations by respecting their different needs and desires, while turning neither sector off their products in the first place.

In this part, therefore, I want to consider the 'added value' to which S. King, the director of J. Walter Thompson, referred in 1973 by analysing how the ideal of youth was connoted in menswear advertising between 1958 and 1978, a period that more or less overlaps with what Arthur Marwick terms 'the long sixties'.[7] In particular, I shall be concentrating on the form and content of publicity for staple garments such as suits, trousers and shirts, as well as the impact of synthetic materials on men's clothing, that appeared in newspapers, magazines, and posters and on cinema and television. But first, it is necessary to give some account of why and how teenagers and youth culture became paramount to the market for and the promotion of menswear, as well as the channels of advertising that were mobilized to circulate such publicity.

Notes

1 'Fashion Post at McCann', *Advertiser's Weekly* (4 September 1959), 9.

2 Arthur Marwick, *British Society Since 1945* (Harmondsworth: Pelican, 1982), 117–18.

3 Mary Quant, 'A Design For Personal Living', *The Listener* (December 1974), 816.

4 *Mens' Wear* (7 July 1956), 15; Alistair O'Neill, 'John Stephen: A Carnaby Street Presentation of Masculinity 1957–1975', *Fashion Theory* 4:4 (2000), 495.

5 *Advertiser's Weekly* (17 March 1967), 55.

6 Nick Tomalin, 'When All the Beautiful People Came to the Aid of the Party', *Sunday Times Magazine* (14 June 1970), 25.

7 Arthur Marwick, *The Sixties—Cultural Revolution in the United Kingdom c.1958–c.1974* (Oxford: Oxford University Press, 1998), 41.

11

SEDIMENTING THE YOUTH MARKET

The novel 'visibility' of the incipient youth market in Britain was a source of contemporary fascination. Writing in 1963, Harry Hopkins remarked, 'Never had "Youth"—with a capital "Y"—been so earnestly discussed, so frequently surveyed, so extensively seen and heard.'[1] In coming to terms with this 'Youthquake'[2] several authors dealt with the way that teenagers set out to transgress the limits of conventional behaviour. Thus T.R. Fyvel attributed the juvenile delinquency of working-class males to the urban 'social wastelands' and unbridled consumerist ethos of the post-war period, while Richard Hoggart homed in on the 'juke-box boys', to whom he referred as a 'depressing group' of 15- to 20-year-old working-class males who frequented milk bars and 'nickelodeons' in the evenings to listen to the latest record releases.[3] Both accounts, however, saw the role of dress as a crucial means of signifying generational difference and carving out a singular social identity. Hoggart, for instance, spoke of the 'drape-suits, picture ties and American slouch' that demarcated the Teddy boy, whereas Fyvel observed a transition to 'the rather attractive "Italian style", which had become normal walking-out wear for the working-class boy'.[4] Since the mid 1950s suits and coats by the Italian manufacturer Balbus had in fact been sold in London by Stein and Sons, and suits by Fratelli Rivetti, costing between £10. 6s. and £27. 2s., were distributed across the United Kingdom by John Buck and Co.[5] It was with such diversity in mind, therefore, that market researchers were preoccupied with finding out how young people spent their income and leisure time, and between 1956 and 1961 several instructive surveys into their earnings and spending power were conducted by Mark Abrams for Research Services Ltd and Stanley Orwell for Market Investigations Ltd. As Orwell posited at the outset: 'Why, then, a youth market? Simply because it is a market in which money is much more freely available for spending on all types of goods than any other.'[6]

According to both Abrams and Orwell, the market of 12- to 24-year-olds had average weekly spending money of 5s. 9d. per capita in 1956.[7] While this sum was meagre, spending among the core market of 16- to 19-year-olds was considerably higher, averaging between 25s. and 30s. a week.[8] In particular,

Orwell's survey revealed that in 1956 and 1957 the youth market was predominantly working-class, with two-thirds belonging to social grades D and E,[9]
and an estimated 60 per cent of expenditure was put down to males, with
young men aged between 15 and 24 spending a mean of 3s. 6d. every week on
clothing and footwear respectively—that is, 30 per cent of their spare income.[10]
By 1960, the spending power of young working-class men was consolidated
with the abolition of National Service and by the fact that the majority of men in
their twenties remained single. This constituency had on average 62s. 8d. free
income per week out of earnings of about £13—25 per cent of which they spent
on clothing and shoes.[11] The average teenage male would also buy one new
suit per annum (the majority made-to-measure and costing around 26 guineas
in 1964[12]) but, writing in the *Sunday Graphic* in 1960 (a popular class C2 and D
newspaper), Peter Laurie cited that he had:

> found a boy who could hang £127 worth of suits in his parents' back yard
> to be photographed, another who earned £5 a week and owned: five suits,
> two pairs of slacks, one pair of jeans, one casual jacket, five white and three
> coloured shirts, five pairs of shoes, twenty-five ties and an overcoat.[13]

These clothing preferences were consolidated in a 1962 survey into the
clothing habits of 603 unmarried men between 15 and 24 years in age, which
was carried out by Courtaulds Ltd and revealed their wardrobe still tended to
gravitate exclusively towards formal wear—for both work and leisure—rather than
including more casual garments such as jeans and thick sweaters. Thus the suit
accounted for 30 per cent of sales with this group, while topcoats and jackets
accounted for 28 and 25 per cent of sales respectively.[14] Equally important,
the survey demonstrated that this age group would save up for clothes rather
than buy a garment on impulse, with the majority shopping for suits, jackets
and trousers at a multiple tailor, which had numerous branches or outlets both
regionally and nationally, or menswear retailer, and many shopping at Marks &
Spencer for shirts and knitwear.[15] (Although, unlike Burton's or Austin Reed,
the company did not rely on advertising at this time.[16]) In this regard it is worth
noting the findings of the 1961 Census of Distribution that, while the number of
menswear shops had dropped from 15,581 in 1950 to 14,095 in 1961, turnover
had increased from just under £200 million to almost £272 million and that the
multiple tailors accounted for more than half the spending on menswear.[17]
By and large, the spending power of young males that had been initially
recognized at the end of the 1950s continued unabated, and earnings managed
to keep pace with the cost of living until the economic recession, rising inflation
and wage freezes of the early 1970s. Between 1955 and 1969, salaries had
increased by some 88 per cent, with the average weekly earnings for men over
21 years standing at £20 in 1966 and £28 in 1970.[18] The affluence of the single

working-class male at this time was particularly striking. In 1965, for instance, fishermen in Grimsby cleared £1,200 per annum and were not averse to spending it.[19] One sales assistant in the local branch of Burton's, for instance, affirmed that 'eight or ten suits a year's not unusual' for the single, teenage deckhands and that they would pay between £12 and £22 for each one.[20] The young Grimsby fishermen also shared a predilection with the correspondents in the 1962 Courtaulds survey for more colourful clothing—pale blue or royal blue gabardine was their favourite fabric for suits. But they had little truck with the Italian-style jackets and sharper, continental styling favoured by the Mods (many of whom had suits made from the luxury Dormeuil Tonik mohair, which advertising is discussed in Chapters 18 and 19), preferring Ted-inspired pleated jackets, worn with either drainpipe or wide trousers. It comes as no surprise, therefore, that Alison Adburgham, fashion correspondent for the *Observer*, began to write about the renaissance of the male dandy, while Shirley Fieldhouse observed in the *Daily Telegraph* that the male peacock, which had been re-emerging since the mid 1950s, was decidedly worldly and media savvy in outlook:

> Flattering the male vanity has become big business and . . . the trend was started by young men who had been abroad, looked at television and had the sense and money to see there is nothing necessarily masculine about wearing drab baggy suits and old school ties.[21]

Consequently, it may be taken as a given that the fashionable youth of the period was manna from heaven to retailers and advertisers alike, and, to cater for the European taste in clothing that Fieldhouse describes, the boutique also began to challenge the more usual outlet of the multiple tailor and menswear specialist.

Cecil Gee, who had opened his first store in London's East End in 1929 and relocated to Shaftesbury Avenue in 1938, was one of the first retailers to latch onto the vogue for patterned shirts and short boxed jackets,[22] and was soon followed in Soho by Vince Man's Shop and John Stephen, and Man About Chelsea on the King's Road.[23] Vince Man's Shop was opened in 1954 by Bill (Basil) Green in Newburgh Street, moving to Foubert's Place sometime in 1961. Green had previously worked as a photographer for men's magazines, shooting wrestlers and bodybuilders in the keynote skimpy posing briefs that he had fashioned by cutting down store-bought swimming trunks. To meet public demand for the garment he began to retail it first by mail order and used the proceeds to open his first shop, where he also sold short Italian-styled jackets (known as 'bum-freezers'), tight-fitting trousers and tops, and black jeans and shirts that he argued 'went like a bomb in those days'.[24] Although Vince's core clientele was gay men, his clothing was popular with young straight men as well.[25] Veronica Horwell remarked that 'pink hipsters walked out of the shop on heteros too', and Green stated in 1960 that Anthony Armstrong-Jones had been a regular visitor, purchasing slim-line slacks.[26] To a large extent, the popularity of Vince Man's Shop was due to word of mouth and personal recommendation, but Green did also produce seasonal catalogues (Sean Connery modelled casual clothes in spring/summer 1957[27]) and advertised in specialist periodicals such as *Films and Filming* and occasionally in mass-circulation newspapers and magazines that were popular with young people; thus publicity for 'Vince' ultra-briefs appeared in the *Daily Mirror* (16 May 1960) and *Weekend* (4–10 November 1964).[28] At the same time, it is possible he would have benefitted indirectly from the advertisements for Lee Cooper jeans that had begun to appear in the *Daily Mirror* in 1958 and for pre-faded and shrink-to-fit Levis that cropped up in *Weekend* from 1964 onwards. His Clothes, another pioneering Soho boutique, was opened in 1957 in Beak Street by John Stephen. He had originally worked as a sales assistant in Vince Man's Shop and by 1966 was running twenty-two shops of his own in the London area.[29] As Alistair O'Neill argues, Stephen sold similar garments to Vince but realized also that, to appeal to a broader teenage market, he would need both to undercut his competitor's prices and to filter 'the homoerotic style . . . for mass consumption'.[30] The shop, His Clothes, however, was not so 'mass market' as to be overlooked by young men—straight or gay—with a more eclectic or idiosyncratic outlook on dress and style, and Stephen's clients included painter David Hockney and fashion illustrator Gerry Richards, who visited his shop for inspiration.[31]

Like Burton's before him, John Stephen initially envisaged the shop window, rather than press advertising, as pivotal in attracting clientele, and to this end he used large-scale photographs by Mike McGrath of well-known straight celebrities, such as boxer Billy Walker, wearing the clothing he stocked as the backdrop to window displays.[32] Similarly, Hogarth Stores in Coventry found that a window display it had devoted to teenage clothing in spring 1960 brought an increased number of young men into the shop.[33] Yet, if boutiques did not need to rely on advertising to sell their merchandise in the late 1950s and early 1960s (Cecil Gee's first publicity appeared in 1963 and the John Stephen Group's not until 1968[34]), the reverse was true of mainstream menswear chains and manufacturers. Comparative figures collated by the *Statistical Review of Advertising* for expenditure on menswear publicity in 1950 and 1959, for example, revealed that spending among men's tailors had increased more than twofold and among casual wear brands by 50 per cent during the period.[35] And, in a speech to the London area members of the Merchant Tailors' Federation in 1960, the director of Hector Powe stated that his firm was currently spending almost 4 per cent of an annual turnover of £2.5 million on publicity and dedicating £23,000 of this to press advertising.[36] Just as they had attempted to ascertain the changes that youth culture had wrought on the market and the shopping habits of young men aged 16–24 years, therefore, so too were advertisers exercised to discover what were their media preferences.

Notes

1 H. Hopkins, *The New Look* (London: Secker and Warburg, 1963), 423.

2 P. Lewis, *The Fifties* (London: William Heinemann, 1978), 177.

3 T. R. Fyvel, *The Insecure Offenders: Rebellious Youth in the Welfare State* (London: Pelican, 1961) 14–15; Richard Hoggart, *The Uses of Literacy* (Harmondsworth: Penguin, 1957), 247 and 248.

4 Hoggart, *The Uses of Literacy*, 248; Fyvel, *Insecure Offenders*, 45.

5 *Men's Wear* (28 September 1957), 9. In 2000, the equivalent of £10. 6s. was £160.32 and of £27. 2s. it was £421.80. These and all subsequent monetary figures for 2000 have been calculated by using Lawrence H. Officer and Samuel H. Williamson, 'Purchasing Power of British Pounds from 1245 to Present', MeasuringWorth (2013). http://www.eh.net/hmit/ppowerbp, accessed 12 January 2013.

6 S. Orwell, 'Selling to the 16–24 Market', *Advertiser's Weekly* (3 February 1961), 25.

7 *Advertiser's Weekly* (28 September 1956), 26–7; Stanley Orwell, 'Survey of the Youth Market', *Advertiser's Weekly* (21 February 1958), 26. The 2000 equivalent of 5s. 9d. was £10.12.

8 Orwell, 'Survey of the Youth Market', 26. The respective 2000 equivalents were £43.98 and £52.78.

9 Ibid., 32, cites figures by Amalgamated Press that revealed out of a total 8,506,000 young people aged 15–24 years, 6,098,000 were from social groups D and E and 2,791,000 lived in London and the South-East; 967,000 in Wales and the South-West; 1,328,000 in the Midlands; 1,150,000 in the North-West; 1,338,000 in the North-East; and 932,000 in Scotland.

10 M. Abrams, 'Selling to the Teenager', *Advertiser's Weekly* (23 January 1959), 31–2. The 2000 equivalent was £6.16.

11 M. Abrams, 'Selling to the Teenager', *Advertiser's Weekly* (12 February 1960), 31; Orwell, 'Survey of the Youth Market', 26. The respective 2000 equivalents were £91.41 and £379.24.

12 D. Beyfus, 'How to Tell a Boy From a Girl', *Sunday Times Magazine* (20 September 1964), 47. The 2000 equivalent was £329.

13 Peter Laurie, *The Teenage Revolution* (London: Anthony Blond, 1965), 20.

14 'Teen Man Market Surprises', *Men's Wear* (1 December 1962), 11.

15 '18 Per Cent Bought Knitwear and 15 Per Cent Shirts from Marks and Spencer', *Men's Wear* (1 December 1962), 11.

16 Ibid. Seventy-four per cent bought their suits, 45 per cent their topcoats, 36 per cent their jackets and 26 per cent their trousers from a tailor. In April 1958, M&S had piloted its first ever clothing advertisement in *Woman*, but did not express any plans to embark on a large-scale national advertising campaign (*Advertiser's Weekly* (2 May 1958), 5).

17 *Men's Wear* (16 February 1963), 9. The respective 2000 equivalents were £4,070.4 million and £3,718.7 million.

18 Arthur Marwick, *British Society Since 1945* (Harmondsworth: Pelican, 1982), 118. The respective 2000 equivalents were £415 and £430.

19   The 2000 equivalent was £26,555.

20   Arthur Hopcraft, 'Grimsby: The Men in Wide-Bottomed Suits', *Sunday Times Magazine* (28 November 1965), 35. The respective 2000 equivalents were £265.55 and £487.

21   Alison Adburgham, 'Renaissance of the Dandy', *Observer* (9 April 1961); Shirley Fieldhouse, 'The Cost of a Shining Image', *Daily Telegraph* (31 December 1962), 7.

22   Francis Wyndham, 'Gee, but It's Great to Be Gee!', *Sunday Times Magazine* (19 January 1969), 18. In an interview with Nik Cohn Gee also stated that he had imported double-breasted suits and shirts with long, pointed collars from the United States. Thus Nik Cohn, *Today There Are No Gentlemen* (London: Weidenfeld and Nicholson, 1971), 19, argues that Gee was 'the first designer to think in mass-market terms'.

23   A. Symes, 'Man About Chelsea', *Men's Wear* (4 April 1959), 14.

24   Shaun Cole, *Don We Now Our Gay Apparel* (Oxford: Berg, 2000), 72.

25   Ibid. In an interview with Cole, John Hardy, who had modelled for the mail-order catalogue, attested that 'a high percentage of *Vince's* clients were gay' (italics in the original). See also Clare Lomas, ' "Men Don't Wear Velvet You Know!" Fashionable Gay Masculinity and the Shopping Experience, London, 1950–Early 1970s', *Oral History* 35:1 (Spring 2007), 82–90. Lomas interviewed three gay men from differing generations to glean some impression of the kind of shops they visited; Peter Viti, who was a student in the 1960s, shopped at Vince Man's Shop, whereas Denis Shurrock, who worked in advertising, found Vince's clothes too unconventional.

26   Veronica Horwell, ' "King of Carnaby Street" Who Changed Attitudes to Male Fashion', *Guardian* (9 February 2004); 'Sleek Line Cruise Clothes for Mr. Armstrong Jones', *Men's Wear* (7 May 1960), 13.

27   Connery was, at that time, working as a French polisher. See *Men's Wear* (21 March 1964), 20.

28   Green states that he had placed an initial ad in the *Daily Mirror* in 1950. See Cohn, *Today They Are No Gentlemen,* 60.

29   By 1975, Stephens had also opened fifty-six Lord John outlets across Britain (*Men's Wear* (12 September 1974), 13).

30   Alistair O'Neill, 'John Stephen: A Carnaby Street Presentation of Masculinity 1957–1975', *Fashion Theory* 4:4 (2000), 489 and 493.

31   Deirdre McSharry, 'The Young Peacock Cult', *Daily Express* (3 April 1965), 14.

32   O'Neill, 'John Stephen', 494.

33   *Men's Wear* (9 April 1960), 23.

34   See *The Times* (26 August 1968) and *Queen* (October 1968). Cecil Gee's first national colour advertising campaign by the agency Cohen Butt, 'One Way or Another, Looks Can Kill', however, did not appear until spring 1979 in the *Observer* and *Daily Telegraph*. It cost £100,000 to produce and featured atmospheric photographs of a man strolling on a beach (*Campaign* (19 January 1979), 2).

35   J. Taylor, 'Wide Scope for Improving the Masculine Approach', *Advertiser's Weekly* (4 March 1960), 38.

36   'Get Wise to Publicity', *Men's Wear* (12 March 1960), 19–20. The 2000 equivalent of £100,000 was £1,367,166 and of £23,000 was £314,448.

12

CINEMA AND TELEVISION ADVERTISING FOR MENSWEAR

It would be easy to assume that by the early 1960s cinema and television publicity had become more strategic than press advertising in reaching wide audiences, but the statistical evidence that exists suggests otherwise and, in the case of television, is somewhat contradictory. In general terms, cinema audiences had been dwindling gradually in Britain, dropping from 30 million per week in 1950 to 10 million in 1960.[1] Yet, a Pearl and Dean survey into the spending habits of cinemagoers in 1956 had revealed that, although cinema attendance was generally in decline, 96 per cent of 16- to 24-year-olds occasionally visited their local cinema and 69 per cent went at least once a week.[2] More particularly, in 1957 Gallup and Group Marketing Ltd undertook research on behalf of Rank Screen Services to chart the extent to which audiences recalled the advertisements that had been screened. After testing an audience of 96 men and 96 women for two weeks in April 1957 at the Odeon in Dudley, the survey revealed that the average adult cinemagoer recalled 60 per cent of the advertisements the day following exposure and 50 per cent one week later.[3]

Early examples of cinema advertising for menswear brands included 'From hanger to husband', an advertisement by Lucien Productions for Rael Brook's Toplin shirt shown in 1,000 cinemas nationwide in July 1956, and 'Uncle Jeff', a two-minute cartoon for Aertex, produced by Pearl and Dean and screened in 260 cinemas in June 1957.[4] But it was not until jeans brands such as Levi's, Wrangler and Brutus began to produce cinema campaigns on a regular basis from 1972 onwards that this form of advertising became more common. The most probable reasons for the dearth of menswear cinema publicity before then were the challenge of television, widely regarded as contributing to the diminution in audiences for film, and cost—in 1960, for instance, the average charge for 30 seconds airtime per venue was £3,000.[5] More economical were commercial tie-ins between clothing brands and cinema chains. Thus in 1960 Clark's shoes were promoted on the picture sleeve of 'Big Beat Boogie', Bert

Weedon's single for Top Rank records, and backed up in turn by choreographed advertising slots in Top Rank cinemas; in 1963 Rael Brook piggybacked Frank Sinatra's latest movie, *Come Blow Your Horn*, with show cards featuring hand-drawn illustrations alongside the slogan, 'Well dressed, a hit success';[6] and the opening sequence of *The Young Ones* (1962), starring Cliff Richard, was shot in front of Cecil Gee's Shaftesbury Avenue branch, while Richard also wore clothes by Cecil Gee throughout the movie.[7] By comparison, the volume of menswear advertising on television was higher in the period 1958–78, largely as a result of the growth in publicity for jeans (see Appendices III and IV) and cheaper airtime. In 1960, for instance, a peak-time 30-second slot (the preferred commercial length) cost £300 in London, while in 1964 it cost £4,772 to buy similar airtime across the entire network.[8] At first, the 'Admag' was the most economical—and thus preferred—method of television advertising: in 1957 Advertising Films Ltd produced a handful of two-minute filmlets, featuring John Collier suits and underwear by Two Steeples, Unwin and Invicta, which were screened in the London, Birmingham, and Manchester regions and in Scotland. And in 1959 a 15-minute advertising magazine, 'Mainly for Men', featuring clothes by Cecil Gee was televised in the London area on 17 June and 26 August, while another, 'Hi There!', presented by teenagers on behalf of teenagers, was transmitted on Tyne Tees Television.[9]

Several menswear labels and retailers, however, did advertise independently: Legget and Nicholson promoted y-fronts in 1958 with the slogan 'For Men on the Go' and a cartoon of a man on safari being pursued by a tiger; Burton's television publicity appeared on an intermittent basis between 1955 and 1979; and Double Two, Rael Brook and Peter England produced 30-second seasonal television campaigns for their shirts on a more regular basis.[10] The biggest player was C&A, which handled its own advertising account and started to promote mens- and womenswear on television in spring 1967.[11] By the close of 1968 C&A was ranked the second highest spending fashion retailer in regard to both press and television publicity, and in spring 1970, at which point it was spending £1,465,000 on publicity, the firm recruited Leo Burnett-LPE as agents for its television campaigns and John Simons Creative Consultants for press and poster advertising.[12] Indeed, by the mid 1970s, several menswear advertisers were spending considerable sums on television publicity. For example, Brutus jeans had a budget of £150,000 for television ad slots in the period June–December 1975 alone;[13] menswear outfitters Hepworth's spent £350,000 on airing a 30-second commercial in spring 1976 for outdoor coats, featuring the football managers Dave Sexton (QPR), Gordon Jago (Millwall), Noel Cantwell (Peterborough), Bobby Robson (Ipswich) and Lawrie McMenemy;[14] and in March 1979 Simon Shirt Co spent £500,000 on a national television campaign, featuring the song-and-dance act, Hot Gossip.[15]

However, the scant evidence we have from the period paints a desultory picture concerning both the frequency of television viewing among young people and the efficacy of menswear television advertising. Between June and November 1960, for example, ATV questioned 1,485 men about their buying habits in clothes and the findings revealed, somewhat speciously, that 32 per cent of commercial television viewers bought a new suit, compared to 23 per cent who either watched BBC only or did not have a television.[16] By contrast, in 1959 Abrams observed that among 16- to 24-year-olds 'viewing of commercial television is relatively low' and in 1960 he argued that, whereas 71 per cent of all teenagers lived in a household within the viewing range of the ITV network, on the average day only 50 per cent of them tuned in to watch it.[17] At the same time, *Advertiser's Weekly* raised the crucial point that commercial television was still uncertain about how to approach male consumers, asking: 'Does every man always want a white shirt? Again, does he always simply accept everything his wife buys?'[18] The magazine proposed two issues of relevance to the menswear retailer or manufacturer: first, that there were too few garments being publicized on television, and second, that the 'honest straight sell that has credibility and is convincing, has the greatest merit'.

To be sure, there was some danger that advertising aimed at men on a more symbolic or emotional level could miss the mark, as the reception of an atmospheric television promotion for Strand cigarettes in 1960 attests. In the ad, a nonchalant Frank Sinatra lookalike, dressed in raincoat and trilby, strolls alone through nocturnal London as he smokes a cigarette. However, the moody *mise-en-scène*, combined with the slogan 'You're never alone with a Strand', was construed by the audience to suggest a sense of urban drift or unpopularity rather than of sociability. Hence, it is hardly surprising to discern from the few descriptions that exist of television advertisements for Rael Brook shirts, produced by Hobson Bates and Partners in the late 1960s and Ogilvy Benson and Mather in the early 1970s, that a no-nonsense, straightforward approach to the male consumer—which also signified the popularity of men with women as a supplementary outcome of such advertising—persisted. In autumn 1968, for instance, publicity for the streamline 'Mr Harry' shirt took the proverbial 'pack shot' (the close-up of the product packaging that usually closed a television commercial) literally at face value by featuring only a white shirt box with the brand name in black letters as a female voice-over announced, 'Mr Harry is a shirt'; while in an advertisement in autumn 1972 a man enters a shop to buy a shirt only to encounter a chorus line of dolly birds who chant 'Rael Brook shirts for men!'[19] And yet, as we also see in Part 3, by the time Levi's aired its 'Bath' and 'Laundrette' campaigns in winter 1985–86, ludic menswear advertising on television had become the rule rather than the exception. More to the point, then, as market researcher Horace Schwerin argued in a paper delivered to advertising delegates at the Royal Festival Hall in June 1959, was whether an advertisement 'contains the right idea, or combination of ideas to produce the desired impression'.[20]

Notes

1   Janet Thumin, 'The "Popular", Cash and Culture in Postwar British Cinema', *Screen* 32:3 (1991): 245–71; Melanie Williams, 'Women in Prison and Women in Dressing Gowns', *Journal of Gender Studies* 11:2 (2002), 13.

2   'Impact of Cinema Ads Is Surveyed', *Advertiser's Weekly* (30 January 1958), 32.

3   Ibid., 33 and 34.

4   'A Shirt Campaign that Was Aimed at Women', *Advertiser's Weekly* (20 July 1956), 24; 'Current Advertising', *Advertiser's Weekly* (30 June 1957), 54.

5   'Talking to Teenagers in Their Own Language', *Advertiser's Weekly* (29 January 1960), 38. The 2000 equivalent was £41,015.

6   *Men's Wear* (10 August 1963), 8.

7   *Men's Wear* (6 January 1962), 24.

8   'Get Wise to Publicity', *Men's Wear* (March 1960), 25; Brian Henry (ed.), *British Television Advertising: The First Thirty Years* (London: Century Benham, 1986), 166. The respective 2000 equivalents were £4101 and £57,444.

9   *Advertiser's Weekly* (4 October 1957), 46–7; 'Big Men's Wear TV Programme', *Men's Wear* (25 April 1959), 11; *Men's Wear* (15 August 1959: 23); Abrams, 'The Teenage Market', (1960), 31.

10 Double Two television campaigns are mentioned in *Men's Wear* (14 November 1959, 2 November 1960, 5 August 1960 and 2 November 1963) and *Ad Week* (4 February 1972), 18. Peter England is mentioned in *Men's Wear* (21 February 1959), vi–vii and *Men's Wear* (26 January 1963), xxx. Rael Brook is mentioned in *Men's Wear* (26 April 1958), ii–iii; *Advertiser's Weekly* (14 November 1966), 12; and *Adweek* (3 November 1972), 16. Double Two spent £85,000 on only two advertisements for its 'White light' shirt, which were screened nationally at peak-time in autumn 1968 (*Men's Wear* (19 September 1968), 11). The 2000 equivalent was £875,871.

11 *Advertiser's Weekly* (25 April 1958), 4; *Men's Wear* (14 June 1958), 14; 'Zip Goes a Million on Men's Wear Ads', *Men's Wear* (28 March 1964), 9; *Men's Wear* (24 September 1966), 35; *Advertiser's Weekly* (20 June 1969), 26. Between April and June 1966, Burton's spent £66,366 on television ads (*Statistical Review of Press and TV Advertising,* London, 1966).

12 *Advertiser's Weekly* (20 December 1968), 17; *Ad Weekly* (8 May 1970), 3. The 2000 equivalent was £13,459,248.

13 *Men's Wear* (22 May 1975), 11. The 2000 equivalent was £747,323,

14 *Campaign* (22 October 1976), 6; the 2000 equivalent was £1,496,802. In spring 1977 Hepworth's spent the same amount on another ad, 'If you lead a full life, you need a full wardrobe', featuring actor Simon Williams (*Campaign* (21 April 1978), 9).

15 *Men's Wear* (23 November 1978), 3. The 2000 equivalent was £1,502,476.

16 'Television Vindicated', *Men's Wear* (17 December 1960), 15.

17   Abrams, 'Selling to the Teenager', (1959), 32; Abrams, 'Selling to the Teenager', (1960), 32.

18   *Advertiser's Weekly* (18 September 1959), 60.

19   *Men's Wear* (6 June 1968), 10; G. Amber, 'Oh Dear, I've Seen this Movie', *Adweek* (3 November 1972), 16.

20   'Schwerin's Findings on "Short" TV Commercials', *Advertiser's Weekly* (12 June 1959), 4.

13

MENSWEAR ADVERTISING IN NEWSPAPERS AND MAGAZINES

From 1967 onwards advertising on television began to compete strongly with press campaigns, although, as a distinct category, television publicity for clothing superseded them in terms of the annual percentage of expenditure on advertising in only 1976, 1982 and 1983 (largely as a result of the consolidation in television publicity for jeans), otherwise averaging 39.5 per cent between 1968–84.[1] Press advertisers were also able to take advantage of the union disputes that took ITV off the air during the summers of 1968 and 1979 and, notwithstanding the impact of industrial unrest on the supply of paper between September 1973 and April 1974, newspapers and magazines continued to exert their hegemony in attracting menswear advertising for the remainder of the twentieth century.[2]

The *Statistical Review of Advertising* in 1957 demonstrated that publicity in newspapers and magazines was holding its own in the face of cinema and television, hitting a peak in expenditure of £96,245,000.[3] Among newspapers, not only was the *Daily Mirror* by far the market leader between 1958 and 1980, accruing more than 5 million readers per issue in 1964, but it also forged ahead in attracting both a youthful readership and a broad range of advertisements for men's clothing.[4] The IPA Readership Survey for 1957 had cited the *Mirror* as the most widely read newspaper among 15- to 19-year-olds and, according to Market Investigations Ltd, by 1960 it was still the most widely read newspaper by teenagers.[5] More precisely, in 1963 Mark Abrams claimed that it was the most popular daily with A-level students and graduates.[6] Its robust circulation also made the *Mirror* an economical channel for advertising such that in 1958 a half-page promotion would cost 6s. 3d. for every thousand readers in comparison to 18s. 4d. for its nearest competitor, the *Daily Express*.[7] And yet, this did not necessarily mean that the *Mirror* always carried the highest volume of publicity for menswear. In a self-promotion the *Express* claimed, for instance, that in October 1962 it contained 3,461 column inches of advertisements for male clothing, while the *Mirror* lagged behind with 896.[8] In fact, several middle-market menswear retailers and brands, notably Austin Reed, Daks Simpson and Alexandre, advertised in the *Express* but not at all in the *Mirror* in spring and autumn 1962.[9] But what is also evident from a sample survey of publicity in each title in the 1960s and 1970s is that many others were prepared to advertise in both of these newspapers. Thus we find advertisements for all of the following in the *Mirror* and the *Express* between 1958 and 1965: Burton's, John Collier, Jackson the Tailor, Hepworth, Wolsey underwear and hosiery, Bri Nylon, Tootal shirts and ties, Rael Brook and Double Two shirts, and Denson shoes.[10] To a large extent, then, menswear advertisers exploited the idea that social class did not necessarily bother young people and that teenagers had 'formed a society of their own'.[11]

Equally buoyant was the market for periodicals. Titles such as the *Radio Times* and *Punch* continued to have a broad appeal and were joined by a cluster of magazines that were targeted at youth culture. Chief among them were *Reveille*, which was launched in 1940 and by mid 1960 had a weekly circulation of 7.5 million readers; *Weekend*, which started in 1957 and was especially popular with 25- to 29-year-olds; and *TV Times*, which went national for the first time in 1968.[12] All three titles were also vehicles for advertising the clothing and brands preferred by young men. *TV Times* claimed it was read by over 1.5 million men aged 16–34 years and thus promoted itself as 'the Junction of Carnaby Street and Savile Row',[13] and publicity for jeans by Lybro, Levi's, Wrangler, Jet and Westcot, and for Denson shoes appeared in *Reveille* and *Weekend* between 1963 and 1968.[14] At the same time, several magazines were published specifically with the fashionable male in mind, including *Vogue for Men*, which ran monthly between November 1965 and September 1968 before being published biannually, and *Man About Town*, founded 1954 but retitled *About Town* in 1960 and *Town* in 1962. More ephemeral were the following magazines: *Man's Journal*, a short-lived supplement of *Woman's Journal* in 1966; the glossy upmarket *man-about* (May–July 1968), aimed at executives and their families; the free sheets *Men of London* (1973–74) and *Man About Town* (1978–79); and the style magazine *View* (1978–79). All of these titles had to compete for readers with longstanding popular men's magazines such as *Playboy*, *Men Only* (originally *Lilliput*, which was promoted as the man's magazine with a readership of over 1 million[15]) and *Penthouse*. The last was aimed at men in the same 18- to 35-year-old demographic as *TV Times'* readership, which, as advertising director Kathy Keeton argued, 'are mainly unmarried and have a larger disposable income'.[16] However, the chief items of clothing that were advertised in their pages were men's hosiery and underwear, the latter frequently resorting to close-cropped photographs that fetishized the garment and to copy that shrouded it in suggestive metaphor, viz. 'What the best undressed men are wearing' by Davis and Page for y-fronts in March–June 1972 (Figure 10).

Figure 10 Lyle and Scott y-front, 'What the best undressed men are wearing', full-page colour advertisement, *Sunday Times Magazine*, 9 April 1972. Permission of Lyle and Scott Ltd.

In fact, although Simpson continued to use hand-drawn illustrations by Max Hoff and Eric Stemp throughout the 1960s and 1970s (Figure 11), by 1960 photography had become the prevalent medium for menswear press advertising. Along with the use of white 'breathing' space and clear-cut type forms, the new photographic advertising was promoted from 1958 onwards in *Neue Grafik*, a trilingual monthly published in German, English and French that became the vehicle for an international graphic style known as the Swiss School because of its association with Emil Ruder, a tutor at the School of Applied Arts in Basel.[17] In Britain it coalesced with the hard-edged, monochrome style of fashion and pop imagery that was pioneered by the likes of David Bailey,

Figure 11 Simpson of Piccadilly, full-page colour advertisement, *Sunday Times Magazine*, 15 May 1963. Permission of Daks Simpson Group.

Brian Duffy and Robert Freeman. By 1962 this approach had started to enliven the pages of *Vogue*, *Queen* and the *Sunday Times Magazine* and was also apparent in newspapers and posters in the atmospheric photographs of Tootal shirts publicity (Figure 13) and the 'top model' promotion for Clarks shoes (*Daily Express*, 2 October 1964). The latter consisted of two high-contrast images by David Bailey—the one on the left representing fashion model Jean Shrimpton,[18] and that on the right a close-up of the new elasticized slip-ons by Hardy Amies— and copy stating, 'Some shoes, some girls, do a lot for a man's prestige.' Hence, it underscored Judith Williamson's idea that 'instead of being identified by what they produce, people are made to identify themselves with what they consume' to such an extent that it even implied that both product *and* woman are the rightful possessions of the male consumer.[19] The Clarks advertisement refers, therefore, to the tendency in consumer culture for human beings and social relations to be reified or transformed into things and how the attributes of people and inanimate objects can be connoted as exchangeable or interchangeable: 'Advertisements thus separate the intrinsic qualities of being human from actual living humans. The link can be restored only by the purchase of the commodity. Human qualities must be bought back, re-appropriated by means of consuming the commodity sign.'[20]

It is in the pages of the newspaper colour supplements, however, that we can discern both the biggest influence of photography on menswear publicity and the way that, alongside eye-catching copy, both colour and black-and-white images could be mobilized to fetishize the commodities advertised and to suggest that they have a personality of their own. Indeed, given the wide variation in the typefaces and layouts used in menswear advertising in the 1960s and 1970s, it is probably photography that above all affords any sense of a unified period style. As Taylor appositely framed it: 'The Sunday colour supplements have been enormously important to the development of advertising—the understated, the elegant, the urbane, the witty, the pleasantest advertising of all to look at and read.'[21]

The *Daily Telegraph Magazine*, published on Fridays, and the *Observer Magazine*, published on Sundays, each began life in September 1964, but more successful was the *Sunday Times Colour Supplement*, launched in February 1962 and retitled *Sunday Times Magazine* in 1963. Although it registered a loss in advertising revenue in its first two years of existence, by autumn 1965 the *Sunday Times Magazine* had rallied, accruing an audited circulation of 4,470,000 readers, of whom almost 50 per cent were men.[22] And in 1971, by which time Donald Barrett claimed its predominantly A, B and C1 readers were 'younger, better off and better educated' than its rivals, the *Sunday Times Magazine* accounted for £5.5 million worth of advertising expenditure, or nearly half of all publicity space bought in the colour supplements.[23] The majority of clothing advertisements in the *Sunday Times Magazine* were either full- or half-page and, in common with the daily newspapers, spring and autumn were the high seasons for menswear publicity. Furthermore, while full-page colour advertisements for Burton's had been inserted in the *Daily Express*, *Daily Mail* and *Daily Herald* in autumn 1962, from the outset both the weekly supplements and magazines such as *Weekend* and *Town* had a distinct advantage over newspapers and television in being able to exploit high-speed web-offset for cheaper colour printing. ITV had started to transmit in colour in November 1969 but it was not until summer 1971 that colour advertising on television became prevalent.[24] Furthermore, given the uncertainty of knowing whether viewers continued to watch television during the commercial breaks, it could prove more economical to advertise in colour in the supplements than on television. In 1970, for instance, it cost £3,300 to produce a 30-second ad in colour and £6,701 to screen it nationwide in a peak-time slot,[25] while a full-page colour promotion in the *Sunday Times Magazine* in 1969 (by which time its circulation stood at 1,435,000) cost £3,731 and in the *Observer Magazine* (circulation, 911,000), £2,004.[26]

The early career of these magazines coincided with the mod cult and the myth of swinging London between 1962 and 1967, a period that Dick Hebdige argues embodied 'the essence of style'.[27] Accordingly, the very first issue of the *Sunday Times Colour Supplement* not only posed the question, 'What do you need to

Figure 12 Sabre Saturday Shirt in C-Nylon, full-page colour advertisement, *Sunday Times Magazine*, 15 May 1966. Private collection.

be of the 1960s?' but also replied with the answer, 'primarily under 30 years old'. Of course, none of the colour supplements were exclusively magazines for young people, but asking such a question did betray the general tendency or preoccupation that they—and many retailers—had with being on trend. This was exemplified in promotions for leisurewear by Sabre and Fred Perry (Figure 12). The latter had been one of the first retailers to realize the demand for more casual clothing shortly after its launch in 1952 with the advertising slogan, 'Dress and Play the Fred Perry Way', and it was this ludic theme that survived into 1960s publicity for the company's branded sport shirts that appeared in the *Sunday Times Magazine*. By contrast, the first advertisement for a boutique chain, Lord John, did not crop up in its pages until 2 December 1973, and by no means was all the menswear publicity in the *Sunday Times Magazine* for brands that teenagers would necessarily buy (viz. Rocola and Viyella shirts; Sumrie and Maenson suits) or retailers where they would shop (viz. Simpson, Burberry and Aquascutum). And yet, with few exceptions, the verbal and visual rhetoric of many advertisements for men's clothing in both the colour supplements and *Town* overlapped with the zeitgeist for youth culture that, as Christopher Booker put it, became 'an almost universal symbol of the sense of innovation and awakening that was affecting every part of society'.[28] Thus an advertisement for a traditional wool worsted suit by Sumrie in the *Sunday Times Magazine* (17 October 1965) also included a girl with a carrier bag bearing the bulls-eye motif, one of the key signifiers of mod culture that Harry Peccinotti had devised as the logotype for the Carnaby Street boutique Top Gear.

Notes

1   The percentage of expenditure for each year was as follows: 1976 (53%); 1982 (56.8%); 1983 (50.9%). The average percentage for 1968–84 was calculated from the figures cited in Appendix L of Brian Henry (ed.), *British Television Advertising: The First Thirty Years* (London: Century Benham, 1986), 514–19.

2   See Henry, *British Television Advertising*, 119 and 193 on these ITV disputes. On paper shortages see: 'Newsprint Crisis Worsens', *Adweek* (5 October 1973), 4; B. Gregory, 'Now More Than Ever a Page Is a Page', *Adweek* (4 January 1974), 12–13. As a result of the rising cost of paper, for instance, *The Times* had increased its full-page ad rate form £2,800 to £3,360 by the end of 1974. *Adweek* (6 December 1974), 1.

3   '1957 Press Spending Hit New Peak', *Advertiser's Weekly* (7 March 1958), 5. The 2001 equivalent was £1,376.7 million.

4   *Advertiser's Weekly* (22 January 1965), 5.

5   Abrams, 'Selling to the Teenager' (1960), 31.

6   'Top Young Minds Read the *Daily Mirror*', *Advertiser's Weekly* (12 April 1963), 1.

7   *Advertiser's Weekly* (30 May 1958), 25. The respective 2000 equivalents were £4.34 and £12.73.

8 *Men's Wear* (10 November 1962), xvii.

9 For example, advertising for Daks appeared in the *Daily Express* on 19 April 1962 and 24 October 1962; for Austin Reed on 12 April 1962 and 11 October 1962; and for Alexandre on 7 April 1962 and 5 October 1962.

10 Advertising in the *Mirror* as follows: Burton's (24 October 1958); Jackson (29 September 1964); John Collier (17 October 1958 and 2 March 1963); Hepworth (13 September 1961 and 2 October 1964); Wolsey (22 October 1958); Bri Nylon (14 March 1960 and 4 March 1963); Tootal (6 March 1959 and 28 September 1964); Rael-Brook (12 December 1962); and Denson (8 March 1960 and 22 September 1964). Advertising in the *Express* as follows: Burton's (13 November 1958); Jackson (1 October 1964); John Collier (7 November 1963 and 2 May 1963); Hepworth (28 October 1961 and 1 May 1965); Wolsey (5 November 1958); Bri-Nylon (5 April 1960 and 5 October 1962); Tootal (24 November 1958 and 3 April 1964); Rael-Brook (12 December 1962); and Denson (8 April 1960 and 24 April 1964). The Wakefield Shirt Company spent £200,000 on a national press and poster campaign for Double Two in winter 1963, taking half-page advertisements in the *Express* and *Mirror*, and posters on 400 Underground stations (*Men's Wear*, 2 November 1963: 9).

11 Peter Laurie, *The Teenage Revolution* (London: Anthony Blond, 1965), 11.

12 *Men's Wear* (23 July 1960), vii; A. H. Davies, 'The Youth Market. The Media: This Is What They Look At', *Advertiser's Weekly* (21 February 1958), 30.

13 *Advertiser's Weekly* (17 March 1967), 74.

14 Denson shoes were publicized in *Reveille*, *Weekend* and *Disc* in April 1963 and June 1963 and September 1965; Lybro ads appeared in the same titles in June 1963; ads for Levis appeared in *Weekend*, *Reveille*, as well as *Melody Maker* and *New Musical Express* in July and August 1964; Westcot jeans ads appeared in *Reveille* and *Weekend* in April and May 1965, and Jet jeans ads between April and September 1965; Wrangler's ads appeared in *Reveille* and *Weekend* in February and March 1967 and March–September 1968.

15 *Advertiser's Weekly* (4 March 1960).

16 Quoted in W. Raynor, 'One Man's Porn . . . Another Man's Pleasure', *Ad Weekly* (14 January 1972), 29.

17 Paul Jobling and David Crowley, *Graphic Design: Reproduction and Representation Since 1800* (Manchester: Manchester University Press, 1996) 161–5.

18 Shrimpton also appeared in publicity for Commodore topcoats in the *Sunday Times Magazine* (26 September 1965).

19 Judith Williamson, *Decoding Advertisements: Ideology and Meaning in Advertising* (London: Marion Boyars, 1978), 13.

20 Robert Goldman, *Reading Ads Socially* (London: Routledge, 1992), 31–2.

21 R. Taylor, '25 Years of the Creative Circle', *Ad Weekly* (30 October 1970), 40.

22 *Advertiser's Weekly* (10 October 1965), 18–19; *Advertiser's Weekly* (29 September 1967), 4.

23 *Ad Weekly* (9 July 1971), 10; *Ad Weekly* (28 January 1972), 21.

24 Henry, *British Television Advertising*, 151.

25 Ibid., 396 and 166.

26 *Men's Wear* (24 September 1970), 50. The respective 2000 equivalents were £30,317, £61,563, £36,462 and £19,584.

27 Dick Hebdige, *Subculture: The Meaning of Style* (London: Methuen, 1974), 9.

28 Christopher Booker, *The Neophiliacs* (London: Pimlico, 1969), 40.

14

POSTER PUBLICITY AND MENSWEAR

Although it lagged behind cinema, television and press advertising in popularity with menswear retailers and brands, poster publicity likewise began to respond to the changing market. In 1964, for example, twenty-five advertising agencies formed the Advertising Agency Poster Bureau (AAPB) to pool resources in buying outdoor space. The AAPB managed to accrue billings of £13 million but announced its break-up early in 1976 after J. Walter Thompson and Collett Dickenson Pearce withdrew their patronage.[1] In comparison to other advertising media, a perennial problem for anyone wishing to use a poster outdoors (rather than an interior public space such as the London Underground) was how to get a reasonable estimate of receptivity, because it could not simply be assumed that someone who had been in the vicinity of a poster had actually paid any attention to it. Interviewing a sample of 319 young people aged 16–24 years as part of a pilot study in 1955, however, Mills and Rockleys Ltd found that the majority of them had taken notice of the billboards they encountered.[2] And mobilizing a similar 'opportunities to see' method as the NRS did in measuring potential audiences for press advertising, a survey conducted by the British Market Research Bureau Ltd in 1964 for outdoor advertising contractor More O'Ferrall not only underscored such findings but also concluded that the best poster coverage was among male audiences.[3] Irrespective of site, the design of a poster was paramount in grabbing the attention of male consumers, and in 1961 W. S. Crawford launched what was to become the first of many hugely successful and notorious photographic press and sixteen-sheet poster (measuring 10 feet by 6 feet, 8 inches (3 metres by 2 metres, 7 centimetres)) campaigns for Tootal's new range of colour shirts designed by Hardy Amies; the campaigns were art directed by Ted Hughes. The girl in the poster, artfully photographed in black and white by David Olins, is clad always and only in a man's shirt; in one version in 1964, having tasted the apple of temptation, which she holds in her left hand, she looks out seductively to the (male) spectator, while the tag line proclaims that the shirts 'Look even better on Adam' (Figure 13).

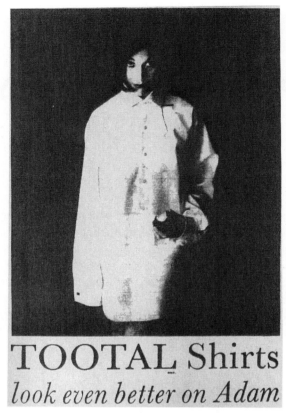

Figure 13 'Tootal Shirts look even better on Adam',
monochrome poster, photograph by David Olins, 1965.
Permission of Morrison McConnell.

Produced by men for men, this campaign allowed Tootal to capitalize on the
success with male audiences of the buxom pin-up that had been objectified
in Rael Brook's 'The Shirt with Eye Appeal' publicity by Lucien Productions,
which had appeared on London buses and Underground station walls in
February 1954. Yet, the girl in the shirt was altogether a more modern and
indeterminate gender stereotype that coincided with contemporaneous debates
on premarital sex, teenage pregnancy and the prominence of young women in
these debates.[4] In evoking the figure of Eve and welding together innocent and
knowing female identities the poster created, therefore, an erotic fantasy that
symbolized sexual availability, if not the idea of transgressive paedophilia (albeit
in a much more elliptical way than Nabokov had in 1961 with his novel *Lolita*).
Thus the shirt simultaneously swamps the teenage model's body and breasts

so as to render her asexual and doubles up as either a nightdress or smock that, combined with her come-to-bed eyes, proffers the male spectator the fantasy of the 'bad schoolgirl', which had loomed large in several press reports as well as the film *A Taste of Honey* in 1961.[5] As the campaign progressed, the trope was eventually dropped and invoked indirectly as a chauvinistic running joke in the changing copy of respective posters, which punned the longevity and propriety of the product ('Tootal—Shirts that stay good a long, long time'), as well as connoting the different attitudes that males and females ostensibly

Figure 14 'Tern Shirts take a timid step towards Carnaby Street', full-page colour advertisement, *Sunday Times Magazine*, 27 November 1966. Private collection.

Figure 15 'Look lithely in Van Heusen Slim Fit', full-page colour advertisement, *Sunday Times Magazine*, 26 November 1967. Private collection. The Van Heusen mark is used courtesy of PVH Corp.

entertained toward clothing. Thus, by winter 1965–66, we observe a woman
sparring with her partner (photographed by Michael Williams), as they dress
for a dinner party; she says to him, 'But darling I can't wear this dress to the
Hutchinson's. I wore it last year,' and he responds, 'Why not. I'm wearing the
Tootal shirt you wore in the last advertisement.'[6]

Poster publicity for Tootal was complemented by campaigns in the press,
and advertising for its shirts also constituted one of the largest categories in the
Sunday Times Magazine, with other key players being Peter England, Double
Two, Tern, Van Heusen, Viyella and Rocola. Although Boar Brand had no need to
advertise its tapered 'Go Man' shirt, targeted at 18- to 30-year-olds, because it

had built up a core market without publicity, Tern and Van Heusen did promote their own slim-fit white and colour models in the press.[7] In particular, the 'Tern shirts take a timid step towards Carnaby Street' campaign by Doyle Dane and Bernbach won a D&AD award, a prize scheme that had been introduced in 1963, for the outstanding use of colour in print advertising in 1966 (Figure 14).[8] And in winter 1967 a Van Heusen advertisement made a double address to men and women alike, representing the male model as a sex object as he reclines on the phallic bonnet of a red E-type Jaguar with a number plate that proclaims both him and the shirt as 'the One' (Figure 15).

Notes

1 *Campaign* (30 April 1976), 1. The 2001 equivalent was £55,595,505.
2 A. H. Davies, 'The Youth Market. The Media: This Is What They Look At', *Advertiser's Weekly* (21 February 1958), 30.
3 'The First Audience Study Carried out by an Outdoor Advertising Contractor', *Outdoor Advertising* (February 1965), 4.
4 Jeffrey Weeks, *Sex, Politics and Society* (London: Longman, 1989), 238.
5 Four reports on the subject appeared in the *Daily Express* in September 1961 alone. See, for instance: Patricia Lewis, 'Wide-Eyed Appeal in Tush's Violet Gaze', an interview with Rita Tushingham, who played the part of unmarried, pregnant teenager Jo in *A Taste of Honey* (7 September 1961), 10; Jane Gaskell, '3 in 5—The Mortality Rate in Teenage *Marriage*' (11 September 1961), 12 and 'Does a Baby Inhibit Teenage Marriage?' (12 September 1961), 10; 'The Party-girl of 15 Who Grew Up Too Fast' (16 September 1961), 4. The last article concerned Hilary Weiswall of Hornsey, London, who killed herself after hosting a round of alcohol-fuelled parties with her £5 per week pocket money, while her mother and stepfather were on holiday. She had confessed to a friend that she had had sexual relations with several boys and believed she was pregnant (the coroner found that she was not).
6 *Outdoor Advertising* (January–February 1966), 23.
7 *Men's Wear* (9 July 1966). See, for example in the *Sunday Times Magazine*: 'Will it ever come to this?' (21 May 1967), 'Tern's bid to end white supremacy' (22 October 1967), 'Tern shirts: further deflationary measures' (1 December 1968) and 'Why should girls get all the fun?' (25 November 1973).
8 *Men's Wear* (24 June 1967), 16. On the D&AD see Jeremy Myerson and Graham Vickers, *Rewind: Forty Years of Design and Advertising* (London: Phaidon, 2002).

15

'YOU BRING THE BODY, WE'VE GOT THE CLOTHES'

PUBLICITY FOR TAILORS

The theme of sexual attraction and flirtation was also a leitmotiv of advertisements for the suit from the mid 1950s to the late 1970s. Almost without exception, the major menswear chains and tailors continued to advertise in mass-circulation newspapers. And, while none of them heeded A.A. Hawker's plea at the 1963 annual conference of Clothing Manufacturer's Federation in Scarborough to produce suits in 'sky blue, sea green, shimmering brown' and waistcoats in 'flaming reds, sunset orange and yellows', the majority did take advantage of advertising in colour in the new magazines and occasionally in newspapers (as Austin Reed had in the *Daily Express* and *Daily Telegraph* in spring 1962).[1] Thus between 1963 and 1977 Austin Reed, Hector Powe, Hepworth's, Simpson's, Burton's, John Collier and Hornes, who coined the phrase 'You bring the body, we've got the clothes' in 1978, all advertised regularly in the *Daily Mirror*, *Daily Express* and *Sunday Times Magazine*.[2] Equally, in spring 1971, the advertising agents Nielsen Williams Harris promoted suits by Mr Harry in the *Evening Standard* and *Sunday Express*, and Lovell and Rupert Curtis circulated advertisements for Magee suits in the *Evening Standard* as well as the *Daily Mail*, *Daily Express*, *Daily Mirror*, and *Times*.

In November 1967, tailors spent £256,600 on press advertising,[3] and between 1969 and 1970 sales of suits constituted 11 million units.[4] By this time also, several chains had begun to advertise on television and in the cinema. In spring 1967, United Kingdom Advertising launched a 12-week campaign to promote Hardy Amies' new designs for Hepworth's, spending £150,000 on full- and half-page press ads and £36,000 on 60-second cinema slots nationwide.[5] Between January to April 1967, Willerby Tailoring aired a series of 30-second television slots conceived by advertising agents Foote, Cone and Belding, and Ridley Scott directed a 30-second cinema advertisement for them, which was screened in winter 1971–72 to promote the introduction of their store card.[6] But the longest running, and one of the most successful, television campaigns for menswear was 'The Window to Watch' for John Collier.

In spring 1954, the Fifty Shilling Tailors had announced its takeover by United Drapery Stores Ltd in a campaign of double-column typographic advertisements in the national and provincial press, which explained that it was no longer possible to manufacture suits for £2. 10s. due to the cost of importing Australian wool. Henceforth, the company would be known as John Collier, but its first advertising campaign proper in April 1954, handled by Greenlys Ltd, included a photograph of a man visiting an in-store tailor to reassure the former Fifty Shilling Tailors' clientele that, although a two-piece suit from John Collier would now cost £10. 10s., it would, as before, be cut by hand.[7] In autumn 1957 John Collier had been featured in a composite television filmlet, but from 1958 'The Window to Watch' press and television campaign, evolved by Greenlys, began to be screened independently and, allowing only for periodic changes in the style of clothing, appeared in a similar format for some 10 years.[8] The theme of the new publicity represented the pleasure of shopping, as a man and a woman gaze into the shop window and point to the merchandise it contains, thereby updating the rhetoric of interwar advertising for the Fifty Shilling Tailors. But it also revived the trope of the male peacock that had been so evident in 1930s advertising for its predecessor, depicting the male consumer as both spectator and spectacle; in other words, as someone who takes pleasure both in looking at his own suited image while simultaneously being admired by his female partner as he does so (Figure 16).

The male peacock appeared in advertising for several other tailors, with Deirdre McSharry commenting in the *Daily Express* that 'boys seem to be better looking . . . snappier dressed . . . no longer bashful about buying new clothes or embarrassed at being stared at—they actually like it'.[9] Some multiples, however, also traded on the idea that a well-dressed man at any age would be capable of attracting the attention of young women. 'Judge a Young Man's Measure', for example, a press campaign for Hepworth's Hardy Amies suits, included a small photograph of a teenage girl looking up in admiration at the man in the advertisement (*Weekend*, 5–11 May 1965); Austin Reed promoted its Gannex town coat in the *Sunday Times Magazine* (14 November 1965) with a photograph of a smartly attired older man turning the head of a young woman as she crosses the road, arm in arm, with her partner (who is truncated by the picture's edge), that is captioned, 'An Englishman expects a coat to do more than keep him warm.' And, as we have already seen in Part 1, the campaign 'You can't beat Burton tailoring!', conceived by W. S. Crawford and running between 1954 and 1962, also represented different types of men receiving the admiring looks of the women in the advertisements (Figure 7).

Burton's was the biggest menswear chain in the United Kingdom throughout the 1960s and 1970s, with one in five men claiming to own one of its suits.[10] Along with John Collier, it was also one of the first multiple tailors to embark on

for your 'Terylene'/wool suit

Record-breaker! This 'Terylene'/wool suit is good to look at, but
needs little looking after. Trouser creases stay put . . . . . others
drop out. Tweeds or plain weaves—you'll find by far the widest choice
at John Collier. Made-to-measure from only £10.10.0.

* For EXTRA warmth, have a MILIUM insulated lining

Figure 16   John Collier Terylene/wool suit,
'The Window to Watch', black and white
advertisement, *Daily Mirror*, 17 October 1958.
Private collection.

television advertising in 1955.[11] By the early 1960s, Burton's was spending more
on advertising than its competitors in the market; in the last quarter of 1963,
for instance, the firm spent £216,000 on press and television publicity, while
Austin Reed and Simpson spent £23,257 and £25,738 respectively on press
advertising.[12] And between August 1996 and August 1997, Burton's was still the
top menswear chain in regard to advertising, spending £1,678,544 compared
to Austin Reed's £581,437.[13] In contrast to such market competitors, however,
publicity for Burton's tended for the most part to be less creative or challenging.
The 'You can't beat Burton tailoring!' campaign may have broken new ground by

putting clothing into situational contexts and representing men in the company of women but, in connoting the idea of masculine pleasure, the copy nevertheless did little to dispel the patriarchal ideal of the active, professional male and the passive female consumer or housewife. Thus, in 'In any design for living', one of the advertisements in Burton's spring 1959 campaign, an architect and his female partner are represented in conversation. In the photograph he is standing up and looking at his design, compass in one hand, the other on his hip, and she is sitting on his desk and smiling admiringly at him, while the prosodic copy states: 'Now, my lord and master-planner . . . if that's my kitchen I'd like a cupboard put in right *there*. Woman, it shall be done, he answers (let him try and get out of it!).'

Furthermore, after Crawford's ceded the Burton account to Hobson, Bates and Partners in 1962, publicity for the company reverted once more to representing the male consumer self-reflexively as his own agent. Hence, a promotion in the *Daily Express* in January 1962 made a deictic appeal to the male consumer with the core message, 'This is your suit, a one-man suit, cut for you, tailored for you. This suit will fit no other man.' The ad-hominem address of such self-reflexive advertising rhetoric was compounded in both press and television campaigns for Burton's until 1970, but Hobson and Bates also made the occasional knowing nod toward the professional and, by extension, class mimicry that Burton's clothing purported to facilitate. Thus a full-page colour advertisement in the *Sunday Times Magazine* (1 June 1969), represented a chauffeur holding open the door of a limousine for a middle-aged businessman wearing a pinstriped suit, while the tag line proclaimed the aspiration, 'You don't have to be a director to wear a Burton Director Suit. You just look like one.' The copy beneath elaborated the point that, although the Burton Director Suit came ready-to-wear for only 22 guineas,[14] it differed from other off-the-peg garments because it was cut by hand and assembled piece by piece: 'The result is it looks, feels and behaves like a costly bespoke suit.' That is to say, not only would the suit pass hegemonic muster in the eyes of the world but so too would the man who wore it, whether he was actually a company director or not. The rhetorical claims that the advertisement made concerning the transformational power of Burton's so-called bespoke tailoring were, however, mythological and, as Frank Mort reminds us, 'There was no direct personal contact between tailor and customer, no hand-finishing, nor was a Burton's suit truly made-to-measure.'[15] Similarly, the self-reflexive personification of the single-minded male consumer in Burton's publicity after 1962 ran counter to the firm's own market research. A 1964 survey of 12,000 women, for example, found that although 50 per cent of Burton's customers bought on average two or three new suits every year, 63 per cent said their male partners always sought their advice when buying one.[16]

That Burton's was struggling to find a consistent brand identity after 1962 or at any rate, one that worked both for it and the public, is manifest in the way the company continued to change advertising agents and, as a corollary, the tack of its publicity. By autumn 1972 it had transferred its £300,000 account to Masius, Wynne, Williams, at that time the second biggest advertising agency in the United Kingdom and the third that Burton's had employed in the space of 10 years.[17] For a while, the association met with some critical success and in spring 1973 was praised for the 'Experience' cinema campaign for the 'Mr Burt' boutique in which scenes of a young man playing a pinball machine were intercut with others of female models zipping and unzipping men's jackets.[18] And yet, by winter 1973, John Edwards, the new publicity director of Burton's, had decided once more to change the company's brand image, and to this end he moved the account (now worth £450,000) to McCormick Richards.[19] This agency was responsible for two initiatives, both of which relied on celebrity endorsement in an attempt to broaden the company's market appeal: a 45-second television campaign launched in autumn 1977 and directed by Terry Bedford, 'Burton on the button for clothes', that starred actor Patrick Mower; and another featuring corpulent comedian Les Dawson, 'The man who could not find a suit to fit until Burton's took up the challenge and made him one', that was screened in the Granada region in 1980.[20] Neither campaign was well received by the critics, however, and Terry King-Smith wrote of the former that the display of different types of clothing for different seasons and occasions was 'too frantic . . . I found myself instinctively turning away from its dazzling pictorial extravagance.'[21] The inconsistency in its approach to publicity and the mixed reviews it received help explain why Burton's took a respite from advertising for a number of years. In 1978 press advertising was dropped until autumn 1985, when 'Dress at Burton, Undress in Bermuda', a £90,000 campaign featuring a male nude viewed from behind, appeared in the *Daily Mirror* and *Daily Express*.[22] And between 1980 and autumn 1984 the company dropped television publicity entirely until 'You get bags more buzz at Burton', art directed by Roddy Kerr for the agency Chuter Morgenthau and focussing on Jim, whose grey life and wardrobe are transformed by Burton's, was screened on the Yorkshire, Midlands, Granada and Tyne Tees networks.[23]

Notes

1   'Plea for the Peacock Look', *Men's Wear* (25 May 1963), 9.
2   Austin Reed advertising appeared between 1963 and 1977 in the *Sunday Times Magazine* as follows: (1963) 15 March; (1964) 5 April, 3 May, 24 May, 20 September, 27 September, 6 December; (1965) 21 March, 4 April, 11 April, 16 April, 9 May, 30 May, 6 June, 12 September, 17 October, 14 November, 12 December; (1966) 6 March, 20 March, 3 April, 17 April, 24 April, 8 May, 15 May, 2 October, 30 October, 13 November; (1967) 10 September, 17 September, 1 October, 15 October; (1968) 24 March, 21 April, 19 May, 15 September, 22 September, 13 October, 20 October, 17 November; (1969) 16 March, 30 March, 20 April, 14 September, 28 September,

5 October, 26 October, 9 November, 12 November, 16 November; (1970)
1 March, 15 March, 22 March, 5 April, 12 April, 26 April, 10 May, 6 September,
13 September, 20 September, 27 September, 11 October, 18 October, 25 October,
1 November, 8 November; (1971) 14 March, 28 March, 11 April, 25 April, 9 May,
10 May, 23 May, 26 September, 24 October, 7 November, 14 November; (1972)
9 April, 23 April, 7 May, 21 May, 11 June, 17 September, 24 September, 1 October,
15 October, 22 October, 29 October, 12 November; (1973) 18 March, 1 April,
15 April, 29 April, 20 May, 9 September, 23 September, 7 October, 21 October,
4 November; (1976) 18 April, 25 April, 9 May, 23 May, 6 September, 17 October,
31 October; (1977) 10 April, 1 May and 22 May.

A representative sample of publicity for these tailors and retailers between 1963 and 1977 can be found as follows: John Collier (*Daily Mirror*: (1963) 2 March; *Daily Express*: (1963) 1 May; (1964) 4 April, 3 October; (1965) 1 May, 27 November; and (1968) 3 May); Burton's (*Daily Express*: (1963) 2 May, 24 May; (1964) 3 April, 2 October; (1965) 7 May and 27 November; *Sunday Times Magazine*: (1966) 30 October; (1967) 5 March; (1969) 16 March, 1 June; (1971) 23 May and 26 September); Simpson and Daks Simpson (*Sunday Times Magazine*: (1963) 5 May; (1965) 2 May; (1966) 22 May; (1967) 30 April, 15 October; (1969) 30 March, 1 June; (1970) 5 April, 20 September; (1971) 5 September; (1972) 12 March, 14 May, 17 September; (1973) 11 March, 9 September; (1974) 10 March, 6 October; (1975) 2 March, 28 September; (1976) 7 March, 10 October; (1977) 13 March and 2 October; *Daily Express*: (1964) 14 April; (1965) 19 May; and (1968) 14 May); Hepworth's (*Daily Express*: (1964) 11 April; (1965) 1 May, 26 November; (1968) 3 May; and (1972) 6 May; *Daily Mirror*: (1964) 2 October and (1970) 5 March; *Sunday Times Magazine*: (1966) 17 April, 6 November; (1967) 12 March, 29 October; (1968) 10 March, 29 September and (1969) 26 October); Hector Powe (*Sunday Times Magazine*: (1964) 20 September; (1965) 7 March, 12 September; (1966) 6 March, 25 September; (1967) 5 April; (1969) 20 April; (1970) 5 April, 20 September; (1971) 9 May, 26 September; (1972) 2 April, 17 September; (1973) 15 April, 7 October; (1975) 13 April, 19 October; (1976) 28 March and 3 October); and Hornes (*Sunday Times Magazine*: (1967) 7 May; (1971) 24 October; (1972) 9 April; (1974) 17 November; and (1977) 15 May).

3 *Advertiser's Weekly* (20 December 1968), 17. The 2000 equivalent was £2,768,111.

4 J. Koski, 'Menswear Market Faces a Big Strategy Shake-up', *Campaign* (5 May 1978), 20.

5 *Men's Wear* (18 February 1967), 9. The respective 2000 equivalents were £1,618,147 and £388,355.

6 'Current Advertising', *Advertiser's Weekly* (27 January 1967), 40; *Ad Weekly* (21 January 1972), 19.

7 The 2000 equivalent was £171.

8 'Current Advertising', *Advertiser's Weekly* (10 March 1967), 53.

9 Deirdre McSharry, 'The Young Peacock Cult', *Daily Express* (3 April 1965), 14.

10 *Adweek* (9 November 1973), 4.

11 'Current Advertising', *Advertiser's Weekly* (2 April 1958): 48.

12 'Zip Goes a Million on Menswear Ads', *Men's Wear* (28 March 1964), 9. The respective 2000 equivalents were £2,685,500, £289,151 and £319,997.

13   'Fashion Report—Who Spends What and Where', *Campaign* (19 September 1997), 6.

14   The 2000 equivalent was £226.

15   Frank Mort, 'The Commercial Domain: Advertising and the Cultural Management of Demand', in B. Conekin, F. Mort and C. Waters (eds), *Moments of Modernity: Reconstructing Britain 1945–1964* (New York: Rivers Oram, 1999), 60.

16   'Woman's Influence: Burton's Plot It', *Men's Wear* (9 January 1965), 7.

17   *Ad Weekly* (6 October 1972), 1. The 2000 equivalent was £2,351,672.

18   J. King, 'This Burton Experience Is Quite Something', *Adweek* (23 March 1973), 16.

19   *Adweek* (9 November 1973), 4. The 2000 equivalent was £3,229,875.

20   *Campaign* (13 October 1978), 7; *Campaign* (14 March 1980), 7.

21   *Campaign* (7 October 1977), 30.

22   *Campaign* (27 September 1985), 2. The 2000 equivalent was £161,994.

23   *Campaign* (30 September 1983), 84.

16

FROM DUMMIES
TO DANDIES

The most withering—and thinly veiled—contumely was reserved for those advertisements that still persisted in using the much derided 'tailor's dummy', the male figure who is depicted wearing clothing in a static pose and, like a cardboard cut-out, devoid of any situational context. Thus, reviewing the campaign for Hector Powe produced by the agency Davis and Page that appeared in the *Sunday Times Magazine*, *Observer Magazine* and *Daily Telegraph Magazine* in spring 1970, the critic M. Daniels unapologetically expressed the patronizing view that 'this advertisement makes the same hilarious error as tailors like Burton; depicting male models who look or pose like spastics'.[1] Hector Powe was one of the oldest bespoke outfitters, opening its first store in 1910 in the City of London and by 1925 owning six shops in the vicinity and one in Westminster. After some initial resistance, the chain embarked on a successful advertising campaign in the London dailies, the *Evening Standard* and *Evening News*, which ran for some 10 years from 1923.[2] From the outset, the 'Pow Wows', a series of advertisements with cartoons by Aubrey Hammond formed a humorous narrative interface between the chain and its clientele, without adopting a superior tone or using copy that would bemuse or confuse the reader: 'I cannot believe that my potential customer is either a dude or professor of psychology.'[3] Indeed, a poster design by Grainger Johnson that appeared on the London Underground in 1923 was singled out for praise by the *Advertiser's Weekly* correspondent, 'Pelican', who opined, 'Here is a real live, clean open-air man.'[4] To be sure, even after the company was acquired by Hope Brothers in April 1954, Powe's maintained a respectable advertising budget throughout the 1960s and 1970s, spending £100,000 on its spring 1971 campaign alone and pioneering radio advertisements on the London Broadcasting Company (LBC) between October and December 1973.[5] And, while its agency Haddons continued to emphasize the practical benefits and quality of materials and manufacture of Hector Powe clothing (referring in one ad to what Powe himself had called in 1932, 'A confident combination of craftsmanship and cut'), and still represented garments worn in a straightforward formal manner, the male models who appeared in their press publicity could scarcely be described in Daniels' condescending terms as 'spastics'.

No such criticism was meted out to Powe's nearest competitor in the middle-class market, Austin Reed. In 1966, C. Forbes lamented in *Advertiser's Weekly* that compared with its 'Men About Regent Street' campaign of the interwar period, in recent publicity, 'the visual situations . . . tend to lack bite'.[6] He also impugned the psychedelic effects in a promotion designed by Alan Aldridge for its in-store boutique, Cue Man (Figure 17), which opened at Regent Street in September 1965 with Colin Woodhead, who had worked on *Man About Town*, at the helm.[7] But apart from such quibbles, advertising for Austin Reed was

Figure 17 Austin Reed, Introducing Cue Man, full-page colour advertisement, designed by Alan Aldridge, 1965. Permission of Austin Reed.

generally singled out as having the creative edge over other menswear retailers. In December 1960, for example, the firm's agents, Clifford Bloxham, rented an illuminated advertising site at the top of the escalator at the Piccadilly Circus Underground station, which was the nearest stop to its flagship Regent Street store, estimating that 28 million people would see it in the course of a year.[8] Like Burton's, Austin Reed was also prone to changing advertising agents on a regular basis in the 1960s and 1970s, though, unlike Hector Powe, rarely— if ever—did it resort to the 'tailor's dummy'. Indeed, the copy of some of its publicity sought to reassure men that they would never leave an Austin Reed store looking 'a fright', even though they did not need the probing eye or helping hand of a female partner to purchase a well-fitting suit, as in 'Has your wife a place in your suit-buying life?' (*Sunday Times Magazine*, 19 May 1968).

Andrew Slater, previously an account executive at Erwin Masey, had joined Austin Reed as advertising manager in 1961, and in 1962 the company's advertising account returned to Pritchard Wood (at that time agents also for the multiple tailor Weaver and Wearer) after an eight-year tenure with Clifford Bloxham.[9] Pritchard Wood promoted Reed as 'the best shops for men across Britain' and, in common with its interwar and postwar publicity, carved out a distinctive and unified commercial identity for the company through the continued use of Bodoni type for copy and the equation of style and taste with the stereotypical image of the English gentleman. Whether he appeared in publicity for the exclusive Albany Club suit, which in 1964 retailed for 40 guineas,[10] or for weekend separates, the gentleman was objectified as the genuine article and no suggestion was made that he was passing as anyone else (as Burton's publicity for its director suit had done). Thus the copy for the former ad tells us that the Albany 'is the suit for the connoisseur, the man at the top' and depicts a middle-aged male enjoying a cigar in a gentleman's club (*Sunday Times Magazine*, 15 March 1964); the copy for the latter ad puns the idea of 'country' being simultaneously a source of rural and national identity, proclaiming, 'We're aware that Englishmen take pride in looking handsomely casual . . . The country expects it of us,' and portrays a gentleman and his pedigree bull in the grounds of a country house (Figure 18).

In personifying the gentleman as quintessentially English, the rhetoric of such publicity for Austin Reed evinces the idea expressed by Jules Barbey d'Aurevilly in 1844 that it was 'the force of English originality, imprinting itself on human vanity' and, in particular, the elegant understated dress of George Brummell that had resulted in the evolution of dandyism.[11] Moreover, represented equally at home in town or country, Austin Reed's fashionable gent both trades on the way that Brummell's so-called 'new look' was in effect a pared-down version of the country garb or riding dress of the English aristocracy and reminds us how the dandy lifestyle coincided with the rise of the landed gentry in the late eighteenth and early nineteenth centuries. In a similar vein, it is interesting to

Figure 18 'Englishmen know they're right with Austin Reed', full-page colour advertisement, *Sunday Times Magazine*, 11 April 1965. Permission of Austin Reed.

observe that in 1973 Burberrys epitomized the class origins of the modern dandy more self-consciously in a series of six advertisements featuring Lord Patrick Lichfield, who was photographed in the grounds of Shugborough, his ancestral country estate in Staffordshire, clad in various garments with Burberry's signature check.[12]

At the same time, several promotions for Austin Reed menswear in the early 1960s resorted to more youthful dandy stereotypes. In spring 1962, for instance, the 'Man's Shop' colour press campaign was launched, with one advertisement in *Town* that depicted a debonair young man buying flowers from a London street vendor as his girlfriend beckons to him from a taxi; it promoted the new Austin Reed fashion concept of 'Twin-Tones', that is, 'the jacket and trousers that don't *quite* match', and which could be worn as leisurewear separates or together to 'create a casual suit-like effect' (Figure 19). Coterminously, the 'Man's Page' campaign was featured in the *Daily Telegraph* (7 May 1963) and *Daily Express* (9 May 1963). The grid layout of these advertisements mimicked the actual fashion features that appeared in such newspapers and

Figure 19 Austin Reed Man's Shop, full-page colour advertisement, *Town*, May 1962. Permission of Austin Reed.

Figure 20 Austin Reed Man's Page, full-page black and white advertisement, *Daily Express*, 9 May 1963. Permission of Austin Reed.

also in magazines such as *Town*, and the sloganized copy, therefore, makes intertextual references to the kind of editorial we would expect to encounter in them. Hence, one advertisement enunciates the phrase 'Blue After Six' to denote the right time to wear a midweight navy suit and defines the new rounded tab collar Summit shirt as the 'Neatest Way to Hold a Collar' (Figure 20). This is the style of performative fashion rhetoric that Roland Barthes called 'written clothing' and that he argued is 'elaborated each year . . . by an exclusive authority', such as the magazine editor or copywriter, in order to dictate to the reader what must be worn and thereby to 'naturalise' the cut or colour of any given garment

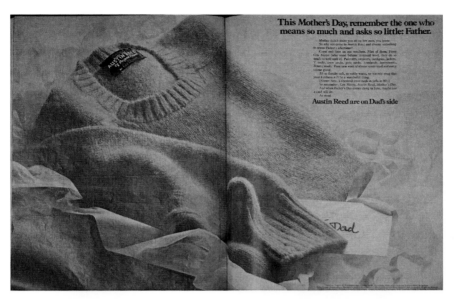

Figure 21 Austin Reed lambswool sweater, double-page colour advertisement, *Sunday Times Magazine*, 16 March 1969. Permission of Austin Reed.

as fashionable.[13] Both the 'Man's Page' and 'Man's Shop' campaigns also broke with the typographic norm in Austin Reed publicity by incorporating a Franklin Gothic sanserif face for some of their straplines alongside Bodoni, used for the copy. But, as Harold Butler had found in sampling one issue of each of the national dailies in October–November 1963, the use of sanserif in display advertising had actually dropped from a high of 87 per cent in 1960 to just over 66 per cent.[14]

From July 1967 until July 1975, Davidson, Pearce, Berry & Spottiswoode (DPBS) took over Reed's advertising account, and it is under DPBS's stewardship that the company's publicity once more hit a winning streak through its lavish use of colour photography. Austin Reed had already won first prize for a colour advertisement in the Layton Awards in 1962 and had ceased using black-and-white photographs in its press campaigns in 1964, but Tony Rule, the advertising manager of DPBS, reinforced the point that colour 'is essential for us because of the 'total look' which we are trying to get across'.[15] Jim Lee was the chief photographer for Austin Reed advertising at the time, and the saturated, sensuous palette of his picture of a crew-neck wool pullover in orange (Figure 21) was singled out for praise by one critic, who commented, 'The photographer deserves all that he earned for that picture.'[16] DPBS also swapped Bodoni for the roman typeface Monotype Plantin to print both headings and copy across the entire spectrum of advertising for Austin Reed, from the £25 ready-to-wear suit to the 40-guinea hand-crafted Chester Barrie suit, and introduced a more democratic and humorous approach to portray the male purchaser as an individual: 'Because having the same body as ten thousand other men is all the more reason for kitting it out differently'.[17] In particular, critics were approving of the way that the male models behaved in such a lifelike fashion in Austin Reed's publicity. Thus T. Johnstone-Cristall spoke of the 'confident authority' and realism that imbued Lee's photographs for the spring campaign in 1972, where the wrinkled sleeves and creased chest signified 'a suit that is going to look good under the stress and strain a living man gives his suits', while Vassie called the 'Wear your jeans to the office' advertisement in spring 1973 a masterpiece of its kind, contrasting it with what he saw as the wooden formality of Hector Powe's advertising (Figure 22).[18]

Figure 22 Austin Reed, 'Wear Your Jeans to the Office', full-page colour advertisement, *Sunday Times Magazine*, 29 April 1973. Permission of Austin Reed.

Notes

1   M. Daniels, 'Chasing the "Brand Vulnerable" Motorists', *Ad Weekly* (10 April 1970), 41.

2   Paul Jobling, *Man Appeal: Advertising, Modernism and Menswear* (Oxford: Berg, 2005), 79.

3   H. Powe, 'What is Advertising? Science or Sympathy?', *Commercial Art* (January–June 1929), 203.

4   Pelican, 'The Month on the Hoardings', *Advertiser's Weekly* (5 October 1923), 25.

5   *Ad Weekly* (30 April 1971), 10; *Men's Wear* (27 September 1973), 14. The 2000 equivalent was £839,781.

6   C. Forbes, 'Advertising Review', *Advertiser's Weekly* (30 September 1966), 35.

7   C. Forbes, 'So Similar It Hertz!', *Advertiser's Weekly* (6 May 1966), 34.

8   *Men's Wear* (3 December 1960), 21.

9   *Advertiser's Weekly* (14 January 1961), 3.

10 The 2000 equivalent was £505.

11 Jules Barbey D'Aurevilly, *Of Dandyism and of George Brummell* [1844], trans. D. Ainslie (New York: PAJ Publications, 1988), 25–6.

12 The six advertisements appeared in the *Sunday Times Magazine* in 1973 on 25 March; 1 and 8 April; and 16, 23 and 30 September. In 1960, the National Trust took over stewardship of Shugborough.

13 Roland Barthes, *The Fashion System* [1967], trans. M. Ward and R. Howard (Berkeley: University of California, 1990), 215 and 49.

14 W. Harold Butler, 'The Types We Use', *Advertiser's Weekly* (7 February 1964), 26.

15 *Men's Wear* (24 November 1962),10; *Men's Wear* (12 August 1971), 5.

16 'The Scanner', 'Triple Suit Attack by Colliers', *Men's Wear* (10 April 1969), 41.

17 This was the caption to a double-page ad in the *Sunday Times Magazine*, 30 April 1969.

18 T. Johnstone-Cristall, 'A Matter of Models', *Ad Weekly* (5 May 1972), 33; M. Vassie, 'Where the Outsider Scores', *Adweek* (1 June 1973), 18.

17

IRONING OUT
THE CREASES

ARTIFICIAL FIBRES AND
MENSWEAR ADVERTISING

By extension, many advertisements for suits, along with those for shirts, trousers and underwear, either underscored the benefits of wool or cotton or demonstrated the impact that synthetic materials had made on the manufacture of menswear. As we shall see below, however, with the exception of a campaign for Terylene in 1966 and another for Dormeuil woollen fabrics in 1973 and 1974, the symbolism mobilized in publicity sponsored by organizations such as the International Wool Secretariat (IWS) and the British Rayon and Synthetic Fibres Federation (BRSFF) did not always stand in marked contrast to each other.

Synthetic fabrics, namely nylons, polyesters and acrylics, had originated in the United States and Britain, contributing to the mass production and expendability of fashion garments from the 1950s onwards.[1] As such they compensated for the lack of natural materials in the post-war period but their popularity also coalesced with the affluence of youth culture so that, as Susannah Handley argues, 'the real fashion potential of the new synthetics was unleashed during the 1960s.'[2] By 1969, Du Pont of Wilmington, Delaware, had invented thirty-one polyesters and seventy nylons, and it is hardly surprising, therefore, to find that the discourse of much menswear advertising after 1960 was concerned with promoting the actual and symbolic benefits of synthetics in regard to both their production and consumption.

It was Du Pont that was responsible for introducing nylon, the world's first totally synthetic fibre, in 1938. Invented by Dr Charles Stine, chemical director at the company, nylon was a polymer made from coal tar derivatives, water and air, which revolutionized the manufacture of clothing after the Second World War because of its versatility. As Stine describes it, 'Nylon can be fashioned into filaments as strong as steel, as fine as the spider's web, yet more elastic than any of the common fibres and possessing a beautiful chemical luster.'[3] Since nylon is a generic term for such polyamides, rather than a brand name, Du Pont began to licence its manufacturer to other companies. Thus in the United States the Chemstrand Corporation was granted a licence in 1951 and went on to produce Blue C-Nylon, which made colours more brilliant, in the early 1960s; in 1958 Bri Nylon was introduced in the United Kingdom by British Nylon Spinners, a company jointly formed by Courtaulds and ICI in 1940; and in the early 1960s BanLon was manufactured by Bancroft. Du Pont had similarly been first to experiment in the development of polyester, but it was two British chemists, John Rex Whinfield and J. T. Dickson, who concocted the first polyester filament in 1941 for the Calico Printers Association, Accrington, Lancashire. ICI in Teesside, England, eventually gained the world rights for the manufacture of polyester, announcing its new brand, Terylene, in the *Manchester Guardian* on 5 October 1946. Polyester also came to be associated with other brand names — Dacron (made by Du Pont), Crimplene (by ICI) and Trevira (by Hoechst) — and was the most important of the man-made fibres for garment production owing to its crease- and sag-resistant properties.[4] Terylene and Dacron came in two forms: as a staple fibre for suits, coats and woollens, or as filament yarn for underwear. The third group of synthetics were acrylic wool substitutes and, again, were usually known by their brand names; for example, Courtelle, Acrilan, and Tricel. Orlon (or 'Fiber A'), was the first of them, pioneered by Du Pont in 1949, and its singular qualities were that it imitated all the lightness and durability of wool, while its resistance to acid initially made it the perfect material for work clothes and uniforms. Like wool, therefore, acrylics could be fluffy or fitted but, unlike wool, they were easy to wash and dry. Moreover, in regard to its ease of care and resistance to moths and perspiration, acrylic was an ideal fibre for the manufacture of sports- and leisurewear, suits and shirts.

In 1953 the BRSFF was formed to promote man-made fibres as acceptable and attractive substitutes for natural textiles, and writing in *Queen* in 1954, Madge Garland, then Professor of Fashion at Royal College of Art, stated in their support: 'The word synthetic is apt to suggest something rather cold and chemical, let me quickly say that one of the joys of "Terylene" is its warm, friendly, "natural" feel.'[5] This was also the challenge that manufacturers and retailers of garments made from synthetic fabrics had to meet in their publicity. The BRSFF would sometimes promote respective synthetics in independent campaigns, as with the distinctive 'Terylene' publicity of 1954–56 by Zéró discussed in Part 1; the 'Terylene talks trousers' advertisements, which appeared in the *Daily Express* and *Daily Mail* in May 1955; and the series of full-page advertisements of 1965–66, comprising colour photographs and telegrammatic copy set in sanserif Futura Display, which put clothing into the context of a bungled romantic escapade (Figures 23 and 24). But a common tactic in the 1960s and 1970s was for the BRSFF to sponsor the publicity of particular menswear brands and outlets and thereby strike up a viable

'TERYLENE': MAINSTREAM OF FASHION

Ordered Janet to make fast. Gave short talk on knots, etc; prepared go ashore, conscious had put up pretty impressive display navigational competence. Had several seconds to contemplate fate as craft swung slowly into midstream. One good thing: wearing 'Terylene' trousers. Would keep knife-edge creases even submerged. Janet sure to notice this when she fished me out. If she bothered.

STRETCH TROUSERS WITH H.C.F. (FOR HIGH COMFORT FACTOR) IN 55% 'TERYLENE' 45% WOOL WORSTED.

Figure 23 ' "Terylene": Mainstream of Fashion', full-page colour advertisement, *Men in Vogue*, 15 March 1966. Permission of Dupont (UK) Ltd.

association with them. In this way the cost of producing and circulating advertising campaigns would be shared and the resulting publicity would work to the mutual benefit of those concerned. Thus Bri Nylon was promoted in advertising for the likes of Fred Perry, Peter England shirts, and Austin Reed; Chemstrand C Nylon in that for Sabre, Mekay shirts, and Kilspindie and Morley knitwear; Terylene in that for Guards and Evvaprest trousers, and Van Heusen and Rocola shirts; Dacron in that for Dhobi raincoats and Rael Brook shirts; Trevira in advertising for several suit labels; Orlon in that for beachwear by Byford; Acrilan in that for coats by Baracuta, Burberry and Hornes and McCaul sweaters; and Courtelle in that for Hepworths. Finally, Vincel 64, a viscose modal fibre developed by Courtaulds in 1972, which had good absorbency and could be woven with cotton in the

'TERYLENE': KNIFE-EDGES ON LEDGES!

Carelessly left front door key in other trousers. Only one way in—
through window. Worked way along ledge, regretted taking 27th
floor apartment. Two strokes of luck—girl sunbathing on roof gave
a hand, prevented nasty fall; and wearing trousers in 'Terylene', so
didn't get frayed, kept knife-edge creases.

TROUSERS IN 30% 'TERYLENE'/65% WOOL, WORSTED.

Figure 24 ' "Terylene": Knife-edges on ledges!', full-page colour advertisement, *Sunday Times Magazine*, 13 April 1966. Permission of Du Pont (UK) Ltd.

production of knitted underwear, appeared in publicity for Lyle and Scott y-fronts (Figures 1, 12 and 25).[6]

The rhetoric of such advertising also represented the wearing of synthetics on different levels. Although there were numerous examples of advertisements since 1945 that referred to the utilitarian aspects of clothing across the spectrum of menswear, many more campaigns for man-made fabrics emphasized the practical and critical valorizations of the product(s) in question. In 1965, for instance, publicity for garments made from Chemstrand C Nylon was orchestrated around the theme of 'Actionwear', which underscored the point that no matter what the activity (from trampolining to judo), or how many times it was worn, the clothing would always retain its original shape. Similarly, the copy of advertisements for

Figure 25 'Take a Man Like You in Bri Nylon', half-page black-and-white advertisement, *Daily Mirror*, 4 March 1963. Private collection.

Guards Lean Line 70 trousers that incorporated Terylene with wool gave a thorough run-down of their practical qualities, including the permanent knife-edge creases and possibility for machine washing. In spite of the economic downturn and devaluation of sterling in 1967, the trouser market had remained buoyant and sales had increased from 29.2 million units in 1966 to 31.7 million.[7]

ICI attributed a significant part of the increase in trouser sales to Terylene blends and, to satisfy market demand for wash-and-wear clothing, had also introduced the Durable Press method in spring 1967. The new process took advantage of the thermoplastic properties of Terylene to bond a permanent crease in the garment, either by using a hot head press in the case of Terylene-wool blends, or by applying a resin treatment such as Koratron to Terylene-cotton mixes and oven curing the fabric at a high temperature.

The copy in publicity for Mekay and Rocola shirts took things a stage further, dealing with the practical valorizations of synthetic fibres but allying them to their critical valorizations by homing in on specific details concerning the manufacture of garments in order to emphasize quality and benefits. Hence, an advertisement for Mekay in the *Sunday Times Magazine* (6 April 1969) featured a close-up photograph of its 57s. 6d.[8] white shirt in C-Nylon Monsanto material overlaid with copy that explained how the collar was constructed as one piece to enhance comfort, the stitching varied according to the weight of the fabric, the cuffs' laminated interlining prevented them from corrugating, and the C-Nylon fabric drip dried and guaranteed 'one full year's normal wear'. More thorough still was the Rocola advertising by Garratt Baulcombe Associates Ltd, art directed by Peter Rose and with copy by Alan Field. 'When we make a shirt. We make a shirt' (*Sunday Times Magazine* 7 May 1967), for example, afforded the reader a critical object lesson in shirt construction with copy that pinpointed everything from the quality of the Terylene fabric to the precise cut of the yoke, the line or slope of the neckband, and the perfect rake across the shoulders. This message is echoed in a series of 1970s advertisements that introduce us to the people who worked behind the scenes to ensure the quality of Rocola shirts. Mary Mitchell, responsible for refining the original prototype for every model that was put into mass production, is the subject of one such ad in the *Sunday Times Magazine* on 19 May 1974. Hence, the advertisement goes against the ludic grain of most advertising insofar as it gives the reader some notion that the shirt is created by human agency rather than appearing ready-made, as if by magic. However, rather than representing Mary Mitchell on the shop floor or giving any realistic indication of her working conditions or earnings, the copy expresses the idea of work as a labour of love, with Mary portrayed as the craftsperson whose expertise is co-opted in order to celebrate a Rocola shirt as superior to other (anonymous) brands: 'Nobody carries out as many inspections as we do.' Even though it cost more or less the same as other mainstream shirts, then, the rhetoric of such Rocola publicity reinforces what Barthes calls the 'total message' of advertising connotation whose final aim, he argued, is to render 'the excellence of the product announced' by suggesting it will have a special place in or transform our lives.[9]

Notes

1 See Amy Sargeant, 'The Man in the White Suit: New Textiles and the Social Fabric', *Visual Culture in Britain* (Summer 2008), 27–54, for an illuminating assessment of the film *The Man in the White Suit* (1951) and its relationship to the textile manufacturer, Courtaulds.

2 Susannah Handley, *Nylon: The Story of a Fashion Revolution* (Baltimore: John Hopkins University Press, 1999), 9. I am indebted to Handley for the factual data concerning synthetic materials included in this chapter.

3 Quoted in Sargeant, 'The Man in the White Suit', 46.

4 Hector Powe even coined the term 'Powelene' to describe its own exclusive blend of Terylene and worsted. See the advertisement, 'Hector Powe sees you're right in fashion', *Sunday Times Magazine* (5 April 1970), 57.

5 Quoted in Handley, *Nylon*, 73.

6 For examples of advertising for such brands involving man-made fibres see the *Sunday Times Magazine* as follows: Austin Reed (10 March 1963); Peter England (13 November 1966); Fred Perry (9 April 1967); Sabre (11 May 1965); Mekay (23 March 1969); Kilspindie (10 April 1966); Morley (9 May 1965); Guards (27 March 1966); Evvaprest (27 May 1973); Van Heusen (27 November 1966); Rocola (9 March 1969); Dhobi (23 March 1967); Rael Brook (21 November 1971); Trevira (9 March 1969); Baracuta (10 November 1965); Burberry (16 March 1969); McCaul (1 March 1964); Hornes (21 March 1965); Hepworth (17 April 1966); and Y-front (30 April 1972).

7 Erica Crome, 'Durable Press Trousers', *Men's Wear* (4 April 1968), viii.

8 The 2000 equivalent was £49.52.

9 Roland Barthes, 'The Advertising Message' [1964], in *The Semiotic Challenge*, trans. R. Howard (Berkeley: University of California Press, 1994), 174.

18

SYNTHESIZING SEX

PUBLICITY FOR ARTIFICIAL
AND NATURAL FIBRES

As Roland Barthes realized there are many different ways of connoting the idea of excellence, as well as convincing consumers of the practical and economic benefits of synthetics; therefore, 'fashion appeal had somehow to be grafted onto the new fabrics.'[1] Accordingly, publicity for man-made fabrics resorted to images of youth lifestyles to connote their ludic and utopian valorizations. The headline to a 1967 print promotion for a Fred Perry sports shirt in Bri Nylon, for instance, likened wearing it to the escapist fantasy of being an 'E-Type type *off* the road'. But, like in the majority of menswear advertising, the most common utopian symbolism across campaigns for different items of clothing composed from synthetic fibres was the idea that wearing them would make men more attractive to women. Not surprisingly, their verbal and visual rhetoric harped on the stereotypical assumption that 'in a world ordered by sexual imbalance, pleasure in looking has been split between active/male and passive/female'.[2] Hence, a 1965 advertisement 'Guards do something to a man!', portrays the woman as the adoring admirer of the man in her life, while an advertisement for a crease-resistant Dhobi raincoat in Dacron in 1967 included a photograph of a woman intimately hugging her partner and copy declaring: 'The girl's mad about that well-cared-for debonair look he always has. He thinks her rather dishy too—so that's one crush that has a sporting chance of lasting' (*Sunday Times Magazine*, 2 April 1967).

Occasionally the tables were turned and a handful of campaigns proffered a less predictable way of looking. A 1966 promotion for Terylene, 'Knife-Edges on Ledges!', tells the story of a man who, having left his door key in another pair of trousers, decides to scale a building to get back in his 27th-floor apartment.[3] The photograph, with short depth of field, represents him perching on a ledge and putting out his hand for help to a girl, who has been sunbathing on the roof (Figure 24). Her attention, however, is not at all with him, and as she gazes off scene at the reader of the advertisement instead, the outcome of the escapade is left in suspension: will she come to his aid or won't she? Equally iconoclastic was the photograph in 'Take a man like YOU' for Bri Nylon in 1963 insofar as it reverses the normative logic of the specular image that, according to Luce Irigaray, usually returns the female body to the male as an object of his own desire: 'a glass for the "subject" to gaze upon himself and re-produce himself in his reflection'.[4] Rather than simply 'doing so much for the man', as the copy implies, therefore, the photograph represents a woman gazing into her compact make-up mirror only to see the putative object of her own desire—a smiling man in a white shirt—captured in miniature for her to possess at will (Figure 25).

The sexual dynamics of visual pleasure were also much in evidence during the 1960s and 1970s in publicity for clothing made from natural fibres. At this time, the International Wool Secretariat (IWS; f. 1937) and the International Institute for Cotton (IIC; f. 1945) supported many cotton and wool manufacturers to respond to the challenge and expansion of synthetics, which tended to cost less, by underscoring the quality, authenticity and comfort of natural cloths, as in, 'Cotton. Something fresh', a promotion for a Double Two printed batiste shirt (*Sunday Times Magazine*, 11 April 1971), and 'You can't fake the real thing', an advertisement for a £32 pure new wool suit by Hector Powe that stated: 'Others may cost a little less . . . But when you're out for that big job. Or the boss is coming for dinner, you want to look and feel your best. You want the real thing' (*Sunday Times Magazine*, 5 March 1967).[5] Just as ICI and Du Pont had sponsored publicity for various brands of clothing, therefore, advertising for many garments in wool incorporated the pure new wool logo of the IWS, which had been designed by Francisco Saroglio in 1964, and those made from cotton the organic tree motif of the IIC (Figures 11 and 15).

An egregious ludic and utopian use of gender stereotypes was Dormeuil's 'Cloth for Men' advertising campaign for two of their fabrics: Sportex, a lightweight wool fabric devised in 1923 for use in the outdoor pursuits of golf, hunting and shooting; and Tonik, a three-ply mohair suiting fabric first manufactured in 1957. The firm initially set up business in Paris in 1842 and by the late nineteenth century had opened a mill in Huddersfield to supply fine woollen cloths to the bespoke tailoring trade, including Savile Row.[6] But the Tonik brand was popular also with the Teds and Mods, the latter having bespoke suits made from it by the tailor Aubrey Morris on London's Holloway Road. The 'Cloth for Men' publicity, produced by the advertising agency Michael Robinson Associates, started life in autumn 1968 and continued well into the 1980s; between 1968 and 1975 alone it would have cost in the region of £206,000 to buy the advertising space for the fifty-eight full-page displays that appeared in the *Sunday Times Magazine*.[7] Art directed by Peter Watson with colour photographs by Alec Murray, Franco Rubartelli, and Victor Skrebneski, the advertisements portray a catholic range of historical female characters—from Eve to Cleopatra—and professional women—from the barrister to the fashion model. For the most part, the male figures in the campaign conform to the trope of the powerful man-in-a-suit, which is mobilized in word and image to bolster a myth of dominant masculinity. Thus in 'Sportex Exotica' a female nude, masked by a giant fig leaf, looks longingly across to the man wearing a plaid suit while the copy puns clunkily, 'Sportex . . . Made for Adam and his *Ev*entualities' (*Sunday Times Magazine*, 29 September 1968); and in a 'Cool Male Case For Tonik', photographed by Alec Murray, a man is admired from left and right by female lawyers with copy stating chauvinistically, 'Tonik, that legendary Mohair; wickedly articulate: a case of inspired pleading that makes women long to settle out of Court' (*Sunday Times Magazine*, 16 March 1969).

Notes

1   Susannah Handley, *Nylon: The Story of a Fashion Revolution* (Baltimore: John Hopkins University Press, 1999), 72.

2   Laura Mulvey, *Visual and Other Pleasures* (Basingstoke: Macmillan, 1989), 19.

3   The building is the Shell Centre on the South Bank, London, which was designed by Sir Howard Robertson and built in 1961.

4   Luce Irigaray, 'The Speculum of the Other Woman', in M. Whitford (ed.), *The Irigaray Reader* (Oxford: Blackwell, 1991), 66.

5   The 2000 equivalent was £345.

6   In a recent interview, Frederick Dormeuil, the company director, stated, 'The strength of the brand is initially the suit' (K. Mirza, 'Dominic Dormeuil', *Draper's* (24 January 2009)). In the 1960s, Dormeuil had also piloted the production of ready-to-wear suits but it was not until 2008 that it entered the market in earnest, with two variations of suits for men aged 35 years and above.

7   J. Mallows, 'Do You Want the Power of Sunday Colour Behind You?', *Campaign* (2 July 1982). Advertisements in the 'Cloth for Men' campaign appeared in the *Sunday Times Magazine* between 1968 and 1975 as follows: (1968) 8 August, 15 September, 29 September, 13 October, 27 October, 10 November, 24 November; (1969) 16 February, 23 February, 16 March, 30 March, 13 April, 1 June, 15 June, 22 June, 29 June, 06 July; (1970) 13 September, 27 September, 18 October; (1971) 7 February, 21 February, 7 March, 21 March, 4 April, 18 April, 9 May, 23 May; (1972) 6 February, 20 February, 5 March, 26 March, 16 April, 23 April, 7 May, 18 June; (1973) 4 February, 18 February, 4 March, 8 April, 22 April, 29 April, 27 May; (1974) 3 February, 17 February, 3 March, 17 March, 7 April, 21 April, 19 May; (1975) 2 February, 16 February, 2 March, 16 March, 6 April, 20 April, 4 May and 18 May.

   The calculated total cost of the campaign between 1968 and 1975 is based on the figure of £3,000 supplied by Media Expenditure Analysis (MEAL) and the Advertising Association and cited by Mallows for placing a full-page display ad for clothing in the *Sunday Times Magazine*. The equivalent of £206,000 in 1970 was £2.03 million in 2000. Unfortunately, the audited accounts for Dormeuil (UK) Ltd for this period that are lodged with Companies House, Cardiff, do not itemize a separate advertising or publicity budget and so it has not been possible to ascertain what the potential production outlay for the 'Cloth for Men' advertising campaign might also have been.

19

'CLOTH FOR MEN'

WOOL AND THE WHISPER OF DARKER THINGS IN DORMEUIL'S TONIK PRESS CAMPAIGN, 1968–75

In 1973 and 1974, a quintet of more utopian and lavish advertisements for Dormeuil, with photographs by Murray, played with masquerade and cross-dressing such that the German model Veruschka von Lehndorff doubles up to perform both 'male' and 'female' parts. One of the characters she portrays is always a suit-wearing dandy, while the other is dressed in unequivocally feminine attire, suggesting a special form of transvestism that Marjorie Garber calls 'a space of possibility' insofar as it contests 'easy notions of binarity, putting into question the categories of "female" and "male", whether they are considered essential or constructed, biological or cultural'.[1] At the same time, all five advertisements can be seen to connote the ambiguity of what Jane Gaines calls the 'homosexual/heterosexual flip-flop', a phrase that she aptly coined to analyse Greta Garbo's performative cross-dressing in Rouben Mamoulian's 1933 film, *Queen Christina*, and it is interesting to note in this regard that Veruschka also bears a passing physiognomic resemblance to Garbo in the Dormeuil campaign.[2] In only one of the advertisements, however—an eclectic postmodern pastiche that combines art deco in the style of dress and use of the Intertype Vogue font with a monochrome op art background—does the copy not just out the person in the white suit as a woman but also portrays her as taking charge: 'She started the revolution and today's male continues it' (Figure 26). Thus the 'she' that the text refers to in this historicist context is on one level the prototype of the 1920s garçonne personified by Coco Chanel, who first wore a suit in 1910 to a society event and whose pared-down, boyish fashion silhouette was the antithesis to the bourgeois 'Women in brocade', whom she derided for looking like 'old armchairs when they sit down'.[3] Chanel's earliest designs included loose-fitting, jersey-knit 'beach pyjamas' and sailor suits, which she sold in Deauville, and it is this style that influenced Yves Saint Laurent when he designed his androgynous 'Le

Figure 26 Dormeuil Tonik, full-page colour advertisement, *Sunday Times Magazine*, 13 February 1974. Permission of Dormeuil SAS, France.

Smoking' women's suit collection in 1966 and that furnishes the second, more contemporaneous revolutionary female in the advertisement.

If the criss-crossing of gender in the 'art deco' promotion ostensibly suggests the fantasy of a lesbian relationship between the woman in the suit on the right and the woman on the left wearing 1930s-styled evening dress, the other four equally eclectic advertisements ('Shadow Play', 'Double Narcissus', 'Like to Like' and 'Charisma') encode sex and gender identities in an even more elliptical and ambiguous fashion (Figures 27 and 28). Thus in each of them, 'she' passes for 'he' in both the illusive images and copy—'This man.

This woman', one of them begins—which, in turn, pay homage to *fin-de-siècle* decadence and androgyny. By extension, as John Reed has argued, one of the hallmarks of decadent art and literature was the establishment of 'character through ornament and decoration' and the *mise-en-scène* that the two figures inhabit in the advertisements is certainly ornate.[4] While the settings contain a diffuse collection of artefacts and furnishings, the overarching stylistic theme of the décor is, however, Gothic Revival rather than late-nineteenth-century aestheticism. 'Double Narcissus' and 'Shadow Play', for example, feature a version of the 'Gothic Lily' wallpaper and wool curtains with a damask pattern, which were originally designed by A. W. Pugin in the mid-nineteenth century. Moreover, given that the same wall and window hangings appear in both bedroom and sitting room alongside carved and painted pre-Raphaelite-style furniture, it is probable that these settings were specially configured for the photo shoot rather than being actual country house interiors—more like a bricolage of period pieces, then, that betrays the early 1970s taste for all shades of brown and complements the photomontage of the two characters portrayed by Veruschka into a unified composition.[5]

Coterminously, both text and photographs abound with many of the common tropes mobilized by nineteenth-century artists and writers to convey a sense of sexual liberation and morbid degeneracy. Accordingly, in three of the advertisements the female character sports long, flowing hair, a sign of the experienced woman and of erotic intent in the work of many artists from Dante Gabriel Rossetti to Aubrey Beardsley and from Gustav Klimt to Edvard Munch.[6] And the tone and content of the lapidary copy, printed in italics beneath each of the photographs, appear somewhat archly to amalgamate the open-ended prose style of Joris-Karl Huysmans and the sensuous, symbolist poetry of Paul Verlaine. Joseph Halpern had described the former's novel *A Rebours* (*Against Nature*, 1884) as 'written against itself . . . its language is that of "untruth (artifice, illusion, *deviation*, *mensonge*) expressed in the idiom of truth'.[7] We can detect a similar air of mythical perversion in the opening stanza of 'Shadow Play', which states, 'Beauty is cruel and cruel is beautiful. The shared decadent lilies of ultimate experience', whilst its concluding line, 'Shadows whispering of darker things, walls pleasured with daemons', evokes the crepuscular 'palace, silk and gold' with 'beautiful demons, adolescent satans' of Verlaine's 1884 poem 'Crimen Amoris'.[8] Furthermore, the portrayal of the lily as a flower of 'ultimate experience' aligns itself with the lily discarded on the carpet in the photograph of 'Shadow Play' as a symbol of debasement. In both religious and secular contexts the lily had long been a sign of purity, but in novels such as Émile Zola's *The Sin of Father Mouret* (1875), as Bram Dijkstra asserts, it had also come to portend the end of innocence as well: 'The search for woman as the lily, the paragon of virtue, had carried within itself the discovery of Lilith, of woman as snake, the inevitable dualistic opposite of the image of virginal purity.'[9]

Figure 27 Dormeuil Cloth for Men, 'Shadow Play', full-page colour advertisement, photograph by Alec Murray, *Sunday Times Magazine*, 4 March 1973. Permission of Dormeuil SAS, France.

Indeed, the Manichean flower forms the veritable topos of another advertisement in the series, 'Double Narcissus'. Thus we witness a 'male' Veruschka, clad in a striped three-piece suit and with slicked back hair, reclining on a bed as 'he' plays a game of cards, and a female Veruschka who—standing at his side and dressed in a white batwing tunic with braided coils that snake around its bodice and waist—is redolent of Rossetti's depiction of 'Lady Lilith' (1868) in the way she wears her flaxen tresses and gazes intently at herself in a shell-shaped hand mirror.[10] And yet, the themes of doubling and reflection elaborated in the advertisement more patently evince the Greek myth

Figure 28 Dormeuil Cloth for Men, 'Double Narcissus', full-page colour advertisement, photograph by Alec Murray, *Sunday Times Magazine*, 4 March 1973. Permission of Dormeuil SAS, France.

of Narcissus, in which the beautiful, though untouchable, youth is pursued by the nymph Echo, who has fallen in love with him at first sight. As with all his suitors, men and women alike, however, Echo repulses him and in revenge one of Narcissus's other suitors imprecates Nemesis, the spirit of divine retribution in Greek mythology, to 'let Narcissus love and suffer/ As he has made us suffer/ Let him, like us, love and know it is hopeless'.[11] Hence, as a punishment, Narcissus is cursed to fall in love with his own reflection, which he first sees in a pool of water. Initially, he fails to recognize the reflexive object of his own admiration, becoming 'the torturer who now began his own torture', but as soon as he grasps that the reflection is actually his, he realizes the impossibility of being consumed by love for himself and fades away. It is the unrequited passion of both Narcissus and Echo, then, to which the 'Languid, doomed narcissi' of the copy could refer. Moreover, in the advertisement it is 'Echo' whom we observe self-absorbed by her own mirror image, compounding the possibility that Narcissus may be female as well as male, an idea that also has its origins in the *fin-de-siècle*. Writing in 1891 about Fichel's painting of a woman kissing her own reflection in a mirror, for example, the poet Armand Silvestre observed: 'The immortal fable of Narcissus has been brought to life again in this graceful painting . . . this woman who is shown so madly in love with her own image . . . has made herself a god.'[12] And in his paper, 'Auto-Erotism, a Psychological Study' (1898), Havelock Ellis described narcissism as 'that tendency which is sometimes found, more especially perhaps in women, for the sexual emotions to be absorbed, and often entirely lost in self-admiration'.[13]

The idea of 'doomed narcissi' that is iterated in the copy and images of all four of the Decadence-inspired advertisements hints, however, at a more subversive and depraved aspect of love and beauty. One version of 'Shadow Play' tells us that 'Shadows whisper of darker things' and sybarites are 'experienced beyond measure' (Figure 27), while another rejoins that the male and female characters are 'hauntingly memorable' and 'wickedly close' (*Sunday Times Magazine*, 8 April 1973). In turn, the copy of 'Double Narcissus' subtends the corrupt atmosphere of the illustration, stating, 'This man. This woman. Sybarites. Wickedly beautiful, illicitly linked instruments of dark and secret intent'. But what could such transgressive intent be? And what kind of link could be regarded illicit? In response I would suggest that the cross-dressing of the female model in a man's suit in this particular advertisement is both historically and sexually more confused than in the other ads. On one level, the 'he' Veruschka embodies is the androgynous aesthete or dandy of the 1890s, who, as the sybaritic setting also connotes, is stereotypically of the leisure class. But the suit 'he' wears is retro-styled to a 1930s silhouette, and on another level, therefore, Veruschka can be seen as symbolizing the bohemian dandy—both male and female—of the interwar period. If we regard the suited character to be a woman, for instance, she typifies the likes of Florence Stettheimer, a New York-based female artist, who portrayed herself in 'Family Portrait' (1933) wearing both trousers and high-heel shoes.[14] In contrast, if we take the character to be male, he invokes the likes of Noel Coward—a point that is reinforced by the fact that one of his own short plays, 'Shadow Play' (1935), about Simon and Victoria Gayforth, a couple on the verge of divorce, not only bore the same title as one of the advertisements but also involved the idea of the 'hauntingly memorable' body double through the device of Victoria's drug-induced dream in which the present, past and future become intermingled (as they are in the advertising campaign).[15] Of course, none of this is to say that men or women with physical characteristics or behaviours assigned to the other gender are necessarily gay;[16] rather the 'secret intent' and 'wicked beauty' that the copy mentions are akin to the way 'same-sex passion always seems on the point of getting said', as Alan Sinfield argues is the case with both Oscar Wilde's writing in the 1890s and Coward's plays in the 1930s.[17]

The nimiety of symbolic detail and double-dealing incorporated in both these advertisements threaten to make them sink under the sheer weight of associations. After all, what we witness here is the grafting of a nineteenth-century sensibility, encoded through the eclectic Victorian interiors, copperplate headings and literary references to Decadence, onto a 1970s one, though which itself nostalgically draws inspiration from 1930s styles in tailoring and clothing. What is more, in allying the ambiguity of dandy identities to a kind of achronicity in dress, the Dormeuil campaign seems to affirm the ideal of youth mattering more than anything else, which as Barthes argued, is how the fashion system ultimately resolves androgyny: 'Both sexes tend to become uniform under a single sign . . . that of *youth* . . . Fashion notably acknowledges the *boyish look . . . the boyish look* itself has more a temporal than a sexual value . . . it is age that is important not sex.'[18] Drusilla Beyfus had already pondered on this phenomenon in the *Sunday Times Magazine* apropos of the fashion-conscious male Mod: 'Is that a boy, or is it a girl? At first glance it seems hard to tell the sexes apart. The skinny young personage before you in dark glasses, with a girlie hair-cut, a coloured shirt, long pants and boots could be either, at a pinch.'[19] But a key question remains: what of the 1970s audience's response to these advertisements? To what extent is it feasible to argue that it would have appreciated such postmodern style raiding and cross-gender identities?

It would be hardly stretching a point to say that some, if not all, of the art and gender connotations of these advertisements would have been recognized by the archetypal class ABC1 'better off and better educated' readers of the *Sunday Times Magazine*.[20] In the same years that the Dormeuil transvestism advertisements appeared, for instance, it contained articles on Edward Hopper (29 April 1973) and Russian constructivism (6 May 1973), and Veruschka was a well-known fashion model for *Vogue* who had already appeared as a cameo in Antonioni's mod-inspired film *Blowup* (1966). Nor is it unlikely that even its straight male readers would have been familiar with acts of androgyny and cross-dressing, if not through Garbo and *Queen Christina* or Marlene Dietrich, who had worn male attire in cult films *Morocco* (1930) and *Blonde Venus* (1932), then more probably through the feminized look of rock artists of the period such as Mick Jagger and David Bowie.[21] In the final analysis, therefore, the Dormeuil campaign transforms what one critic was to call a 'potentially unglamorous product',[22] blending high and low culture (or the serious and the frivolous), and dealing with transvestism, style and visual décor in such a knowing way that it bears many of the hallmarks and tropes of the camp sensibility that Susan Sontag enumerated in her seminal essay of 1964, namely: exaggeration, artifice, aestheticism, 'Being-as-Playing-a-Role' (travesty, impersonation, theatricality), 'gestures full of duplicity', corrupted innocence and the perverse 'new-style dandy', who 'sniffs the stink and prides himself on strong nerves'.²³ As she contends, 'Camp taste turns its back on the good-bad axis of ordinary aesthetic judgment. Camp doesn't reverse things. It doesn't argue that the good is bad, or the bad is good. What it does is to offer for art (and life) a different — a supplementary — set of standards.'²⁴ And it is androgyny and Garbo that she singles out for special attention in this regard, arguing:

> The androgyne is certainly one of the great images of Camp sensibility . . . the most refined form of sexual attractiveness (as well as the most refined form of sexual pleasure) consists in going against the grain of one's sex. What is most beautiful in virile men is something feminine; what is most beautiful in feminine women is something masculine . . .²⁵

Notes

1   Marjorie Garber, *Vested Interests: Cross-dressing and Cultural Anxiety* (New York: Harper Collins, 1993), 10.

2   Jane Gaines, 'The Queen Christina Tie-ups: Convergence of Show Window and Screen', *Quarterly Review of Film and Video* II (1989), 43.

3   Anne Hollander, 'The Great Emancipator, Chanel', *Connoisseur* (February 1983), 84.

4   John R. Reed, *Decadent Style* (Athens, OH: Ohio University Press, 1985), 22.

5   For Pugin, see A. V. Sugden and J. L. Edmondson, *A History of English Wallpaper, 1509–1914* (London, 1926), and P. Atterbury and C. Wainwright (eds), *Pugin: A Gothic Passion* (New Haven: Yale University Press, 1994). C. Wainwright, 'Pre-Raphaelite Furniture', in J. M. Crook (ed.), *The Strange Genius of William Burges, 'Art-Architect', 1827–1881* (London: John Murray, 1981), 67–70, uses the term 'pre-Raphaelite furniture' in his discussion of the architect-designer William Burges, who produced his first piece of decorated furniture, the Yatman cabinet, in 1858 and, as Wainwright argues, 'by integrating joinery, architecture and painting in miniature form . . . revolutionised furniture design'. I am grateful to Colin Cruise for the suggestion that these Dormeuil ads could be more like stage sets than actual domestic interiors.

6   See, for instance, Rossetti's 'Bocca Baciata' (1859); Beardsley's illustrations for Oscar Wilde, *Salome* (1891); Klimt's 'Veritas' (1898); and Munch's 'Madonna' (1895).

7   Joseph Halpern, 'Decadent Narrative. *A Rebours*', *Stanford French Review* (Spring 1978), 100.

8   C. F. MacIntyre, *Selected Poems* (Berkeley: University of California, 1970), 323.

9   Bram Dijkstra, *Idols of Perversity: Fantasies of Feminine Evil in Fin-de-Siecle Culture* (Oxford: Oxford University Press, 1986), 216.

10 Dijkstra (ibid., 141) claims that in the 1890s Arts and Crafts 'designers everywhere . . . were turning out massive numbers of elaborately carved oval hand mirrors decorated with wood nymphs, cupids, Ophelias, Venuses, and so on'. At the same time he contends that the 'provocative vulval shape' of the oval mirror heightened the personification of vanity as female.

11   Ted Hughes, *Tales From Ovid* (London: Faber and Faber, 1997), 78.

12   Quoted in Dijkstra, *Idols of Perversity*, 143–4.

13   Quoted in ibid., 145.

14   Susan Fillin-Yeh (ed.), *Dandies: Fashion and Finesse in Art and Culture* (New York: New York University Press, 2001), 136. Some working-class women, such as female miners in Lancashire, and some middle-class politicized American feminists such as Madame Bernard Trouser (who lent her name to the eponymous pants worn by women) did wear male styles of dress in the 1860s and 1870s. Colette in *The Pure and Impure* (1932) records that gay women in interwar Paris masked their masculine attire with 'Lady Bountiful' coats when they took to the streets to agitate for the right to vote. In general, therefore, new women and gay women simply did not wear suits or trousers until well after the Second World War. See Elizabeth Wilson, *Adorned in Dreams: Fashion and Modernity* (London: Virago, 1985), 162–4.

15   Noel Coward, 'Shadow Play: A Musical Fantasy' [1935] (London: Samuel French Trade, 2010). 'Shadow Play' is one of ten one-act plays in Coward's cycle *Tonight at 8.30*, first performed in Manchester in 1935 and in which he played the role of Simon and Gertrude Lawrence that of Victoria.

16   A. Sinfield, *The Wilde Century* (London: Cassell, 1994), 90. 'To be sure, the aesthete was regarded as effeminate—but not . . . as distinctively homosexual.'

17   Ibid., 104; A. Sinfield, 'Private Lives/Public Theater: Noel Coward and the Politics of Homosexual Representation', *Representations* 36 (1991), 44.

18   Roland Barthes, *The Fashion System* [1967], trans. M. Ward and R. Howard (Berkeley: University of California, 1990), 257–8, italics in the original.

19   D. Beyfus, 'How to Tell a Boy From a Girl', *Sunday Times Magazine* (20 September 1964), 46.

20   *Ad Weekly* (9 July 1971), 10.

21   Mick Jagger, for instance, had worn trousers and a short white dress with ribboned bodice and flouncy skirt, designed by (Michael) Mr Fish, for the Rolling Stones' Hyde Park concert in 1969. Playing the part of the reclusive rock star Turner in Nic Roeg's *Performance* (1970), he also wore lipstick and eye shadow along with decorative robes. Bowie had caused a stir in 1971 with the release of his album *Hunky Dory*, featuring a close-up shot of his pale, androgynous face. John Mendelsohn, 'David Bowie? Pantomime Rock?', *Rolling Stone* (1 April 1971), www.rollingstone.com/archive, accessed 26 September 2010, commented about Bowie at the time: 'in his floral-patterned velvet midi-gown and cosmetically enhanced eyes, in his fine chest-length blonde hair and mod nutty engineer's cap that he bought in the ladies' hat section of the City of Paris department store in San Francisco, he is ravishing, almost disconcertingly reminiscent of Lauren Bacall, although he would prefer to be regarded as the latter-day Garbo.'

22   J. Koski, 'Ad of the Week', *Campaign* (11 May 1979), 24.

23   Susan Sontag, 'Notes on "Camp"', in *Against Interpretation and Other Essays* (London: Picador, 2001), 108–11 and 117.

24   Ibid., 114.

25   Ibid., 108.

20

LOOKING GOOD, FEELING GOOD

MATERIALITY AND THE INTERPLAY OF THE SENSES

It is surprising to note that the critics for *Adweek* and *Men's Wear* totally over looked the camp sensibility of Dormeuil advertisements, if not their slippery gender symbolism. Nonetheless, it is equally interesting to see Johnstone-Cristall praising the critical valorizations in Dormeuil's 'Cloth for Men' campaign of 1971 and 1972, which is to say he was struck by the way both the male models managed to convey an air of naturalness and the photographs by Franco Rubartelli gave the impression of garments as actually worn (Figure 29). Thus in one review he opined that 'the result is that the suit looks as if it would go on looking as good as it does, even if a living human being goes on wearing it', and in another, 'I know I can never look like he looks . . . I know that I could feel how he looks.'[1] Linking the sensations of looking and feeling as he did in describing the ludic scenes of amorous intimacy between the male model and Veruschka in various Italian cities, his comments once more raise the dialectic of haptic visuality and pleasure, which I identified at play in Lyle and Scott's 1954 publicity for y-fronts in Part 1 (Figure 9), and through which Maurice Merleau-Ponty argues there exists 'an inscription of the touching in the visible, of the seeing in the tangible—and the converse'.[2] Thus cloth, and in particular cloth worn on the human body, obviously has an instrumental part to play in such an imbrication of touch and sight—not only for the person who wears it, sees and feels him- or herself wearing it and is seen wearing it, but for the spectator as well who, as Johnstone-Cristall implies, in looking at how the cloth is worn can sense what it would also feel like to be clad in it him- or herself.[3]

In fact, many advertisements set out to appeal to the sense of touch that technically they were not able to represent.[4] Thus they portrayed the texture and tactility of fabrics through close-cropped photographs that used seductive lighting

Figure 29 Dormeuil Tonik, 'The Legendary Ones', full-page colour advertisement, *Sunday Times Magazine*, 21 March 1971. Permission of Dormeuil SAS, France.

and a saturated colour palette, such as Austin Reed's promotion for an orange wool sweater (Figure 21); deliberative exhortations such as 'Handle rough' for Smedley Bancora machine-washable wool underwear (*Sunday Times Magazine*, 31 October 1965), or phatic statements like 'It's a soft touch' for an Acrilan sweater (*Sunday Times Magazine*, 1 March 1964). A set of five advertisements for upmarket Viyella lambswool and cotton blend garments, originated by Alan Field, creative director of Garratt Baulcombe Associates, with photographs by Andrew Kim that appeared in *Town* and the *Sunday Times Magazine* was exceptional in this regard. David Smith proposed that in looking at the ads, 'the reader's eye performs what the rag-trade calls "the schmutter's handshake" ',[5] while Johnstone-Cristall commented with pink enthusiasm about one of the campaigns (Figure 30): 'This is impeccable product presentation. The shirt is at the same time the subject and background . . . The crumpling of the cloth recalls the texture of Viyella perfectly . . . this presentation is in some respects better than seeing the product itself. If ever an advertisement had breeding, then it is this one.'[6] In fact, so seduced was he by the conception and perception of the fabric's texture that he failed to realize the advertisement was for a dressing gown. What is more, the ad also reveals that Viyella relied on text as much as it did image to connote the breeding and luxury of its product; 'Only an old Viyella is nicer than a new one', the promotion nostalgically tells us, while another states that Viyella 'is the

Figure 30 'Only an old Viyella is nicer than a new one', full-page colour advertisement, *Sunday Times Magazine*, 6 December 1970. Permission of Morrison McConnell.

international choice of those who care how they feel and how they look' (*Sunday Times Magazine*, 17 March 1963).

Likewise, the interplay of sensory perceptions was reiterated in the copy of much publicity for natural and artificial fibres. Thus men were repeatedly told wool 'looks and feels more comfortable', and even that it has 'the special feeling only pure new wool can give' (*Sunday Times Magazine*, 20 October 1974 and 12 November 1978), while campaigns for Acrilan allied the sensation of wearing clothing made from it to sexual fantasy. Hence, the advertising copy for a warm coat by Swallow stated, 'Her hungry eyes lingered over the soft down that covered his powerful shoulders, his magnificent body' (*Sunday Times Magazine*, 11 September 1966), while a shirt for Peter England was reified as possessing the 'warmth and good looks and friendliness and feel' that 'girls are very

Figure 31 'What's a suit without Dormeuil?', full-page colour press advertisement, 1989/1990. Permission of Dormeuil SAS, France.

susceptible to', even when the spectacle-wearing nerd in the advertisement inverts the normative advertising stereotype of the alpha male (*Sunday Times Magazine*, 24 April 1966). Dormeuil, too, once more inverted the expected norm of looking and feeling, when its ad agency BBDO launched the 'What's a suit without Dormeuil?' campaign in December 1989 at a cost of £1.5 million.[7] In a series of ads that appeared in *Vogue* and the colour supplements, therefore, not only does the male model appear naked in the delectable soft-toned photographs—and in one of them his pert buttocks are on show—but the haptic relationship of clothing to bodies is also suggested by the metonymic buttons superimposed on and touching his bare skin (Figure 31). At the same time, the ad illuminates another kind of doubling that a trans-sensory aesthetic involves; that is, its erotic charge and the giving over or immersion of selfhood to pleasure and desire—either one's own or that of another—that it evinces and that after 1985 were also much in evidence for several campaigns for Levi's 501, to which I shall return in Part 3.

Notes

1 T. Johnstone-Cristall, 'Tailors Don't Need Ad Dummies', *Ad Weekly* (9 April 1971), 26; T. Johnstone-Cristall, 'A Matter of Models', *Ad Weekly* (5 May 1972), 3.

2 Maurice Merleau-Ponty, *The Visible and the Invisible*, trans. A. Lingis (Evanston, IL: Northwestern University Press, 1968), 143. He strengthens the point, arguing, 'Since the same body sees and touches, visible and tangible belong to the same world. It is a marvel too little noticed that every movement of my eyes—even more, every displacement of my body—has its place in the same visible universe that I itemize and explore with them, as, conversely, every vision takes place somewhere in the tactile space. There is double and crossed situating of the visible in the tangible and of the tangible in the visible' (134).

3 Clare Pajaczkowska, 'On Stuff and Nonsense', *Textile* 3:3 (2005), 242, argues a similar point about clothing as a liminal or interstitial membrane that simultaneously conceals and reveals identity: 'As cloth in clothing is the most tactile of surfaces, always in contact with skin and body, it carries the contradictory meanings of being an external surface turned outward towards the gaze of the viewer.'

4 Laura Marks, *The Skin of the Film* (Durham, NC: Duke University Press, 2000), 129, also explores how cinema can appeal to the senses of touch and smell through the notion of the 'haptic eye'.

5 D. Smith, 'Shirts, Volkswagen and Christmas Pudding', *Ad Weekly* (13 March 1970), 32.

6 T. Johnstone-Cristall, 'Getting Too Clever by Half', *Ad Weekly* (8 January 1971), 35.

7 *Campaign* (1 December 1989), 14.

21
GETTING MORE FOR YOUR MONEY

MENSWEAR PUBLICITY AND THE 1970s RECESSION

According to *The Young Market*, Citron and Murray's survey for Pearl and Dean, although the estimated disposable group income of unmarried males was some £2 million per week in 1971, men under 21 years old, the largest segment of the male market, had average net weekly earnings of only £13.65.[1] At the same time, the National Economic Development Office recorded a 100 per cent increase in menswear prices between 1966 and 1975.[2] And while Daniels could comment in *Ad Weekly*, 'Very few customers wish to see themselves as choosing a tailor because of price alone,' price had always mattered in a market saturated with choice, and several tailoring chains were keen to emphasize for consumers the critical valorizations of the merchandise in their publicity.[3] Thus in 1963 John Collier promoted its Terylene-wool mix suit, costing £10. 19s., under the banner 'Get the 1963 suit with the 1957 price tag', and Burton's cited exactly the same price for its all-wool worsted suit with the competitive slogan 'so much more for your money'.[4] Moreover, with the onset of the recession, inflation and rising consumer prices, it is probable that a professional such as London primary-school teacher Joe Rea, who earned £28 per week in 1971 (and was designated one of the 'unofficial poor' in a *Sunday Times Magazine* report), may have entertained forking out £16 for Burton's cheapest ready-to-wear suit.[5] Yet, in comparison to London bank manager Anthony Adair (the actual rather than putative Burton's director in a suit), who earned £65 per week, it is doubtful that Rea had sufficient wherewithal to contemplate purchasing a Chester Barrie suit from Austin Reed at £60.[6]

Coupled with the rationing of newsprint in 1973, the volatile economic situation of the early 1970s forced some menswear advertisers to take stock. Hence, Jackson the Tailor shifted its £100,000 advertising account from

Garland-Compton to the Tyneside-based agency Redhead Advertising in autumn 1972 since Graham Peacock, the company's promotional director, argued, 'We could not take the chance of working with an agency in London when a postal strike or power cuts could screw things up.'[7] And in 1974 some agencies, which generally aimed to make 3 per cent profit on each of their billings, were also forced to relinquish unprofitable accounts. From a high of seventeen full-page colour advertisements for Austin Reed in the *Sunday Times Magazine* in 1970, for instance, in 1973 there were ten and in 1974 none, and so DPBS terminated business with the outfitters.[8] Generally, however, expenditure on consumer advertising managed to remain constant in the face of such economic ups-and-downs and material constraints, with newspaper publicity increasing by 53 per cent, magazine publicity by 25 per cent, and television publicity by 46 per cent between 1971 and 1973.[9]

In fact, as in the Great Depression of the 1930s, many retailers regarded advertising as instrumental in helping the consumer market to tick over. Thus it is instructive to acknowledge that just as Hepworth's was suffering losses of £800,000 during the recession of 1973–74,[10] its agency French, Gold Abbott produced a four-page colour promotion that appeared in *Radio Times* on 13–19 April 1974. Featuring Radio 1 and 2 disc jockeys Ed Stewart, Terry Wogan, Noel Edmonds, Emperor Rosko and Tony Blackburn under the banner 'If a Hepworth's made-to-measure suit can satisfy this lot, think what it could do for you', the campaign helped the company to turn its finances around, with sales increasing by 24 per cent and Hepworth's planning seventeen new shop openings by March 1975.[11] All in all, consumer spending on boys- and menswear rose from £606 million in 1966 to £1,254 million in 1974, and between 1972 and 1975 the number of households earning £3,500 per annum increased threefold.[12] But by 1975 also inflation in Britain reached nearly 27 per cent, and a report by Phillips and Drew concluded that consumer spending on men's clothing had dipped by almost 8 per cent between 1973 and 1977.[13] The spectre of unemployment also loomed large for the male workforce, although with variation according to region and age. Thus by January 1978 the unemployment rate was heaviest in the North and Scotland (just over 10 percent) and for men over age 40 across the United Kingdom (just over 39 percent), and lowest in the South-East (nearly 6 percent) and for men under 20 (about 13 percent).[14] Nonetheless, if young men were still prepared to splash out on clothing it was not exclusively formal attire that they desired, and this was a challenge that advertising for menswear retailers met with variable success. Stylistically tasteful and unified as it was in regard to text and image, for example, advertising for Austin Reed signified a more fragmented identity, embracing at one end of the generational spectrum young men in denim suits and publicity for Cue Man, and at the other older, grey-haired professionals, many of whom were not averse to patronizing Cue as well (Figures 17, 22 and 32).[15]

Figure 32 Austin Reed wool v-neck jumper, full-page colour advertisement, *Sunday Times Magazine*, 1 April 1974. Permission of Austin Reed.

The changing of the guard from suits to casual styles in clothing was neatly highlighted in a double-page colour ad for 'Man at C&A' in the *Sunday Times Magazine* on 21 March 1971, which represented a line of longhaired models wearing a panoply of reasonably priced garments from wet look and leather jackets, costing respectively £6.95 and £18.50,[16] to two- and three-piece suits at £15.95 and £26.50.[17] Indeed, by 1976 sales of suits were down to 7.5 million units in comparison to 11 million in 1970. Burton's closed more than eighty shops as a result and in 1980 Mintel reported that Burton's share of the suit market was diminishing year on year; for instance, in 1976 it stood at 17 per cent and in 1979 at 14 per cent.[18] It was not for nothing that the Burton Group launched the first two of its teenage-oriented Top Man outlets in spring 1977 in Kingston-on-Thames and Watford and backed them up with a £200,000 publicity campaign by the Creative Business advertising agency in the *Evening Standard*.[19] By the mid 1970s, therefore, the tide had definitely turned in favour of more casual clothing, something that had already been adumbrated in the informal and unkempt dress codes espoused by the prevailing counterculture. But, as the 'Man at C&A' promotion reveals and, as we shall see in the next part, the anti-consumerist ethos of the hippy movement was prone to incorporation and commoditization by the mainstream, and the change in youth culture fashions from 1972 onwards was also accompanied by a renewed emphasis on television and cinema publicity, particularly for jeans. Thus Simon Broadbent, vice-chairman of Leo Burnett, and Mike Townsin, media director of Young Rubicam, both lamented the fact that by the late 1970s the heyday of exceptional magazine advertising was over, insisting that it was television 'where the best creative work can be produced'.[20]

Notes

1 'The Young Ones—What Are They Worth?', *Ad Weekly* (19 November 1971), 33–4. The respective 2000 equivalents were £27,629,242 and £193.

2 'Men's Underwear Prices Heads Clothing Price-Rise Chart', *Men's Wear* (5 August 1976), 5.

3 M. Daniels, 'Chasing the "Brand Vulnerable" Motorists', *Ad Weekly* (10 April 1970), 41.

4 *Daily Mirror* (2 and 5 March 1963). The 2000 equivalent was £136.

5 P. Gillman, 'The Unofficial Poor', *Sunday Times Magazine* (27 February 1972), 36. The respective 2000 equivalents were £387 and £134.

6 R. Lacey, 'Their Weekly Bread', *Sunday Times Magazine* (1 October 1972), 59. The respective 2000 equivalents were £898 and £504.

7 *Adweek* (3 November 1972), 52. The 2000 equivalent was £783,891.

8 'The Loss Makers', *Adweek* (27 June 1975), 12–13.

9 J. Treasure, 'What 1974 Holds in Store for the Ad Business', *Adweek* (4 January 1974), 11.

10 The 2000 equivalent was £5,741,999.

11 'The Men's Wear Sales Battle Looms', *Adweek* (7 February 1975), 11.

12 'Men's Underwear Prices', *Men's Wear* (5 August 1976), 5; *Campaign* (5 March 1976), 9. The respective 2000 equivalents were £6,700 million, £7,758 million and £37,734.

13 H. Sharman, 'The Ups and Downs of Consumer Spending', *Campaign* (10 February 1978). 11.

14 Kevin Hawkins, *Unemployment* (1979), cited in Arthur Marwick, *British Society Since 1945* (Harmondsworth: Pelican, 1982), 203.

15 B. Ritchie, *A Touch of Class: The Story of Austin Reed* (London: James and James, 1991), 118.

16 The respective 2000 equivalents were £58.40 and £155.

17 The respective 2000 equivalents were £134 and £223.

18 J. Koski, 'Menswear Market Faces a Big Strategy Shake-up', *Campaign* (5 May 1978), 20.

19 *Campaign* (17 March 1977), 1. The 2000 equivalent was £738,105.

20 N. Mawer, 'Supplementary Benefits and Drawbacks', *Campaign* (13 January 1978), 16.

PART THREE

LEADER OF THE PACK

JEANS ADVERTISING SINCE THE 1960s

A fabric that was designed by Levi Strauss to be practical garb for the working man has become—heaven help us—chic. (*Campaign*, 15 August 1975)

When advertising's grey-haired historians gaze back at the Eighties, the campaign most likely to have 'seminal' stamped on it is Bartle Bogle and Hegarty's rose-tinted homage to the Fifties on behalf of Levi's. (Alexander Garrett, *Campaign*, 19 January 1990)

Introduction

Simon Broadbent's assertion that, by the late 1970s, television publicity had started to overtake press and poster advertising must be applied with some moderation to menswear in general, as only a handful of outfitters had resorted to television publicity at this point in time (see Appendix III).[1] Hepworth, for instance, advertised on television from autumn 1976 till autumn 1978 and Burton's between 1977 and 1979. In spring 1977 the International Wool

Secretariat's 'Man in Wool' 30-second advertisement by Davidson Pearce Berry and Spottiswoode, with visuals of a ram running toward a ewe intercut with those of a man running toward a woman and the tag line, 'There's nothing like it', made its debut alongside the first of the 'Man at C&A' 30-second spots, directed by Eddie Vorkapitch, which ran until 1985.[2] Only when it comes to publicity for jeans, however, does the balance tip towards television advertising from 1976 onwards (see Appendices III and IV). Certainly, in comparison to other items of dress, jeans were exponentially ascendant throughout the period and by the 1970s had begun to challenge the clothing hegemony enjoyed by the suit. Bucking economic fluctuations in income and expenditure, in 1970 6 million pairs were sold and in 1980, 25 million pairs.[3] The two instrumental players were Levi's and Wrangler, but campaigns for most brands had started to appear in the cinema and on television by 1972; one of the first television jeans advertisements was for Lybro in March 1972, which was shortly followed by Dingo in May 1972 and Brutus in June 1974.

Even so, cinema and television promotions were not to have everything their own way. A Target Group Index Survey of 24,000 television viewers in 1982, for instance, indicated that during peak slots between 7 and 8 p.m., only 35 per cent of viewers on weekdays and Sundays were men, and only 28 per cent on Saturdays.[4] Just as the colour supplements had challenged the hegemony of television and cinema publicity in the 1960s and 1970s, therefore, so too did advertising for jeans appear in the music press and a cluster of new youth culture titles such as *The Face* (founded 1980), as well as on poster hoardings.

Accordingly, in this final part I want to concentrate on the publicity for jeans that appeared across the advertising spectrum from the early 1960s until 2000. From tentative beginnings, by 1980 jeans constituted the largest share of the men's clothing market according to a Mintel report, with sales of £324 million,[5] a position they maintained right up to the turn of the century, with the two top brands Levi's and Wrangler racking up sales of £4,154,320 and £2,297,498, respectively, in 1997.[6] From the outset, jeans also became popular with both men and women, and across the generational divide. In regard to age, for example, it is worth mentioning that, after brand leaders Levi's and Wrangler, Marks and Spencer were grossing the same percentage of sales for their own jeans in 1980 as were Falmers and Brutus.[7] However, I shall only be concerned here with analysing those brands such as Levi's, Wrangler, Lee and Brutus that represented jeans as male or masculine attire in their publicity, which they did until the early 2000s, and whose advertising rhetoric also targeted a youth audience. As we shall see, several predominant themes will be addressed in the process: the impact of youth culture, new man and new lad; gender and race identities; the role of hyperreality and simulation; and the part played by the pop music soundtrack in relaying the advertising narrative.

Notes

1 N. Mawer, 'Supplementary Benefits and Drawbacks', *Campaign* (13 January 1978), 16.

2 C&A spent some £744,000 on television publicity in 1977 (*Campaign* (31 March 1978), 45). See also *Campaign* (15 April 1977), 35.

3 *Campaign* (28 August 1981), 8.

4 D. Wood, 'Who Will Watch The Most Television Later Tonight?', *Campaign* (30 April 1982), 31.

5 The 2000 equivalent was £825m. This and all subsequent monetary figures for 2000 have been calculated by using 'Lawrence H. Officer and Samuel H. Williamson, 'Purchasing Power of British Pounds from 1245 to Present', MeasuringWorth (2013). http://www.eh.net/hmit/ppowerbp, accessed 12 January 2013.

6 According to Mintel sales for leisure clothing, including knitwear, accounted for £919 million of the total £2714 million spent on menswear in 1980. Jeans formed the largest share of the leisure market, with 54 per cent of sales. 'Fashion Report—Who Spends What and Where', *Campaign* (19 September 1997), 6. The data cited in the article were from a report into fashion retailing prepared by Media Monitoring Services.

7 Ibid. The Progress Agency masterminded the 'Falmer Genius' campaign. In spring 1979, an ad shot in Paris by Terence Donovan also appeared on television (*Campaign* (30 March 1979), 2).

22

THE JEANS MARKET AND ADVERTISING BETWEEN 1950 AND 1985

More than any other form of attire jeans came to symbolize the universal image of youth after the Second World War. Thus a utilitarian garment, which Levi-Strauss had originated during the Californian Gold Rush of the 1850s and which was worn subsequently and exclusively as working gear, became a fashion item almost a hundred years after its invention. We can detect this shift and the association of jeans with youthful rebellion in the play *Blue Denim* (1955) and the film *The Wild One* (1954); in the latter Marlon Brando wore jeans with a white T-shirt and black leather jacket. From this point onwards, as Richard Martin and Harold Koda argue, jeans were established as 'the most influential clothing in contemporary dress'[1] and were even worn by teenagers in some Iron Curtain countries as a status symbol and a means of emulating the freedom of youth in capitalist societies (a message that Bartle, Bogle and Hegarty went on to exploit in their 'Airport' cinema and television campaign for Levi's in spring 1985).[2]

The first Levi's factory in Britain was established in Acton in the early 1950s (the company eventually relocated to Northampton in 1973), while Wrangler jeans, which had been launched in America in 1847, were being produced in four factories in Scotland by 1964.[3] Although the two brands became internationally hegemonic in the jeans market by 1975, in post-war Britain they had to compete with the popularity of trousers and slacks such as 'Guards' and 'Bucks', of which almost 32 million units were sold in 1967.[4] One of the first British jeans labels was Texsun, manufactured by Wescot in Egham, Surrey, and initially publicized in 1952 as 'the latest vogue . . . smart and gay for all the family at work or play. Made in fine deep tone blue denim with orange decorative stitching'.[5] However, alongside Slikfit, Jet and Lybro, all of which advertised in youth culture and music titles such as *Reveille*, *Weekend*, *Fabulous* and *Rave*, by the mid 1960s, Westcot were also targeting the 16–25 age group with its advertising campaigns.[6] Lybro, manufactured in Liverpool, was probably the most versatile of these British brands in terms of cut and colour, producing jeans in various shades such as pewter, tobacco, barley, bronze, black, ice-blue, blue-grey and swinging (navy) blue. In one campaign in summer 1963, 'Go Merseyside! Go Lybro!', it capitalized on the origins and popularity of the product by associating its jeans with the onset of the Liverpool music scene. Here, a sketch of the four members of the Beatles (who had already scored number one hit singles in 1963 with 'Please Please Me' and 'From Me to You'), representing each of them with improbably attenuated legs and wearing a different style and fit of Lybro jeans, is collaged with press cuttings proclaiming the rise of Beatlemania (Figure 33).

Figure 33 'Go Merseyside! Go Lybro!', monochrome advertisement, *Reveille*, 1963. Private collection.

The relationship of jeans to music is, of course, most associated in the postmodern imaginary with Levi's 501 advertising since 1985 (see Appendix IV), but it was also evident in the first publicity for the label in Britain, which appeared in the summer of 1964 in *Weekend* and the pop music press (viz. *Melody Maker*, *Record Mirror*, and *New Musical Express*). Levi's retailed at 49s. 11d. in 1966,[7] and by 1968, at which point demand was outstripping supply, the musical theme was compounded in a series of radio and press ads masterminded by Young and Rubicam that tied up with Radio Luxembourg's *Top Twenty Chart Show*.[8] At the outset, however, Levi's were quite often advertised as a unisex product as much as they were exclusively for men; witness a promotion in *Weekend* (1–7 July 1964) that featured an illustration of a man and woman wearing blue jeans as they listen to their record collection. This dual appeal to male and female audiences enabled Levi's to become brand leader by 1971, with a 15 per cent share of the jeans market and sales of £40 million,[9] and is most notoriously—and literally—embodied in its 1972 cinema ad, 'Bottoms', shot by John Alcock (who had previously been cinematographer for Stanley Kubrick).

Its soundtrack 'Tutti Frutti' had been a minor rock and roll chart success for Little Richard in Britain in 1957.[10] But the iconography of the advertisement trades on the 'summer of love' and carnivalesque situationism of the American counterculture between 1968 and 1972, which aimed to puncture the 'hypocrisy' of mainstream lifestyles by, amongst other things, expressing itself through peaceful methods of protest and a playful and unbridled interest in sex.[11] Thus fetishistic close-ups of men's and women's behinds, clad in various styles of striped and denim Levi's that are sometimes decorated with 'V-sign' and 'Smile' patches, are intercut throughout the ad, which also includes snapshots of bottom patting and pinching. Shortly afterwards a cinema campaign for Brutus jeans, directed by David Saive for London Advertising and Jennie and Co, cribbed the general idea of 'Bottoms'.[12] The Brutus advertisement was, however, simultaneously more sexualized (its closing shot depicted a young man and woman naked above the waist as they caress each other's buttocks) and represented the product as a catalyst for male desire (the *mise-en-scène* conjures up the fantasy of what *he* would like to do with her as he tries the jeans on).

The appeal of the moving image for the jeans market was recognized in an 1976 editorial in *Campaign*: 'Cinema is a particularly good medium for jeans advertising because audiences are generally in the prime 15 to 34 age group.'[13] This was borne out not only by the fact that many brands resorted to cinema ads but also by product tie-ins such as that between the Odeon, Leicester Square, and Levi's in summer 1974 to promote the film *For Pete's Sake* (dir. Michael Sarrazin), in which Barbara Streisand wears Levi's blue jeans.[14] And yet, by the autumn of 1974 and throughout 1975, both Levi's and Brutus had also moved into advertising on television, the former spending £189,000 and the latter £500,000 on national campaigns of 45- and 60-second spots.[15] At this time the

UK jeans market was estimated to be worth some £250 million, and in 1979 the Price Commission declared there were over 200 different brands on sale.[16] Even Daks Simpson launched its own brand of blue denim jeans in 1976 that, retailing at £14, were four pounds dearer than the average cost of a pair of jeans,[17] and in 1979 Austin Reed's Cue boutique began to stock Midnight Blue and Hoofer jeans. In the same year, a Mintel survey of 229 adults also found that the 6 per cent of them who bought at least two pairs of jeans a year did so at Marks & Spencer, prompting Ian White to comment: 'It would appear from research that there is also a small band of trendy age-old pensioners who can be seen rushing down to their local boutique at least two or three times a year for the latest in jean fashion.'[18] While universal consumer demand for jeans had resulted in a worldwide denim 'famine',[19] nonetheless their promotion continued unabated from the mid 1970s onwards. For instance, in 1976 Wrangler, who was second in the market to Levi's and had dedicated its £500,000 ad budget mainly to poster publicity, produced its first cinema and television campaign, 'We make more than just blue jeans,' and Falmer its first cinema ad in 1977 (see Appendix III).[20]

Given that the market for jeans was also demographically diverse, the key challenge facing advertising agents, as Robin Dilley of Collett Dickenson and Pearce avowed in an interview in 1980, was 'to pitch the image of the innovatory group, without alienating other target markets'.[21] To this end, much publicity for jeans between 1976 and 1985 centred on the practical and critical valorizations of the brands in question by emphasizing the quality of their manufacture and the durability and versatility of their everyday use. Typical of this approach are the following: Brutus's 1976 'Jeans on' television and cinema campaign by Saatchi (which won a D&AD award for the best use of music[22]) and its £500,000 cinema campaign of 1979–80 by WCRS, 'From Texas', whose tag line stated, 'The longer it takes you to put on a pair of Brutus jeans, the more satisfaction you get from wearing them'[23]; Levi's 1978 'Not a patch on them' poster campaign, photographed by Jack Bankhead and designed by Roger Manton for McCann Erickson (which won a Design Council award[24]), and 'Rivets', its 1983 cinema and television campaign, filmed in New Mexico by Nick Lewin for Bartle, Bogle and Hegarty and costing £1 million to produce[25]; and Wrangler's 'Mr Rickenbacker' 1978 television campaign by Wasey Cambell-Ewald and its 1983 poster 'What's going on?' by Collett Dickinson and Pearce.[26]

Concurrently, and more significantly, however, a discernible shift toward the lifestyle values of the 'innovatory group' (that is 13- to 20-year-olds, according to Dilley) rather than the practical and/or critical valorizations of jeans also took place in advertising, which has persisted until the present day. Levi's led the way in 1976 with the 60-second television and cinema campaign 'Leader of the Pack' directed by Ridley Scott, which strayed into the subversive milieu of biker culture and went on to win the first of the brand's Gold Lion awards at Cannes in 1977.[27] It was followed by Wrangler in 1980 with 'The Diary of a Pair of Jeans' and in 1981 by Lee Cooper with 'On the Streets'. The former, a 60-second television campaign scripted by John Kelley for Collett Dickenson and Pearce, represented the laddish fantasy of how a pair of Wrangler jeans transformed the life of its male purchaser, who in the space of a week wears them to a football match, is mistaken for a rock star by teenage schoolgirls, and starts dating a girl whom he meets in the Marquee club. The ad also enabled Wrangler to take over as brand leader in 1980, taking a 15 per cent share of the market of 11- to 17-year-olds in comparison to Levi's, which had 12 per cent.[28] The ad, 'On the Streets', was a futuristic poster and cinema campaign produced by Zetland for Lee Cooper, which had been founded in 1908 and stood at the elite end of the jeans market with a share of 3 to 4 per cent.[29] The dystopian scenario of the cinema ad in particular, shot in moody, tenebristic tones at Shoreditch railway station by Willi Patterson, underscored the idea that Lee Cooper would set you apart from the crowd, as a cyberpunk with green eyes and spiked hair sets his dogs on a gang of urban street fighters; the ad went on to win Pearl and Dean's cinema advertisement award in 1983 (Figure 34).[30]

In 1981 some 55 million pairs of blue jeans had been sold in the United Kingdom,[31] but critics were also quick to point out that advertising across all brands seemed to be dipping into the same shallow pool of ideas and, as a result, confounding public perceptions. Thus Jack Bridges protested that:

Much more to the point, however, is the question of the *memorability* of adverts which make overt use of sexual images . . .This is the paradox of

Figure 34 Lee Cooper, 'On the Streets', still from colour television advertisement, 1981. Permission of Lee Cooper Brands.

'sexy advertising'; if everyone's doing it for profitable purposes, nobody is doing it; a relentless tide of bosoms and bottoms leaves the reading public completely bemused . . . with no clear memory of which bottom was advertising which product. This has certainly always been the danger with jeans advertising . . . Whatever Oedipus would have felt (to this observer at least) one shapely rear view, clothed or unclothed, is much the same as any other.[32]

There is obviously something to this point when one considers the similarity between advertisements for Levi's, Brutus and Wrangler that display the garments being tried on and zipped up, or bottoms being patted (viz. 'Tutti Frutti', 'Jeans On', 'From Texas' and 'What's going on?'). But it also overlooks the more innovative approach of campaigns such as 'Diary of a Pair of Jeans' and 'On the Streets'. At any rate, Levi's, whose market share fell from 18 to 14 per cent between 1981 and 1984,[33] seemed to be especially stung by this criticism as well as the results of a 1981 survey of 2,000 female and 1,500 male viewers in the London ITV area that revealed its advertising was trailing Wrangler's in regard to consumer awareness.[34]

Hence, in July 1982 the company moved its British advertising account to one of the new breed of independent-minded agencies, Bartle, Bogle and Hegarty (BBH), which they held until summer 2010.[35] The agency's creative director John Hegarty, who had begun his career in advertising in 1965 with Benton and Bowles and went on to work for Saatchi & Saatchi, asserted: 'We want to establish Levi's as a more avant-garde company and make them more attractive to the young consumer.'[36] By the close of 1991, BBH had billings of almost £84 million, including accounts for Boddingtons and Häagen-Dazs alongside Levi's.[37] BBH made its debut for Levi's in November 1982 with a poster promotion for black jeans that cost £180,000 to produce and that was displayed on 800 different sites.[38] The publicity was organized around an apothegm coined by copywriter Barbara Noakes, 'When the world zigs, zag', and featured an eye-catching photograph of a flock of white sheep walking in one direction as a black sheep walked in the other (Figure 35). Noakes was one of only a handful of women to find success in the male-dominated world of the post-war advertising agency creative department, with only 18 per cent of females being employed in creative jobs as late as 2000.[39] Although the poster campaign she worked on did not halt Levi's dip in popularity, it did herald a more imaginative and visually arresting style of jeans advertising. This new style was reinforced by BBH in its cinema and television campaigns, 'Rivets' and 'Stitching' in 1983 and 'Airport' in spring 1985, and to more iconoclastic effect with the pan-European campaigns 'Bath' and 'Laundrette'.

Costing £4 million to produce, the 50-second television and cinema spots 'Bath' and 'Laundrette' for Levi's Red Tab 501, directed by Roger Lyons and

Figure 35 Levi's black jeans, 'When the world zigs, zag', colour poster, photograph by Alan Brooking, 1982. Permission of BBH Partners.

scripted by Barbara Noakes, made their debut in Britain on 26 December 1985 and ran for three months on ITV and Channel 4.[40] BBH had initially publicized 501s during David Bowie's 1983 tour with in-store photographs of him wearing the brand, which had also already accrued a dedicated following with trendsetters in France.[41] Retailing on average at £28 per pair in 1986, sales of 501s eventually increased by 700 per cent after BBH's creative advertising initiative.[42] But the two advertisements were not just significant for turning around the economic fortunes of Levi's; they were also a milestone in menswear publicity for several other important iconographical reasons and went on to win Gold Lion awards at Cannes in 1986.[43]

Notes

1 Richard Martin and Harold Koda, *Jocks and Nerds* (New York: Rizzoli, 1988), 47.

2 'Jeans Continue Their Climb up the Fashion Ladder', *Men's Wear* (4 July 1964), 20–1. The anonymous author remarked with some surprise: 'In Prague—they even wear them to church.'

3 *Men's Wear* (25 January 1973), 32; Ian White, 'The Jeans Phenomenon', *Campaign* (27 April 1979), 49.

4 Erica Crome, 'Durable Press Trousers', *Men's Wear* (4 April 1968), viii.

5 Advertisement in *Men's Wear* (26 July 1952), 3.

6 Ads for Slikfits jeans and casuals appeared in *Rave*, May 1964; for Jet in *Men's Wear*, 20 March 1965 and in *Fabulous*, *Rave*, *Reveille*, *Weekend*, and *Photoplay* between April and September 1965; and for Westcot jeans in *Weekend* between April and May 1965.

7 Advertisement in *Weekend* (23–29 March 1966), 9. The 2000 equivalent was £27.60.

8 'Jeans Importer Explains His Problem', *Men's Wear* (1 February 1968), 12.

9   *Campaign* (27 August 1971), 4. The 2000 equivalent is £336m.

10 The song entered the record chart at no. 29, for one week only, on 23 February 1957. See R. Osborne, *40 Years of NME Charts* (London: Boxtree, 1992) 44. In 1972 Saatchi had used another 1957 hit by Little Richard, 'Good Golly Miss Molly' in a television ad for Lybro jeans (*Ad Week* (8 November 1974), 1).

11 A good round-up of such developments can be found in Michael Brake, *The Sociology of Youth Culture and Youth Subcultures* (London: Routledge and Kegan Paul, 1980), 86–114.

12 J. King, 'Borrowed Bottoms Invite Criticism', *Adweek* (24 November 1972), 16.

13 'Wranglers Looks Around From DDB', *Campaign* (4 February 1976), 1.

14 *Men's Wear* (29 August 1974), 9.

15 *Adweek* (8 November 1974), 1; *Adweek* (10 January 1975), 23; *Campaign* (21 May 1976), 1. The respective 2000 equivalents of £189,000 and £500,000 were £1,170,000 and £3,090,000.

16 Ian White, 'The Underlying Appeal of Jeans Is That They are Classless', *Campaign* (27 April 1979), 47. The 2000 equivalent of £250 million was £751 million.

17 *Men's Wear* (1 January 1976), 7; *Men's Wear* (3 June 1976), 5; T. Douglas, 'Why Jeans Manufacturers Are Enjoying Record Sales', *Campaign* (6 August 1976), 9. The 2000 equivalent of £12 was £51.30 and of £16, £59.90.

18 White, 'The Underlying Appeal of Jeans', 47.

19 *Men's Wear* (1 January 1976), 7.

20 Douglas, 'Why Jeans Manufacturers Are Enjoying Record Sales', 9. In 1977, Levi's share of the market stood at 14 per cent, Wrangler's at 12 per cent and Brutus' at 7 per cent (*Campaign* (8 December 1978),10). The 2000 equivalent of £500,000 was £2,140,000.

21 Quoted in Ronnie Roter, 'Wrangler: The Real Reason for Our Split with Waseys', *Campaign* (15 August 1980), 20.

22 *Campaign* (18 February 1977), 30.

23 The ad featured five glamourous women trying on their jeans in front of a cowboy. *Campaign* (6 June 1980), 4.

24 *Campaign* (17 March 1978), 42–3.

25 *Campaign* (5 October 1984), 11. The 60-second ad, with a score by Midge Ure, was screened between March and October 1983. This television ad may be viewed in the Arrows Archive at the History of Advertising Trust website: www.hatads.org. uk. The 2000 equivalent was £2 million.

26 *Campaign* (14 April 1978), 2 and *Campaign* (11 October 1985), 42.

27 *Campaign* (1 July 1977), 18–19. The ad also won a Creative Circle Award and D&AD silver award for outstanding film photography in 1977. *Campaign* (18 February 1977), 30 and *Campaign* (10 June 1977), 20.

28 *Men's Wear* (9 April 1981), 4. These figures were collated by Mintel in their 1980 report *The Teenage Market*. According to their research this age group spent £315 million on clothes.

29 In 1979, its share of the jeans market was 3 to 4 per cent. White, 'The Underlying Appeal of Jeans', 49.

30 *Campaign* (22 April 1983), 28–9.

31 *Campaign* (29 November 1985), 45.

32 Jack Bridges, 'Sexism in Advertising', *Men's Wear* (8 January 1981), 24.

33 *Campaign* (18 October 1984), 14.

34 *Campaign* (11 July 1980), 6. In the survey, 55 per cent of viewers recalled Wrangler advertising and 52 per cent Levi's. It also revealed that Lee Cooper's punk cyborgs ad was generally found confusing, with only 31 per cent of viewers taking any notice of it.

35 For an overview of BBH's early achievements in advertising see J. Claridge, 'Agency of 1986', *Campaign* (9 January 1987), 32; Frank Mort, *Cultures of Consumption— Masculinities and Social Space in Late Twentieth-Century Britain* (London: Routledge, 1997), 107–13; John Hegarty, 'Why Levi's Proved to Be Such a Good Fit for BBH', *Campaign* (23 July 2010), 11.

36 *Campaign* (22 October 1982), 3.

37 'Top 300 Agencies Report', *Campaign* (28 February 1992), 27.

38 The 2000 equivalent was £377,000.

39 Donna Klein, *Women in Advertising, Ten Years On* (London: IPA, 2000). 9.

40 The 2000 equivalent was £7,200,000.

41 *Campaign* (18 October 1985), 14; *Men's Wear* (26 May 1983), 3.

42 L. O'Kelly, 'Levi 501s: Why Hegarty Knew the Time Was Right for a Denim Revival', *Campaign* (25 April 1986), 16. The 2000 equivalent of £28 was £48.70.

43 *Campaign* (4 July 1986), 8.

23
LEVI'S 501

BACK TO THE FUTURE?

When it came to promoting 501s to a British audience, BBH intermeshed the practical and ludic valorizations of the brand in two advertising scenarios that espoused the postmodern aesthetic of style revivalism or hyperreality about which Baudrillard contends: 'It is no longer a question of imitation, nor duplication, nor even parody. It is a question of substituting the signs of the real for the real.'[1] Hence, the 1985 simulacral British television campaigns for Levi's 501 stood in marked contrast to '501 Blues' in the United States, which emphasized the media savviness of a range of jeans wearers by connecting audiovisually, as Goldman has argued, 'the meaning of "Blues" as a musical genre expressing solitude and alienation with the meaning of "personal blues" as jeans'.[2] By comparison, the loose narrative motif of 'Bath' is orchestrated to Sam Cooke's 1960 soul single, 'Wonderful World', which at the outset we observe being played on a Dansette record player as if to connote that the ad is taking place in real time; it is centred on model James Mardell, a muscular James Dean lookalike, trying on his 501 shrink-to-fit jeans for size (which first became available in 1873) in a 1950s-styled urban apartment. Wearing only white boxer shorts, he performs pull-ups on the window casing before slipping into his jeans and squatting to ensure a perfect fit on his buttocks. Next, he checks himself out in the mirror, chooses a shirt, checks the time on his watch and glances momentarily at a photograph of (presumably) his girlfriend before eventually sliding into the bath with a bottle of cola to mould the 501s to his reciprocally well-cut body.

The second ad, 'Laundrette', which promoted stone-wash 501s, was likewise 1950s-inspired in regard to its milieu and dress codes. Set in an American laundromat, it starred olive-skinned model Nick Kamen, whose dark hair is styled to look like Elvis Presley's slick quiff. However, it was also orchestrated to a 1960s soundtrack—Marvin Gaye's 1969 no. 1 Motown single, 'I Heard It Through the Grapevine' (though here covered by Tony Jackson)—and, in contrast to 'Bath', Kamen divests his T-shirt and jeans. Thereby his striptease glamorizes the mundane act of visiting the laundrette, uniting in astonishment both the viewers of the ad and his own personal audience. The latter encompassed two teenage girls with high pony-tails, one wearing a flared skirt, the other pedal pushers; two mischievous young boys in red baseball caps, worn back to front, and their stressed mother; a young woman in rimmed glasses, reading a magazine; an older bespectacled woman eating a cream cake; and an obese man with a cane, who glances bemusedly at Kamen as he sits down in his white boxers and socks to read a magazine while he waits for the jeans that he has put into the washing machine along with some rocks literally to attain a stone-washed effect.[3]

Although the advertising brief that Levi's gave to BBH did not specify the use of such historicist imagery,[4] justifying the 1950s and 1960s style raiding elaborated in both ads, Hegarty has averred:

> In the end advertising is all about the leap from brief (the marketing proposition) to creative execution . . . I thought it would be more interesting to do an ad with a period look . . . We had to talk to a young market in a way it would respond to. It's a fickle market . . . The integrity of the product demanded that we draw on the 501s heritage, but the heritage had to be relevant to what's going on now. America, these days, is guilty until proven innocent in the eyes of the young, and our strategy was to restore the appeal of innocence. The past can be very acceptable, but it has to be played air-conditioned.[5]

Hegarty's summation of the youth market portrayed the idea of a mythological 'rebel without a cause' and several commentators were also quick to make a similar point, seizing on the way that the simulacral retro styling of the ads collapsed the past and the present. Thus for Sarah Mower, the 'lethal combination of sex and nostalgia' plied in the ads was convenient shorthand to connote the escapist fantasy that in 1980s Britain there was no such thing as a uniform youth movement (as there had ostensibly been in the 1950s and 1960s) and that therefore, 'People are only too ready to look backwards and clutch on to the ethos surrounding Levis 501s.'[6] In contrast, Janice Winship refuted any simplistic notion of postmodern escapism in images or depoliticization through style in the 501 ads—and other simulacral campaigns such as posters for Brylcreem by Grey Advertising in 1986—asking more trenchantly: 'But why in 1986 should it be necessary to travel back to the future? Why more specifically should it be the 1950s which are providing the memories and images through which to explore being young in the 1980s?'[7]

In answering her own questions, Winship argued that it was not so much the case that there was not a 1980s youth movement, rather that 'in the 1980s, the struggle of being young has paradoxically turned around'.[8] She posited a more convincing ideological link between style revivalism and social reality, realizing that in the process of trying to denigrate—indeed to erase—the history of all post-war youth movements, the Thatcher government had ironically reinforced style revivalism not as a means of escapism but of protest for young people in the 1980s. Thus the 1950s, viewed as a golden age of youth hedonism and rebellion, spoke 'both of possibilities contemporarily denied the young and of problems experienced today'—problems such as unemployment topping more than 3 million by the start of 1983[9]—but in such a way that this vision of the 1950s should be regarded 'not as desire to return to the past but as a wish for a better present, and one means by which to create a different future'.[10]

Notes

1   Jean Baudrillard, 'The Precession of Simulacra', in *Simulacra and Simulation*, trans. S. F. Glaser (Ann Arbor: University of Michigan Press, 1994), 2.

2   See Robert Goldman, *Reading Ads Socially* (London: Routledge, 1992), 179–201, for an illuminating analysis of this campaign in the United States.

3   This television ad may be viewed in the Arrows Archive at the History of Advertising Trust website: www.hatads.org.uk.

4   H. Green, 'How Creative Minds Work', *Campaign* (20 September 1996), 23.

5   *Campaign* (29 November 1985), 39. See *Creative Review* (December 1983), 19 for a discussion of Levi's style-raiding practices generally.

6   L. O'Kelly, 'Levi 501s: Why Hegarty Knew the Time Was Right for a Denim Revival', *Campaign* (25 April 1986), 16.

7   Janice Winship, 'Back to the Future', *New Socialist* (July/August 1986), 49.

8   Ibid.

9   Alan Sked and Chris Cook, *Post-War Britain, A Political History* (Harmondsworth: Pelican, 1984), 435.

10 Winship, 'Back to the Future', 49.

24

HERE COMES NEW MAN—AGAIN

Evident in both Levi's 'Bath' and 'Laundrette' is the phenomenological dialectic of haptic visuality and 'the inscription of the touching in the visible, of the seeing in the tangible' expounded by Merleau-Ponty and that I addressed in Parts 1 and 2 in regard to publicity for Lyle and Scott, Dormeuil and Austin Reed. But whereas these press campaigns symbolize such a trans-sensory aesthetics by way of both text and image, in the Levi's ads it is left to the moving image alone, rather than the combination of music soundtrack and visual narrative, to convey the relationship between touching and seeing, clothing and skin. This is an instructive point, as the music not only replaces the use of dialogue but also totally obliterates the other sound effects, such as the rustle of the clothing being donned and discarded, we might expect to hear in the televisual jeans ads, to evoke a sense of material pleasure. It is by means of such a visual economy, therefore, that 'Bath' and 'Laundrette' represent not only the erotic charge of denim but also the giving over or immersion of selfhood to desire (whether one's own or that of another) that its aesthetic relationship to human skin evinces and that Laura Marks illuminates through her concept of the 'haptic eye': 'What is erotic about haptic visuality, then, may be described as the . . . loss of self, in the presence of the other'.[1] Thus, in the context of BBH's Levi's 501 campaigns, not only are the jeans positioned as a sensual product for the new man that he could mould to his body or whose material texture he could alter through stone-washing but so too is this sense of tactility imbricated with the pleasure he takes in looking at himself as he does so (viz. 'Bath') or looking at and being looked at by others as he does so (viz. 'Laundrette'). Indeed, Winship maintained in particular that the way Kamen performed his seductive striptease in 'Laundrette' engendered a 'new sex object'.[2] And explaining her choice of Kamen, casting director Ros Hubbard attested that what singled him out was 'sheer sexuality. A kind of animal magnetism. All the girls, and the boys for that matter, seemed to be drawn to him.'[3] As we have seen, the male peacock had already been put on display and objectified for the spectatorial pleasure of both men and women many times in menswear advertising since the 1920s, from promotions for the

Fifty Shilling Tailors and Austin Reed to Guards slacks and Van Heusen and Bri Nylon shirts (Figures 15, 19 and 25). In fact, 'Bath' and 'Laundrette' had inherited the sexualization of the male body in underwear campaigns such as those for Lyle and Scott y-fronts in 1972 (Figure 10) and the 1982 traffic-stopping billboard in New York's Times Square of a buff *gymnos* wearing his Calvin Kleins. But, as Winship, Chapman, Mort, Edwards and Nixon have all contended, by the mid 1980s this kind of objectification had not only intensified but also became more sexually ambiguous.[4]

Some female advertising critics saw this change as liberational and prog-ressive; as early as 1971 Erica Crome had commented that 'today underwear is very much a fashion area',[5] and in 1973 Cathy Goldhill stated: 'There is no better sign of the growing equalisation of the sexes than the interest men now take in their underwear.'[6] It is not for nothing, then, that in both 501 ads the display of underwear also had a prominent part to play through fetishistic close-ups of the male torso either dressing or disrobing, and indeed that they contributed to the popularity of boxer shorts with men between 16 and 30 years old.[7] But male critics found this kind of voyeuristic display of the male body in advertising troubling to patriarchal values. Writing about the same trend for the French-inspired, tight-fitting, colourful underwear hailed by Crome and Goldhill and inspired by the arrival of the Hom Brand in the United Kingdom, male advertising critic M. Vassie cavilled: 'Now the joke's on us . . . whether you fancy yourself in them is not the issue; what matters is whether she fancies you in them.'[8] And Mark Jones rejoined about the Levi's campaign:

> The Nick Kamen 'Laundrette' commercial represents the decade's low point for masculinists. The thought of that poor, misguided youth being leered at by millions of sex-obsessed women is just too awful to contemplate. The IBA gave agencies a charter to demean and exploit men's bodies by allowing this to go on air.[9]

Jones's comments bring us to consider the vagaries of the debate concerning masculinity and consumerism in the 1980s that had coalesced once more around the trope of new man. New man had previously been enlisted on two occasions to herald a singular type of twentieth-century fashionable male: first by Selfridge's advertising manager, Sidney Garland, in *Advertiser's Weekly* in 1919 and then, as we saw in Part 2, by head of menswear and styling for the House of Jaeger, Geoffrey M. Gilbert, writing in *Man and His Clothes* in 1953.[10] Suffice to say, new man was adland's dream male subject, and during the 1980s, therefore, various marketing studies probed more systematically the consumerist ethos of a certain constituency of British males (arguably, white-collar professionals, aged 18–35 years old). These studies were influenced by consumer lifestyle surveys, such as the Values and Lifestyles System (VALS) originated in 1978 by the Stanford

Research Institute to supplement the A–E economic classifications of the IPA/ NRS. VALS, which inherited Dichter's thinking, categorized consumers according to their motivation and temperament and coined types such as actualizers, who were well off and had the ability 'to take charge', and strugglers, who were in comparison poor, despairing and passive. By this measure, young fashionable males were ideally achievers (work-oriented conspicuous consumers) or experiencers (impulsive, rebellious and seeking variety).[11]

In a similar vein, the term 'new man' ended up being somewhat ambiguously and loosely defined, and was eventually used to sum up several different masculine typologies, from style leaders in fashion to the more emotionally centred, caring-sharing partner or father figure. In 1984, for example, the advertising agency McCann Erickson published its *Manstudy Report* and concluded that new man constituted 13.5 per cent of all British males. This percentage was made up of three distinct types: 'avant-guardians' or nurturers, who were strongly contemporary and politically iconoclastic in regard to patriarchal notions of masculinity; self-exploiters, who were at the forefront of social and cultural trends; and innovators, who were style leaders in fashion and clothing.[12] Several reports on menswear retailing and youth lifestyles by market research organization Mintel also pinpointed just how dominant an interest in fashion had become for young men. The first report in 1986, edited by Maurice Cheng, revealed how the menswear market had increased by 80 per cent between 1980 and 1985 and that in 1985 the total market was worth £3.4 billion.[13] The second in 1988, edited by Frank Fletcher, found that among 1,000 15- to 24-year-olds, 63 per cent had elected clothing as their top spending priority (indeed that 67 per cent of those unemployed declared it to be so), with jeans accounting for 73 per cent of all clothing expenditure.[14] And the final report in 1991 stated that between 1985 and 1990 consumer expenditure on menswear (excluding jeans) had increased by 32 per cent and advertising expenditure by menswear retailers had risen almost threefold from £981,000 in 1986 to £2,836,000 in 1990.[15]

In reaching their target new man audience, jeans and other menswear advertisers also relied very much on press publicity and especially on a cluster of style monthlies dedicated to a youth and/or male readership: *The Face*, *i.D*, and *Blitz* (all founded 1980); *Teenage Kicks* (eventually *Kicks*, founded 1981); *Unique* (July 1986–December 1987); *Arena* (founded 1986); *FHM* (founded 1987); and the British edition of *GQ* (founded 1988). Before the new man-in-bath motif appeared on television, for instance, a prototype of it had appeared in 'It's Still the Best Way to Get Fit', a two-page ad for 501s in *The Face*, October 1983. Similarly, during the summer of 1986, alongside *i.D*, *Tatler* and *Smash Hits*, *The Face* ran a series of ads photographed by Stak in which 501s were customized by various cult fashion designers such as Crolla and Paul Smith. In February 1986 *The Face* also featured 'Nuff Said', the first promotion by Fred Perry in 20 years for a polo pique shirt, art directed by Clive Norris at Wiscombe Baptie

Norris and with a striking photograph by Spencer Rowell. In fact, the polo shirt was one of the staple accoutrements of what the magazine had christened the ubiquitous 'matt black street urchin', whose style choices also included 501 jeans and a black or green bomber jacket.[16]

The Face first appeared in May 1980, the brainchild of Nick Logan, who had formerly edited *New Musical Express* and *Smash Hits*, and was published by Wagadon on (allegedly) a shoestring budget of £4,500.[17] Along with *i-D*, founded by Terry Jones and published by Levelprint Ltd, and *Blitz*, founded by Carey Labovitch and published by Jigsaw, it was one of three youth culture magazines launched during the recession of 1980–81 to tap both the imagination and wherewithal of young adults who had grown up in the shadow of punk. This was achieved by emphasizing music, club culture and, more notably, the idea of street style as a way of mixing, for example, army surplus store items with the accoutrements of high fashion.[18] Indeed, the avowed aim of Logan was to emulate the look and production values of the glossy fashion magazines but to break away from their more hidebound and exclusive convention of lionizing haute couture.[19] From a creditable first issue sale of 56,000 copies, the circulation of *The Face* peaked at 92,000 copies between 1985 and 1987 before settling down to an average circulation of around 50,000 copies.[20] During the 1980s it also went on to garner various design awards and to be the focus of several exhibitions. In 1983 it was elected Magazine of the Year in the Magazine Publishing Awards; in 1985 it was the subject of an exhibition at the Photographer's Gallery in London; and in spring 1988 the work of its chief designer Neville Brody, who was responsible for the magazine's distinctive style between 1981 and 1986, was showcased in the Boilerhouse at the Victoria and Albert Museum. As a result of this activity, the professional journal *Design and Art Direction* went on to claim that 'from a design point of view (*The Face*) is probably the most influential magazine of the 1980s'.[21]

Since its launch in November 1986 *Arena*, the stablemate of *The Face* that was targeted at males between 25 and 35 years old, likewise relied heavily on apparel advertising for the likes of Levi's 501; Katharine Hamnett's men's clothing line, which was featured in Hamnett's recently opened flagship store on London's Brompton Road, which was designed by Sir Norman Foster; and Clarks desert boots, which cost £30 and were publicized in an iconic campaign by BMP Davidson Pearce in 1988 and 1989, initially costing £75,000 to produce and circulate in the style press.[22] *Arena* attained a circulation of 60,000 copies for its first two issues,[23] and, from the outset, it also peddled an all too familiar eclectic perspective concerning new man: witness publisher Nick Logan's contention that:

I don't have any big philosophy of the new man . . . Take people like myself who became interested in fashion as mods in the sixties, or the soul boys and

Bowie fans of the 70s and 80s. If you become involved in fashion with that intensity I think it stays with you.[24]

Thus its editorial policy tended to stick to a tried and tested formula in terms of content that, until the early 1990s, made a deliberate appeal to the self-styled politics of new man and usually included many, if not all, of the following items: interviews with well-known personalities; articles concerning politics, culture, travel, cars, fitness, health, and sex; reviews of music, books, film and food; a section called 'Vanity' (later known as 'Eye') concerning matters of grooming, style and sartorial details; and, last but by no means least, fashion advertising and themed fashion spreads.

Hence, throughout the 1980s and into the 1990s, new man could be found in campaigns not only for Levi's 501 and others for clothing and grooming products but he also began to appear in advertisements for financial services (Nat West and Halifax), alcohol (Stella Artois), and health (most notably, Health Education Authority (HEA) campaigns for HIV/AIDS and related promotions for condoms). As Rowena Chapman went on to define him, therefore, new man was culturally diverse, the ubiquitous 'child of our time',

rising like Venus from the waves or Adonis from the shaving foam, strutting his stuff across posters, calendars, magazines and birthday cards, peering nonchalantly down from advertising hoardings, dropping his trousers in the launderette. He is everywhere. In the street, holding babies, pushing prams, collecting children, shopping with the progeny, panting in the ante-natal classes, shuffling sweaty-palmed in maternity rooms, grinning in the Mothercare catalogue, fighting with absentee mums and the vagaries of washing machines in the Persil ad.[25]

Yet, just as important was the ambiguous sexual charge of new man, something that clearly troubled Mark Jones and that Mort suggests, 'as a form of visual coding . . . eroticised the surfaces of the gay body'.[26] Patently, many advertisers at this time were intent on exploiting the hedonistic lifestyle of the gay scene and what came to be defined as the 'pink pound'.[27] In fact one such, Sports Locker (a mail-order service set up by Graham Haines in 1979 to sell American cult brands Devaney, Sub 4, Dolphin and Etonic), aimed its products and publicity at affluent gay men in the class A–B income group. Advertising from April 1980 in general titles such as *Time Out* and *The Stage*, and in niche ones like *Gay News* and *HIM*, Haines argued that 'there are many gay people who take more pride in their appearance and are prepared to put more effort into it than the conventional sports-conscious man . . . Everything we sell is geared toward people who look after themselves—ordinary people with good bodies— not perfect faces.'[28]

D. A. Miller, in his highly imaginative essay, *Bringing Out Roland Barthes*, has maintained that, while there does exist a mutual pursuit of the mesomorphic body beautiful by both straight and gay men, nonetheless:

> Only those who can't tell elbow from ass will confuse the different priorities of the macho straight male body and the so-called gym-body of gay male culture. The first deploys its heft as a *tool* (for work, for its potential and actual intimidation of other, weaker men or of women) — as both an armoured body and a body wholly given over to utility . . . whereas the second displays its muscle primarily in terms of an *image* openly appealing to, and deliberately courting the possibility of being shivered by, someone else's desire.[29]

Certainly, as Alan Klein has demonstrated, the gym is a border territory that permits a kind of institutionalized homosexual 'hustling' and the potentiality of sexual transgression.[30] But the difference between the body as *tool* and the body as narcissistic *image* is not necessarily as easy to distinguish in the way that Miller describes. In contrast, Mort maintains that the 'overall effect' of the cross-pollination that was evident in both the dress codes and youth identities of the late 1980s 'was deliberately to disrupt sexual meanings',[31] and several of the straight and gay male subjects he interviewed about their consumption practices reflected this point of view. For example, Andrew, a chef at the First Out gay café in London in 1987, attested, 'When I walk around I find it very difficult to tell who's gay and who's not,'[32] while Jonathan, a film studies graduate who was working as a barman in the Soho Brasserie, described male identities in terms of camp and performance: 'And you find yourself playing up to that . . . It's that front — sort of flirtatious. You're always flirting with the customers.'[33]

It is instructive that Jonathan refers to camp, playing a part, and flirting, since these strategies were firmly embedded in menswear publicity such as Levi's 'Bath' and 'Laundrette'. As we have also seen, however, they are evident in advertising for Dormeuil Tonik in the 1970s and afterwards in publicity for Russell & Bromley shoes and Yves Saint Laurent Rive Gauche (Figures 36 and 45). The former ad is redolent of the way many men were represented in the illustrations in British interwar publicity for pants and vests such as Aertex (*Punch*, 29 May 1929). Moreover, as I have argued elsewhere,[34] the homosocial iconography of some interwar underwear ads, such as a 1932 promotion for 'Celanese' (Figure 37) that represents men sharing a cigarette, reinforces the camp sensibility remarked on by Jonathan and, in particular, Eve Kosofsky Sedgwick's idea of camp as a gambit for projective fantasy — an opportunity for the ads' spectators to negotiate ambiguity by pondering, 'What if the right audience for this were exactly me?'[35] Thus, in co-opting the new man's body in fashion and clothing publicity on television and in magazines aimed at straight and gay readers alike, many advertisers strategically adapted a generic 'dual marketing' approach so as to 'speak to the homosexual consumer in a way that the straight consumer will not notice'[36] and, thereby, to acknowledge that taking an interest in one's appearance could be an acceptable and feasible project for all men, regardless of their sexual orientation. In the case of press publicity in 2004–5 for Dolce & Gabbana, this publicity also addressed age and in photographer Steven Meisel's homosocial bar scenes at least one of the men included has grey hair. For Levi's as well, this meant transcending the popularity that 501s had already accrued by the mid 1970s with the macho gay clone for showing off 'his bulging calves, his tantalising thighs, his perfect buns, and of course, his notorious basket' (the button flies and construction of the crotch in 501s produce a codpiece effect),[37] in order to make a wider appeal to a younger generation of style-conscious males, whether gay or straight.

The new man of the 1980s, therefore, has to be placed in the wider historical context of debates on gender and sexuality, although we should be wary of

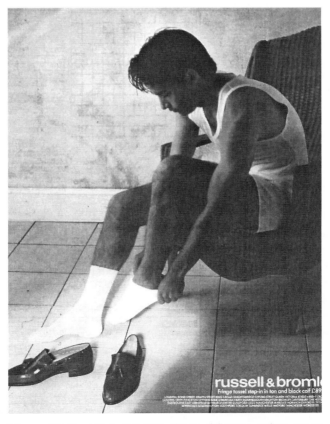

Figure 36 Russell & Bromley shoes, full-page colour press advertisement, 1986. Permission of Russell & Bromley Ltd.

Figure 37 Celanese underwear, full-page colour press advertisement, *Man and his clothes*, April 1932. Private collection.

simply regarding him as of a piece with his antecedents, not least in terms of his
attitude towards narcissism and style culture. Indeed, for many commentators it
is precisely on account of such consumerist values that the epiphany of new man
during the 1980s can be explained away as nothing more than a fiction or case
of media hype that had but little impact on patriarchal power structures or on
the way that the average male treated his body. Style guru Peter York called him
an advertiser's invention, who was driven by 'greed, corruption and treachery',[38]
and Judith Williamson, who in the Radio 4 programme *The Stylographers* in
1988 had lamented the vapid economy of capitalist chic that the style press
had engendered, concurred: 'the key fact about the new man is that he doesn't
exist.'[39] This perspective on new man is borne out by findings in Mintel's *Men
2000* report, published in 1993, in which only 18 per cent of those consulted
admitted that men were contributing to domestic chores and matters of child
raising, and was also sent up by Häagen-Dazs in one of their ads in 1999,

representing a suited and booted male vacuum cleaning his designer apartment along with the parodic copy, 'New man, once in a blue moon. A new flavour, every season. At least Häagen-Dazs is 100% Perfect.'[40] It is in this regard that we seem to be dealing with new man as a form of popular mythology or media hype. But even if this is the case, we would still have to make sense of new man as a cultural construct, however limited that may be, and to argue whether and to what extent we are dealing with the redefinition of masculinities, if not in reality, then idealistically in media texts like advertising. Chapman realized this much, arguing aptly: 'Men change, but only in order to hold on to power, not relinquish it . . . the new man ideal is . . . co-opted into the service of patriarchy.'[41] To put it another way, then, new man made manifest the social process that Barthes called inoculation. For, as he argued, it is through such acts of inoculation, which admit only a controlled amount of change or subversive activity to take place, that society immunizes 'the contents of the collective imagination', and thereby maintains its original hegemonic order.[42]

Notes

1   Laura Marks, *The Skin of the Film* (Durham, NC: Duke University Press, 2000), 193.
2   Janice Winship, 'Back to the Future—A Style for the Eighties', *New Socialist* (July/August 1986), 49.
3   Cited by Jim Davies, 'Campaign Craft: Profile', *Campaign* (18 October 1996), 22–3.
4   Winship, 'Back to the Future'; Rowena Chapman, 'The Great Pretender: Variations on the New Man Theme', in R. Chapman and J. Rutherford (eds), *Male Order: Unwrapping Masculinity* (London: Lawrence and Wishart, 1988), 225–48; Frank Mort, *Cultures of Consumption—Masculinities and Social Space in Late Twentieth-Century Britain* (London: Routledge, 1997); Sean Nixon, *Hard Looks: Masculinities, Spectatorship and Contemporary Consumption* (London: University College Press, 1996); Tim Edwards, *Men in the Mirror: Men's Fashion, Masculinity and Consumer Society* (London: Cassell, 1997).
5   Erica Crome, 'Underwear Circus', *Men's Wear* (22 July 1971), 12.
6   Christine Goldhill, 'Under-wares', *Men's Wear* (4 January 1973), 13.
7   This was confirmed by Danny Hughes, the brand manager of Jockey who is cited by M. Billet and S. Lynn, 'Below the Belt', *Men's Wear* (7 June 1990), 12–13.
8   Quoted in *Advertiser's Weekly* (1 September 1972), 21.
9   Quoted in *Campaign* (19 February 1988), 43.
10 Sidney T. Garland, 'Advertising Causes an Evolution in Men's Wear', *Advertiser's Weekly* (4 July 1919), 5–6: 'Generally speaking the average man to-day is paying much more attention to the question of clothing . . . and evidence shows that the "new man" is a keener buyer than he was before the war'. Gilbert, 'Meet the New Man', 26–7.
11 VALS consists of the following chief eight types: Actualizers (successful, well off; emerging leaders in business and politics; people with the ability to 'take charge'),

Fulfilleds (mature, retired people with a disposable income), Believers (conventional, patriotic, safe), Achievers (work-oriented people who value stability; conspicuous consumers who seek out products to demonstrate their success to others), Strivers (want the approval of others; who they want to be or what they want to buy is usually out of reach), Experiencers (young, impulsive, rebellious, seek variety), Makers (practical and self-sufficient; only interested in function and utility, and unimpressed by material possessions), and Strugglers (cautious consumers who are poor, badly educated, despairing and passive).

12 These typologies were foregrounded in McCann-Erickson's *ManStudy Report*, which was presented by Colin Bowring at the Institute of Practitioners in Advertising on 18 June 1984, and subsequently promoted by Marplan. See S. Marquis, 'The Publishing Conundrum: How to Reach the "New Man"', *Campaign* (26 July 1985), 39. Indeed, the nurturer can be seen as similar to the husband, whom William Cobbett acknowledged should contribute to domestic tasks in his treatise *Advice to Young Men*, 167.

13 'The Facts Behind the Theories', *Men's Wear* (27 November 1986), 9.

14 India Knight, 'The Teenage Rebel Is Dead', *Campaign* (13 May 1988), 58–9.

15 Mintel, *Clothing and Footwear Retailing Report* (London: Mintel, 1991); N. Compton, 'Campaign Trail', *Men's Wear* (29 October 1992), 15.

16 'Review of 1986', *The Face* (January 1987), 68.

17 The 2000 equivalent was £11,500.

18 By the late 1980s only *Blitz* remained independent. *The Face* was by then backed by Condé Nast and *i.D* by *Time Out*. See M. Honigsbaum, 'Blitz—No Time to Grow Up', *The Guardian Media* (2 September 1991), 23.

19 '*The Face* That Launched a Hundred', *Media Week* (22 July 1988), 29.

20 Paul Jobling, *Fashion Spreads* (Oxford: Berg, 1999), n.3, 46.

21 Dick Hebdige, 'The Bottom Line on Planet One—Squaring up to THE FACE', *Ten.8* 19 (1985), 41.

22 R. Johnson, 'Bona Fide Desert Boot That Enjoys A New Cult Status', *Campaign* (15 May 1987); 'A Step Back In Fashion', *Sunday Times* (20 November 1988). Clarks had an international turnover of £604 million for the year ending 31 January 1987, but only 9 per cent of the UK shoe market.

23 Jobling, *Fashion Spreads*, 50.

24 Quoted in *Campaign* (15 August 1986), 18.

25 Rowena Chapman, 'The Great Pretender: Variations on the New Man Theme', in R. Chapman and J. Rutherford (eds), *Male Order: Unwrapping Masculinity* (London: Lawrence and Wishart, 1988), 225–6.

26 Frank Mort, *Cultures of Consumption—Masculinities and Social Space in Late Twentieth-Century Britain* (London: Routledge, 1997), 178.

27 See H. David, 'In the Pink', *The Times Saturday Review* (13 June 1992), 10–11. David cites gay tourism as the prime indicator of the 'health of the pink economy'; in 1991, for example, the International Gay Travel Association grossed £247 million. At the same time, however, in the wake of HIV/AIDS and the implementation of Clause 28 in 1988, which banned the promotion of homosexuality by any local government agency, gay consumerism could be regarded as an act of political solidarity, a way of expressing one's individuality and existence in protest against marginalization and victimization by heterosexual society.

28 Quoted in M. Cockburn, 'Selling Sports Wear with a Difference', *Men's Wear* (14 August 1980), 24–5.

29 David A. Miller, *Bringing out Roland Barthes* (Berkeley, CA: University of California Press, 1992), 31.

30 See A. M. Klein, 'Little Big Man: Hustling, Gender Narcissism and Body-building Culture', in M. A. Messner and D. F. Sabo (eds), *Sport, Men and the Gender Order* (Champaign, IL: Human Kinetic Books, 1990), 127–40.

31 Mort, *Cultures of Consumption*, 179.

32 Ibid., 184.

33 Ibid., 192.

34 Paul Jobling, *Man Appeal: Advertising, Modernism and Menswear* (Oxford: Berg, 2005), 130–1.

35 Eve Kosofsky Sedgwick, *The Epistemology of the Closet* (Harmondsworth: Penguin, 1990), 156.

36 Danae Clark, 'Commodity Lesbianism', in H. Abelove, M. A. Brale and D. M. Halperin (eds), *The Lesbian and Gay Studies Reader* (New York and London: Routledge, 1993), 188.

37 C. Henley, *The Butch Manual: The Current Drag and How to Do It* (New York: Plume, 1982), 55.

38 Peter York quoted by C. Bowen-Jones, 'Adman Finds a New Woman', *The Times* (16 March 1988), 26.

39 Judith Williamson, 'Short Circuit of the New Man', *New Statesman* (20 May 1988), 28.

40 Mintel, *Men 2000* (London: Mintel, 1993). Mintel interviewed 1,576 men and women for their survey. Later research by Healey and Baker demonstrated that the number of men who did the main food shop had risen to 26 per cent during 1997. However, the increase was mainly among high earners under 24 years old living in London, while only 11 per cent of men with families admitted to shopping for groceries every week. See 'Shopping New Man', *Guardian* (20 January 1998), 14.

41 Chapman, 'The Great Pretender: Variations on the New Man Theme', 235.

42 Roland Barthes, 'Myth Today', in *Mythologies*, trans. A. Lavers (London: Paladin, 1973), 164.

25
A SOUNDTRACK FOR CONSUMERISM

MUSIC, IMAGE AND MYTH

Last, but by no means least, 'Bath' and 'Laundrette' brought renewed impetus to the role of music in generating or emphasizing the visual meaning of Levi's ads, something that had initially been achieved with 'Bottoms' in 1972. Indeed, as Hegarty himself attested: 'The music accounted for at least 50 per cent of the effect.'[1] It was this holistic approach that helped BBH to win a British Television Ad Silver Award and a Gold Lion Award at Cannes,[2] and for the songs 'Wonderful World' and 'I Heard It Through the Grapevine' to re-enter the British charts in 1986, peaking at no. 2 and no. 8 respectively. Levi's was not the first brand to make a successful commercial link between music and image, as 'Jeans On', David Dundas's song for Brutus's eponymous television campaign by Saatchi, had been a hit single in the summer of 1976 and also led the agency to win a D&AD award in 1977 for the best use of music in an advertising campaign.[3] But Levi's did set a singular trend, within its own publicity and that of other jeans manufacturers, for mobilizing iconic pop tunes in advertisements that cost a fortune to produce and screen (see Appendix IV): in 1990, for instance, the agency Simon Palmer spent £2 million on a television and cinema campaign for Wrangler (to which I shall return) that was shot by Roger Lyons in New York City with Jimi Hendrix's 1969 hit single 'Crosstown Traffic' as the soundtrack;[4] and in 1992 Grey Advertising spent £5 million on a television campaign for Lee that was directed by Steve Ramser and featured John Lee Hooker's 'Baby Lee', and the following year $10 million to produce a pan-European 60-second television and cinema campaign, directed by Michael Mann and with an original soundtrack, 'River Come Down', by Dave van Ronk.[5] What set these campaigns apart, therefore, was the way that the pop music soundtrack completely replaced the use of the jingle, dialogue or voice-over that had been expressly composed for a particular advertisement. In the use of music on such an associative level we are dealing with what Roland Barthes calls *l'écriture*, a form of writing whereby language—and by extension music—does not just convey its own meaning(s) but becomes a support for supplementary meanings as well.[6] This is also what philosopher Richard Wollheim refers to as 'tokens' of music performances, so that the recording (itself an allographic token of the original score, performance or autographic type[7]) in turn becomes another token by virtue of its interpretation, indeed its performance, in the commercial context of jeans advertising.[8]

On many occasions, the quotation of the music token in such publicity had little to do with relaying narrative, although it was used to express an emotional or aesthetic correspondence between the aural and visual components. This is evident with Levi's television campaigns 'Entrance' in 1987 and 'Surfer' in 1990. The first, directed by Steve Hopper and Dennis Lewis to promote black 501s, cost £3 million and starred stunt rider Eddy Kidd as a replacement for Nick Kamen (who was dropped after 'Laundrette' since the £70,000 fee he had requested just to appear in the new campaign was regarded as exorbitant by BBH).[9] But its music soundtrack, 'Stand by Me', first recorded by Ben E. King in 1961, was deployed to set the moody tonal atmosphere and complement the critical valorization of the ad (the black denims allow Kidd to circumvent the 'No blue jeans' bar to the night club) rather than for any appreciable diegetic effect. The second ad, 'Surfer', also costing £3 million, was directed by Tony Scott and used Bad Company's 1974 hit 'Can't Get Enough' as a soundtrack to illustrate the scenario of a dog stopping a bikini-clad girl from stealing the 501s of his owner, a surfer on a Hawaii beach. Tim Mellor, creative director of Publicis, lamented, however: 'It is a plot that is weak even by Just Seventeen standards . . . The kids don't look great, the photography is average and the track is bland.'[10] On other occasions, in close association with the image, the pop soundtrack was both the non-physical code and the mode of expressing some (often abstract) meaning about the physical product itself. Brutus's 'Jeans On' achieved this association on a very obvious level—the message of the lyric literally illustrating and underscoring the donning of different types of jeans by the male and female actors in the ad. But, as Roland Barthes also contended, the age of 'post-serial music has radically altered the role of the "interpreter"', such that the listener—as much as the performer—'is called on to be in some sort the co-author of the score, completing it rather than giving it "expression"'.[11] This is significant when it comes to interpreting the use of the pop record in postmodern advertising like that for Levi's 501, where 'the text is very much a score of this new kind: it asks of the reader a practical collaboration'.[12]

In the case of 'Laundrette', for example, the meaning of 'I Heard It Through the Grapevine' seems to be out of synch with the overall 1950s visual aesthetic of the ad's *mise-en-scène*. Yet, from the outset, the opening bars of the song, in a pulsating minor key, draw the spectator into the ad by creating a sense of suspense or anticipation as we also see Kamen's hand in close-up opening the door of what turns out to be a laundrette. And although the lyric, which tells the story of a man being the last to know that his lover is cheating on him, has no ostensible connection with blue jeans, the title and lyric of the song have much to do with the practical and ludic messages the ad conveys. Thus, as we hear Tony Jackson (who covered the original for the ad) sing, 'I bet you're wondering how I knew about your plan to make me blue', we observe Kamen remove his sunglasses to survey the laundrette and, unpredictably, to put the rocks, which will subsequently change the shade of his blue jeans, into the washing machine. The next line, 'With some other guy you knew before', overlaps with the image of the two teenage girls whispering conspiratorially behind their hands, while 'You took me by surprise, I must say' coincides with the segment of Kamen stripping off in front of his startled audience. Finally, in conjunction with the 1950s-inspired imagery, the 1960s Motown soundtrack provides a timeless ideal that reinforces the dual myth of youth culture's 'golden age' and the idea that blue denim is an American invention rather than originating, as it did, in Nîmes, France.

A similar mythology was portrayed in the iconic 1986 press ad by Yellow-hammer to promote Lee Rough Rider, 'The jeans that built America', which represented a muscular, topless new man from behind. He holds a scythe in a wheat field, as if he were a latter-day sharecropper (the name Rough Riders had actually been coined in 1898 to refer to the First U.S. Volunteer Cavalry) and his pose and body evoke George S. Evans's chauvinistic ideology that 'the wilderness will take hold of you. It will give you good red blood; it will turn you from a weakling into a man'.[13] The rural or Wild West theme was compounded in Lee's parallel cinema and television advertising, directed by Hugh Hudson, as well as several subsequent campaigns, including 'River Come Down' and 'Cowtown' in 1990, the latter filmed by Tim Pope in Phoenix, Arizona, and costing Yellowhammer £2 million to produce and air.[14] But in September 1991 a pan-European 60-second television and cinema campaign by Grey, costing £5 million, recodified the idea of the 'Jeans that built America' by locating the product in an urban milieu.[15] Directed by Roger Lunn, the ad was aimed at the market of 15- to 34-year-olds and portrayed the World Trade Center in New York City being clad in a giant pair of Lee jeans, which have been constructed by an army of buff new men. As we watch them carry out their task we also hear a classical music soundtrack, the 'Anvil Chorus' from Verdi's opera *Il Trovatore* (1853). In the opera, a chorus of male gypsies, working at forges, rhapsodize the love of a putative gypsy maid and sing 'To work, to work' as they swing their hammers and bring them down on clanking metal in rhythm with the music. A similar sense of biometric synchronization is manifested in the ad, where the movement of the new men's bodies as they 'build' the jeans echoes the tempo and rhythm of the music. The notable connotation of the ad is that the jeans are built (a masculine profession) rather than stitched (a feminine one), even though the men are portrayed carrying an enormous needle aloft.

At one and the same time, the audiovisual rhetoric of the campaign perpetuates a kind of timeless myth about the origins and construction of Lee jeans, which were first manufactured in 1889 in Kansas and became popular as work clothes during the 1930s, and as casual wear after 1954. Thus past and present seem to merge together seamlessly, though ambiguously, in the ad. The music is Italian and from the mid-nineteenth century, while the urban setting is late twentieth-century New York City, and the army of men creating a giant pair of jeans recalls and updates the Lilliputian tailors who fashioned some clothing to fit the giant Gulliver in Swift's utopian story, first published in 1726. Only now it is not for a human body the garment is made but a quondam architectural symbol of Western corporatism. Although it mobilizes a different set of cultural symbols from publicity for Levi's 501, the Lee campaign nonetheless ultimately promotes and legitimizes the idea that jeans are the result of both American industry and masculine heroism, in common with its competitor. To borrow a trenchant idea from Barthes: 'A conjuring trick has taken place; it [the campaign] has turned reality inside out, it has emptied it of history and has filled it with nature' — to the extent that the jeans magically clad the World Trade Center the right way up.[16] It comes as no surprise, therefore, that by 1991 several critics began to upbraid and satirize what they identified as the somewhat hackneyed lingua franca of jeans advertising, and even the agency WCRS had spoofed 'Laundrette' in an advertisement for Carling Black Label lager in 1986. For instance, S. Rice opined, 'To say that the public now expects a certain formula from jeans commercials might well be the understatement of the year. Since Nick Kamen set the tone in the laundrette in the middle of the decade, the groove has been fairly sharply defined.'[17] And Mike Court, joint creative director at Young and Rubicam, quipped:

How very simple it must be to do a jeans commercial these days.
Here are the guidelines:

1 Fill your commercial with young, moodily attractive people.
2 Occasionally pit them against old, fat repellent people.
3 Shoot in grainy black and white or oversaturated colour.
4 Buy the rights to an old track which can be plugged into becoming a number-one single.

It's very simple—and predictable as hell.[18]

In light of much jeans publicity between 1985 and 1991 such criticism was to a large extent justified. In 1991 BBH's annual advertising budget for Levi's 501 was £7 million, and it produced three more television campaigns that relied on an old pop track: 'Pool Hall', 'Camera' and 'The Swimmer' (see Appendix IV).[19] The tactic was, of course, a winning formula and aided the brand's hegemony in the jeans market until the winter of 1997, by which time sales of jeans in general had dipped, with Levi's down by 17 per cent.[20] Between 'Bath' and 'Laundrette' in 1985 and 'Flat Eric' in 2000, Levi's television and cinema campaigns had enlisted a pop soundtrack, with the exception of 'Fall' (1994), 'Kung Fu' (1997) and 'Kevin the Hamster' (1998). And yet, this was not always an unproblematic tactic. In 1996, for example, Tom Waits won damages of $20,000 from BBH for the 'distress and embarrassment' caused when a cover by Screamin' Jay Hawkins of his song, 'Heart Attack and Vine', was used to orchestrate 'Procession' (1993). The television campaign, shot in New Orleans and directed by Tarsem (Tarsem Dhandwar Singh), a graduate of the Art Center College of Design, Pasadena, who started his career in 1990 in music video, focussed on a young man commemorating the 'passing' of his 501s as he carries them to their place of burial.[21] At the same time, between 1985 and 1997, many of their campaigns mined a boy-meets-girl plotline, notably, 'Refrigerator' (1988), art directed by Marcus Vinton and starring pro-basketball player Bruce Hulse and Swedish-born model Tatyana Patitz; and 'Cinderella' (1992), directed by Tarsem and starring male model Cameron and Norwegian model Renate Karlsen. But there were also occasional subtle variations on this theme, such as 'Great Deal' (1990), 'The Swimmer' (1991) and 'Drugstore' (1995), and some that eschewed it entirely, such as 'Pawnbroker' (1989) and 'Pool Hall' (1990). Accordingly, we need to take a more balanced view of jeans advertising than Rice and Court propound and to take account also of those campaigns for Levi's and other brands that did not simply or entirely conform to their stereotypical formula.

Notes

1   Quoted in *Campaign* (29 November 1985), 43.
2   *Campaign* (25 April 1986), 5 and *Campaign* (4 July 1986), 8.
3   *Campaign* (10 June 1977), 20.
4   A. Garrett, 'New York Taxi Driver Blues', *Campaign* (19 January 1990), 30.
5   *Campaign* (9 October 1992), 37 and *Campaign* (12 November 1993), 4.
6   Roland Barthes, 'Blue Is in Fashion This Year' [1960], in *The Language of Fashion* (Sydney: Power Publications, 2006), 47.
7   The terms 'allographic' and 'autographic' are used by Nelson Goodman, *Languages of Art* (Indianapolis: Hackett, 1976), 113–22, to distinguish between art forms that are either 'two-stage' (music) or 'one-stage' (painting). Thus he argues: 'One notable difference between painting and music is that the composer's work is done when he has written the score, even though the performances are the end-products, while the painter has to finish the picture. No matter how many studies or revisions are made in either case, painting is in this sense a one-stage and music a two-stage act' (113–14).
8   See Richard Wollheim, *Art and Its Objects* (Harmondsworth: Peregrine, 1975), 90–100, for a wider discussion of different types of art (including music and poetry) and their contextual tokens.

9   *Campaign* (7 November 1986), 5 and *Campaign* (21 November 1986), 21.

10 Quoted in *Campaign* (19 January 1990), 12 and 13.

11 Roland Barthes, 'From Work to Text', in *Image Music Text* (London: Fontana, 1977), 163.

12 Ibid.

13 Cited in R. Nash, *Wilderness and the American Mind* (New Haven: Yale University Press, 1979), 14.

14 *Campaign* (30 March 1990), 7.

15 *Campaign* (6 September 1991), 7.

16 Roland Barthes, 'Myth Today', *Mythologies*, trans. A. Lavers (London: Paladin, 1973), 155.

17 R. Rice, 'Young, Trendy and Bland?', *Campaign* (11 April 1991),12.

18 Court quoted by ibid., 13.

19 *Campaign* (11 January 1991).

20 *Men's Wear* (5 February 1998), 1. AGB Fashion Track recorded a drop of 13 per cent in jeans sales in the eight-week period leading up to 22 November 1998.

21 'Levi's—the Golden Decade', *Campaign* (5 February 1993), 36–7; *Campaign* (3 May 1996), 43. In fact, 'Procession' was an updated version of a 1972 cinema ad for Levi's, 'Better to have had Levi's and lost 'em than never to have had Levi's at all', produced by Young and Rubicam, in which a bearded old cowboy buries his jeans and places his name tag on the grave. S. Stein, 'The Good, the Bad and the Ugly . . . Mostly Good', *Ad Weekly* (21 April 1972).

26
MORE THAN JUST A NUMBER

A NEW STYLE OF ADVERTISING FOR THE 1990s

A significant milestone in achieving the change from retro styling was the shift to gritty realist, or left-field, jeans advertising and it was introduced in 1990 not by Levi's but by its nearest market competitor, Wrangler. According to Marc Cox, director of the advertising agency BBDO, the bedrock of support for Wrangler was in the north of England, and in 1987 it spent £1 million on a poster campaign targeted exclusively at this constituency. Nationally, however, Wrangler played second fiddle to Levi's; in 1989, for instance, it had a 9 per cent share of the jeans market (on a par with Pepe Jeans) in comparison to Levi's 16 per cent.[1] The brand had evolved some interesting advertising campaigns with 'Diary of a pair of jeans' (1980) and 'Bus' (1988), a 30-second television and cinema ad directed by Andy Lawson for BBDO to the tune of £1 million in which a double-decker bus hurtles through the air over a row of twenty-seven motorbikes. But, by and large, Wrangler had struggled to find a consistent identity in and for its publicity, changing agents no less than six times between 1973 and 1990.[2] Thus, when the advertising agency Simons Palmer Denton Clemmow and Johnson took over the Wrangler account in 1990, it realized the need to craft an image for the brand that would put clear water between it and peers such as Pepe, which in 1989 had espoused a surreal-style of advertising directed by Tony Kaye and starring performance artist Leigh Bowery.[3]

Costing £2 million to produce and with Jimi Hendrix's 'Crosstown Traffic' as the soundtrack, the plot of the resulting Wrangler television and cinema campaign is about a taxi driver played by 40-year-old actor Paul Garcia, who had actually worked a stint driving a cab in New York between appearing in *Jaws 2* (1978) and *Trading Places* (1983). Fed up with his job and the sleaziness of life in the Big Apple, he abandons his cab midtown, rides a train to the airport and flies away to the sunshine. The storyline was written by Chris Palmer and filmed by Roger Lyons in Manhattan with a hand-held 16-mm Super-8 camera.[4] Although the campaign symbolized a utopian fantasy of escapism (evident in British advertising since the mid 1960s in promotions such as 'Getaway' for National Benzole with its emphasis on speed and motoring), its realist aspects went against the general ludic grain of most contemporaneous postmodern publicity, and certainly that for jeans. In the final cut, set-piece locations were montaged together with vérité snippets of provisional incidents from everyday city life, such as a knife fight that was caused by a mugger snatching another man's bag in a deli, and pictures of the real-life denizens that Garcia encountered on the streets of New York: a drunk, a cop, a businessman, a middle-aged transvestite and several black and white male vagrants and beggars. The edgy lyrics of 'Crosstown Traffic', about a sadomasochistic relationship between the singer and his girl, were not an exact match for what was going on in the ad, but they did complement the emotional turmoil of the taxi driver: 'Crosstown traffic/ I don't need to run over you/ Crosstown traffic/ All you do is slow me down/ And I'm tryin' to get to the other side of town'. This was definitely an advertising campaign that did not dodge the seamy side of the urban experience and was appositely aimed at a market of 15- to 25-year-olds that since 1986 had been repeatedly warned about the dangers of modern life and HIV/AIDS in the rhetoric of HEA propaganda such as 'This ad isn't meant to spoil your sex life'.

So convincing and innovative was the campaign that it won immediate critical acclaim. Alexander Garrett enthused that 'Wrangler's slice of cinema vérité is indeed unlike the image that most advertisers would look for in urban America. It plays *Mean Streets* to their *West Side Story*; street life to their high-school jinks,'[5] while Craig Smith heralded the campaign as 'a hard-hitting trendsetter for future style ads'.[6] The stylistic and rhetorical departure that Simons Palmer had taken in the audiovisual of the ad did, in fact, resonate with its target audience and the tag line, 'Be more than just a number', was underscored in 1991 when Brad Pitt appeared in *Thelma and Louise* wearing Wrangler's (although in 1991 he did also appear as a newly released jailbird in 'Camera' for Levi's 501[7]). Moreover, as much as Levi's publicity had revived an interest in old pop music, 'Taxi Driver' led to fresh demand for Hendrix's back catalogue and in October 1990 a special one-off television tribute, featuring graffiti-artist Denny Dent, was produced by Wrangler to commemorate the twentieth anniversary of Hendrix's death.[8]

Within the space of two years, the company had once more changed advertising agents—to TBWA Holmes Knight Ritchie—and, in keeping with Lee, had also decided to emphasize the association of jeans with the Wild West. Nonetheless, the tension between escapism and realism represented in 'Taxi Driver' was upheld in the series of 'Ranching Out' campaigns of 1993–6, which were masterminded by Trevor Beattie and focussed on the freewheeling and macho aspects of cowboy culture. This masculinism reached its apogee one year later with an exceptional campaign created by Nick Worthington and John Gorse for Abbott Mead Vickers BBDO as part of Wrangler's £16 million pan-European advertising strategy.[9] The six ads, unscripted and shot in a documentary style by director Spike Jonze at rodeos in Texas and Arkansas, featured actual riders talking in graphic detail about the risks they had taken and injuries they had sustained for the sake of their profession. Here cowboy culture is represented unequivocally as a type of independent masculinity that overlaps with Michael Kimmel's summation: 'He moves in a world of men, in which daring, bravery and skill are his constant companions. He lives by physical strength and rational calculation; his compassion is social and generalized, but he forms no lasting bonds with any single person.'[10] At the same time, the new style of advertising pioneered by Wrangler began to influence significantly the appearance and themes that were elaborated by BBH in its publicity for Levi's between 1993 and 1995. Ditching the boy-meets-girl formula, the agency decided to refocus on the product's American heritage in a series of pivotal press, poster and television campaigns.

With the advent of satellite television in the early 1990s, advertisers could gain maximum exposure on an additional fifteen channels, and Levi's 'Settler's Creek', which first aired in February 1994, was one of the first to achieve such high-profile visibility. (Arnell) Vaughan and Anthea (Benton), who had collaborated between 1982 and 2004 producing music videos and television advertisements, were its directors; the musical soundtrack, 'Inside' was specially composed by Peter Lawlor of Scottish band Stiltskin; and Worthington and Gorse were responsible for the plot and visualization.[11] It was filmed in atmospheric black and white, and the ad's nineteenth-century sensibility aimed to reaffirm the original connection of Levi's to the Californian gold rush; the ad went on to garner numerous creative prizes, including a D&AD silver award and the RSA Advertising Grand Prix.[12] In effect, the ad is a promotion for shrink-to-fit 501s and in it we witness a similar criss-crossing between the pleasure of seeing and touching as in 'Bath' in the close-up of the young male squatting to ensure a tight fit for the jeans around his buttocks. Moreover, the historicist plot of the ad is similar to 'Laundrette' on two counts: Peter Lawlor's timeless music soundtrack enlists a classically inspired choral chant at the outset that segues into a contemporary rock guitar solo, while its visualization also hinges on the act of male undress and the pleasure of the female spectator, though with a parodic sting in the 'tale'.

Two daughters on a family picnic in the Yosemite Valley of the Californian High Sierra decide to go for a stroll to the banks of the Merced River, where they spy, from behind a tree, a buff young pioneer bathing. The erotic tension and surreptitious pleasure of the situation are connoted through both the funky electric guitar solo and close-up shots of water trickling down the male's taut skin and chest intercut with others of the girls' pouting lips and keen eyes. Meantime, one of the sisters finds a pair of jeans at the water's edge, which they both (mis)take as his, their anticipation (and ours) mounting as he starts to make for the shore, ostensibly naked. With the denouement of the ad, however, their (and our) bubble is burst, as he is already wearing a pair of shrink-to-fit jeans and we discover that the jeans the girls have found belong to a grizzly, bearded old-timer in long johns, who has also been bathing in the river.

The ad conterminously subverts the usual dynamics of the keyhole aesthetic and plays a joke on the spying girls in the ad, as well as the equally complicit spectators of it, such that, as Barthes contends, in the name of fashion we 'no longer know what we can or should look at'.[13] It is also striking for the way it pays homage to the poetic photographic vision of Ansel Adams and the patrimony of the American land. Adams was born in San Francisco in 1902 and first visited the Yosemite Valley in 1916. His passion for the location was bolstered by involvement with the Sierra Club, an organization that had been founded in 1892 by the Scottish conservationist, explorer and mountaineer John Muir with the aim of studying and protecting the great wilderness areas of the United States. During the early 1920s, while still an amateur, Adams submitted several of his landscape photographs to the Sierra Club Bulletin, but his career really took off with the publication of the portfolio *Parmelian Prints of the High Sierra* by art patron Albert Bender in 1927. The prints included one of his most iconic images, 'Monolith, the face of the Half Dome, Yosemite National Park', which adumbrated the signature photographic style of his 'Zone System', encompassing a graphic range of monochrome tones between saturated blacks and incandescent whites.[14] It is this precise tonalism and the pristine super-realism of the images Adams printed on glossy paper, such as 'El Capitan, Merced River' (1938), that the producers of 'Settler's Creek' have emulated, and in such a way that—save for the fact the land in the ad is populated—it looks as if Adams could have directed it himself. To a certain extent, then, we can regard the ad as another act of postmodern simulation or quotation, portraying the timeless myth of a pre-lapsarian Eden or, as Joan Didion described the land in John Wayne's westerns, 'another world, one which may not have existed ever but in any case existed no more: a place where man could move free, could make his own code and live by it'.[15] And yet, it is altogether a more consistent and considered pastiche than 'Laundrette' or Lee's 'Rough Riders', which more self-consciously graft a 1980s sensibility onto an earlier historical period. Rather, in the way that it sympathetically harnesses time and space, the mytho-poetic *mise-en-scène* of 'Settler's Creek' embodies Mikhail Bakhtin's concept of the chronotope, through which he argued, 'spatial and temporal indicators are fused together into one carefully thought-out, concrete whole', and 'time, as it were thickens, takes on flesh, becomes artistically visible; likewise, space becomes charged and responsive to movements of time, plot and history'.[16]

BBH achieved an equally successful simulacral chronotope with 'Drugstore', which was directed by Michel Gondry in Texas and won multiple prizes in 1995, including a Gold Lion at Cannes and the British Television Advertising Award for best ad.[17] Alongside Gondry, Worthington and Gorse once more contributed to this critical acclaim. Worthington furnished the storyline, which had a safe sex subtext as a young boy visits a drugstore to buy some condoms to put in his jeans' watch pocket (a feature introduced by Levi's in 1873), only to discover when he calls on his girlfriend that her father is the pharmacist who sold them to him in the first place. And Gorse provided the visualization, which was inspired by the 1930s documentary photography of Walker Evans (a significant factor in BBH winning the Kodak Eastman Award in 1994 for the best use of craft in advertising). In point of fact, the years 1993 through 1995 marked an intense interest in different photographic styles in Levi's publicity and came littered with prizes. Thus in spring 1993 a series of posters and press ads promoting different styles of Levi's mobilized Bill Brandt's monochrome photographs of biomorphic female nudes. Initially shot in the late 1950s on the East Sussex and Normandy coasts, these photographs played on the tension between the animate and inanimate, homing in on body parts in order to make them look like stacks of rocks or pebbles. Mobilizing these photographs enabled BBH to make a deliberate association between advertising and art photography—as much as they did with 'Settler's Creek' in 1994—and to win a *Campaign* award for the best advertising poster of 1993.[18] But at the same time, BBH set out to reinforce the artistic pedigree of Levi's advertising by commissioning original work from several high-profile American photographers.

The trend kicked off in 1990 in the style press with a set of detachable postcards by *Vogue* photographer Herb Ritts, renowned for his fashion images of heroic male bodies, and the 'Best' press campaign by another celebrated fashion photographer, Richard Avedon, who was employed by *Harper's Bazaar* in the 1940s and 1950s and produced seminal work such as 'Dovima with the Elephants' (1955) that brought a sense of the extraordinary to the fashion shoot. Like Wrangler's neorealist 'Taxi Driver' ad, however, Avedon's campaign for Levi's featured ordinary professional types—a welder, a plumber and a fisherman—rather than fashion models. The photographs, therefore, emulated the hallmark style of Avedon's project *In the American West*, a series of uncompromising portraits that he took between 1979 and 1984 representing a cross-section of blue-collar workers and the unemployed. Hence, the subjects in the Levi's ads were shot in stark monochrome against a white background, their clothing and bodies smeared with the sweat and grime from their daily toil. And, in keeping with Wrangler's slogan 'More than just a number', they were invited to epigrammatize their individuality with a handwritten caption explaining why they preferred Levi's, which was printed alongside their portraits. Thus, Ling

Li, a photographer's assistant wrote, 'Every pair I ever had was different,' and Robert Horton, a fisherman, 'Because they fit . . . eventually'. According to Roy Edmundson, then marketing services manager for Levi's UK, 'People are far more likely to relate to people who have had real experiences, as opposed to some perfect bland face.'[19] The ads were indeed well received, winning two *Campaign* awards in 1991: gold for best press ad and silver in the fashion and clothing category.[20]

The success of this realist tactic was compounded in spring 1993, when art director Rosie Arnold commissioned another notable American photographer, Mary Ellen Mark, to shoot some portraits of the denizens of Miami. Beginning in the late 1960s Mark had carved out a reputation as a photojournalist, becoming a member of the Magnum cooperative between 1977 and 1981. In 1976 she produced *Ward 81*, a novel photoessay about female patients in a mental institution in Oregon, about which she later commented: 'I wanted to show their personalities—that was the thing that drew me to them.'[21] It was this consciousness that also led to her involvement with Miami, which she visited for the first time in 1979 and where she encountered a different kind of eccentricity. Mark later said, 'In many ways the reality of Miami is exceptional and extraordinary . . . I have this theory that the edges of countries will always cultivate far more weirdness than the centres.'[22] This antithetical vision of Americanness was precisely what BBH wanted to encapsulate in its advertising: 'We feel the crassness of the city is essentially the complete flip-side of the Levis' American mythology.'[23] To represent the flip side, then, and in contrast to the earnest workers in Avedon's photographs, Mark was asked to use colour film and to concentrate on the kind of people who would not be seen dead in jeans. Finally, to underscore their antipathy, captions by copywriter Chas Hendley such as, 'I hate them because they look so scruffy', were pasted on top of her images. Mark has professed that she did not ever set out to ridicule the people she photographed in Miami,[24] and that one of the problems with colour photography is that 'it becomes merely decorative'.[25] But this is precisely the point of the Levi's campaign, where both the captions and saturated colour palette of Mark's images caricature the excessive and ostentatious lifestyles of the subjects portrayed. By implication, therefore, the 'Miami' press campaign served to legitimize the street credibility of Levi's core market of jeans wearers, the so-called independent and sceptical Generation X of the early 1990s, which emerged as the economy went into recession yet whose spending power in Europe was estimated to be a considerable £260 billion per annum.[26] But, if BBH had set out to represent the plurality of American society in its campaigns between 1993 and 1995, at the same time this publicity had also tended to marginalize a significant part of the youth jeans market, namely those whose ethnic and racial identities were non-white.

Notes

1   *Campaign* (10 April 1987), 8 and *Campaign* (20 January 1989), 2.

2   In 1973 JWT ceded the Wrangler account to Doyle Dane Bernbach. Wasey
    Campbell-Ewald held it between 1976 and 1978, and in January 1979 Collett
    Dickenson Pearce took it over until 1987, when BBDO inherited it until 1990.

3   A. Garrett, 'New York Taxi Driver Blues', *Campaign* (19 January 1990), 12.

4   Ibid., 30.

5   Ibid.

6   Quoted in *Campaign* (23 February 1990), 31.

7   *Campaign* (11 January 1991).

8   When it was re-released in 1990, 'Crosstown Traffic' had a picture sleeve with
    some stills from the ad. *Campaign* (12 April 1990), 28.

9   *Campaign* (28 March 1997), 8. The 'Rodeo' campaign itself cost £2.5 million
    in 1997 at which time Wrangler still had only an 8.2 per cent share of the jeans
    market.

10 M.S. Kimmel, *Manhood in America: A Cultural History* (Oxford: Oxford University
    Press, 2006), 100.

11 This television ad may be viewed in the Arrows Archive at the History of Advertising
    Trust website: www.hatads.org.uk.

12 *Campaign* (6 May 1994), 4; *Campaign* (9 December 1994).

13 Roland Barthes, 'Fashion: A Strategy of Desire' [1966], in *The Language of Fashion*,
    (Sydney: Power Publications, 2006), 88.

14 Two detailed assessments of Adams's photography are Therese Thau Heyman
    (ed.), *Seeing Straight, Group f.64* (Oakland, CA: Oakland Museum, 1992) and
    James Alinder and John Szarkowski, *Ansel Adams: Classic Images* (Boston: Little,
    Brown, 1987).

15 Quoted in Gaby Wood, 'Western Hero', *Observer Review* (30 June 2002), 5.

16 Mikhail Bakhtin, 'Forms of Time and of the Chronotope in the Novel', in M. Holquist
    (ed.), *The Dialogic Imagination: Four Essays by M. M. Bakhtin*, trans. by C. Emerson
    and M. Holquist (Austin: University of Texas Press, 1981), 84.

17 *Campaign* (10 March 1995), 15–26.

18 *Campaign* (16 October 1993), 4.

19 Quoted in A. Holden, 'This Year's Models', *Guardian* (20 August 1990), 31.

20 *Campaign* (22 March 1991), 22.

21 E. La Bar, 'Conversation with Mary Ellen Mark', *Photographer's Forum* 2 (February/
    March 1980), 8.

22 Quoted in Ashley Heath, 'Kitsch 'n' Pink', *The Face* (July 1993), 59.

23 Ibid.

24 Ibid.

25 La Bar, 'Conversation with Mary Ellen Mark', 8.

26 'Generation X Advertising', report by Jane Robins, *The Money Programme* (BBC2,
    2 April 1995).

27
RACIAL SAMENESS AND RACIAL DIFFERENCE

Ethic and race minorities were not entirely absent from jeans publicity, rather, as with much advertising in general, there were significant colour-blind spots in the way they were objectified. As early as 1959, the Institute of Practitioners in Advertising (IPA) had sent the Home Secretary, R. A. Butler, storyboards and designs by several agencies for a public service press campaign promoting racial harmony, but he turned them down. Posing the question, 'If people are prejudiced and talk of "coons, coloureds, wogs and niggers" will advertising change their opinions?' the IPA proposed a similar initiative 10 years later for a national press and television campaign, but once more it came to nothing.[1] These projects throw into sharp relief, therefore, the dilemma that agencies faced right up to the turn of the millennium regarding inclusion of black people in British advertising. It was not until the mid 1990s that black people appeared in publicity for washing-up liquid or coffee and a survey of ads on ITV and Channel 4 between June and August 1997 by the Glasgow University Media Group calculated that not only were 90 per cent of actors white but that white actors also got more lines and more diverse roles. Even today, blue-chip companies such as British Airways, BMW and Marks & Spencer do not buy banner space on websites such as Blackbritain.co.uk. As Werbane McIntyre, co-owner of WM and P, the first advertising agency for black people founded in 1984, concluded: 'British companies are scared to use blacks because they assume that whites will decide that product x or y is strictly for blacks.'[2]

One of the most persistent considerations cited by the advertising industry for such colour-blindness, then, is grounded in class and economics: in 1973, for example, the wages of blue-collar West Indians, between £1,500 and £3,000 per annum, were less than what teacher Joe Rea, one of the 'unofficial poor' discussed in Part 2, had earned in 1971, and certainly could not match the earning power of the lucrative and desirable A–C1 target audiences that most advertising addressed.[3] And while a report by the Campaign for Racial Equality in 1997 contended that there had been many positive changes in race relations since its inception in 1977, it found in comparison to the white British majority that both the Irish and black ethnic communities still suffered from higher than average unemployment rates and were also less likely to own either a car or their own home.[4] Yet this fiscal argument was flawed when it came to the retail of jeans. Since the late 1970s, for example, Levi's had been sold at considerable discount in London outlets such as J. Mart and Dickie Dirts, where they cost as little as £8.50 in comparison to Selfridges' £18.50.[5] And in 1997, Tesco started to sell Levi's 501 imported from the United States for £30 (they cost £52 at Levi's own stores) until the European Court of Justice banned them from doing so in November 2001.[6]

An additional problem in the promotion of clothing has been the dearth of black models. David Mainman tried to rectify the situation when in 1969 he set up a British agency called Black Boys,[7] yet even by 1996, only four of the ninety-six male models represented by Boss were non-white: Gary Dourdan, Robbie Brooks, Asio and Rod Foster.[8] This very low number could be put down to two factors: first, the general misconception that fashion was exclusively a job for gay men, as averred by (white) male model Pete Avey in 1972: 'I had the opinion that most of the public have, that all male models are queers';[9] and second, the express homophobia and heteronormativity of many black communities that, according to Horace Griffin, paradoxically originated as an antidote to the obscenities of slavery: 'Given the majority culture's racism and sexual attitudes, African Americans soon learned their very survival depended on distancing themselves from "sexual perversions."'[10] Indeed, not one of the five male models interviewed by the *Sunday Times Magazine* in 1977 about their skin- and hair-care regimen was black, and while they all responded positively to a question about homosexuality and the fashion industry, shrugging it off as inconsequential, interestingly, the question of racial prejudice did not surface.[11]

A significant way round the problem of exclusion has been the use of 'black' sportsmen, or more accurately photogenic males of dual heritage. Thus John Conteh, light heavyweight boxing champion in 1974 whose parents were Irish and Sierra Leonean, appeared in a press ad for Austin Reed in 1976 (though clad in training gear rather than the Safari look merchandise being promoted) and in poster ads by JGA Partners for Hom underwear in 1979 (Figure 38). In 1996, Liverpool's Anglo-Jamaican goalkeeper David James appeared in press ads for Armani underwear and jeans to the extent that not only do the silvery monochrome photographs make his skin look white but their 'sculptural code' also 'turns black male flesh to stone'.[12] At the same time, the use of the competitive black athlete in menswear and jeans advertising panders to the stereotype that sporting achievement is often the only way for race and ethnic minorities to assert or express any kind of power in postcolonial societies: 'the dreams of the native are always of muscular prowess; his dreams are of action and aggression.'[13]

Figure 38 Austin Reed, full-page colour advertisement, *Sunday Times Magazine*, 1976. Permission of Austin Reed.

Accordingly, the sexualized depiction of the black athlete was an entirely different affair from the more buttoned-up and staid representation of white sportsmen in menswear publicity, such as former England football captain Bobby Moore for Hornes in 1967, or Alex 'Hurricane' Higgins (snooker), Eric Bristow (darts), and Fred Trueman (cricket) in John Collier's press campaign in spring 1981.[14] Thus the fact that black role models conformed to the hegemonic stereotype of what being black or non-Caucasian means has served to bolster the ideological fantasy of 'commodity racism', a term that Anne McClintock coined in her assessment of nineteenth-century soap advertising.[15] Similarly, while some advertising appeared to address race discourse in straplines such as 'Tern's bid to end white supremacy' (*Sunday Times Magazine*, 22 October 1967), in the final analysis their rhetoric was nothing more than a hollow parodic gesture, in this instance co-opting a political message for the commercial gain of promoting colour shirts. If, then, as bell hooks has argued, 'Ads are a primary vehicle for the dissemination and perpetuation of white-supremacist and patriarchal values,'[16] the question remains: how representative is this view of jeans—and by extension menswear—advertising in Britain since the 1950s? As we have already seen, the likes of Levi's and Wrangler did not represent black sportsmen or celebrities in their advertising. Nonetheless, from 1972 onwards they did vicariously rely on the voices of such culture by mobilizing the records of black soul and blues musicians as the soundtrack for many of their campaigns. It was not until some time later, however, that non-white subjects began to appear in British publicity for various jeans brands and in such a way that overlaps with the two contradictory tendencies of racial sameness and racial difference that Susan Willis has identified at play in postcolonial commodity culture.[17]

In the three BBH television and cinema campaigns for Levi's in 1993, 'Tackle', 'Procession' and 'Campfire', non-white subjects make only a token appearance. 'Tackle' was directed by Carlton Chase and went on to win silver for Best International Commercial at the 1994 British Television Advertising Awards.[18] The tag line, 'In 1922 Levi's did the decent thing and added belt loops', denotes another of the practical valorizations of 501s, just as 'Drugstore' did in the case of the watch pocket. But as the latter had also imbricated this message with another concerning safe sex, so too did the narrative of 'Tackle' orbit around the familiar boy-meets-girl plot. The ad deals with a game of rugby and is set in California in 1921, one year after the US national team (nicknamed the Eagles) had won gold at the Olympic Games. From the sidelines of a muddy playing field a young woman in a white dress looks longingly at one of the players, who loses his jeans as he scores a try, while a black infant appears fleetingly as he makes mischief by sending a dog onto the pitch to fetch the ball. 'Campfire', directed by Tarsem, is set sometime in the 1930s and its plot (such as it is) concerns a female photographer, who seems to be modelled on the photojournalist Margaret Bourke-White, taking a plein-air group portrait of cowboys and fur traders, whose number includes an American Indian.[19] But the soundtrack, Johnny Cash's 'Ring of Fire', specifically illustrates the humorous scene where one of the cowboys overheats his jeans by crouching too close to the campfire and thereby it also promotes the practical valorization of the tag line, stating that Levis' removed the 'notorious crotch rivet' from 501s in 1941. By contrast, 'Procession', directed by Tarsem and Martin Galton, was set in contemporary New Orleans, but the black people in the ad appear more or less as extras to the main event; thus a group of them—some playing in a jazz band—follow the young tanned man, who is carrying a pair of worn-out 501s to their place of rest.

With 'Taxi' (1995), however, conceived by Roger Beckett and directed by Baillie Walsh in New York City, the black subject is very much centre stage (as he had been in Wrangler's 'Crosstown Traffic') and the idea of racialized sexuality is the central concern. The egregious ad represents a cross-dressing black male, who may also be a transsexual, and like 'Drugstore', it could not be screened on television before 9 p.m. due to its subversive content.[20] The ad's story takes place on a rainy night in New York City, where an elderly couple hail a cab in Times Square. To their consternation, the driver ignores them and picks up someone that he—and we—take for a glamorous black female, wearing jeans and a cropped red top. As the journey proceeds, he keeps looking at 'her' in the rear-view mirror, and she checks out her make-up in a compact mirror. Suddenly, to the horror of the driver, she takes an electric razor from her handbag and starts to shave her chin. In this case, the soundtrack, Freakpower's 'Turn On, Tune In, Cop Out', with its lyric about transgression and transformation, provides a reciprocal ekphrasis to the corresponding images, involving what Françoise Meltzer has called a free exchange and transference between visual and verbal art: 'You gotta know who's driving your car/ Or else you're starring in "a cruise too far"/ Turn on, tune in, cop out/ Let it flow now mama/ Let it flow become a woman.'[21]

This is an entirely different kind of gender-bending, therefore, from the white middle-aged transvestite in Wrangler's 'Crosstown Traffic', who is obviously a man wearing black tights and skirt, or the carnivalesque masquerade in Levi's 'Girls' press ads of 1994, in which two young white men are photographed with bad make-up and clothes—one of them sporting an ill-fitting blonde wig—as if to reinforce the sense of parody. Furthermore, the depiction of polymorphous perversion in 'Taxi' is not dissimilar to that in Neil Jordan's film *The Crying Game* (1992). In this complex tale about the Troubles, a young black man passes successfully as both a female hairdresser and a torch singer called Dil and has two male lovers: Jody, a black British soldier serving in Northern Ireland, who has been kidnapped by the IRA and is killed by accident during an attack on their hideout in Armagh; and Fergus, one of his kidnappers who flees to London after the attack and seeks to protect Dil, having already been shown a photograph of her by Jody. Fergus, however, begins to fall in love with Dil, eventually discovering her/his liminal sexual status when they spend their first night together. He is shocked and repulsed initially, but decides to stay with Dil and it is around this gender ambiguity that the remainder of the film's plot hinges. In 1994, a cinema ad for Hom, directed by Eugene McGing for Young and Rubicam, also ripped off and debased this plot, depicting a 'strange' female who picks up a man in a bar and who reveals 'herself' to be a man wearing Hom underwear before his very eyes when 'she' undresses in the bedroom.[22]

Of course, the narrative of Levi's 'Taxi' does not in any way contain the political complexity of *The Crying Game*. Nonetheless, it does centre around what Eila Rantonen has called 'the mystery of the black woman's sexuality',[23] proffering a challenging view of the intersection of race and gender identities and the Manichean ambiguity of being 'the same but not exactly the same'.[24] In this regard, we need to consider what is at stake in the ad by representing such a border crossing between race, gender and sexuality, as much as Rantonen does about *The Crying Game*: 'Fergus's and Dil's fascinating relationship also refers to the possibility of two kinds of readings: either as a warning against inter-racial and non-heterosexual love or as a vigorous defence of inter-racial and queer love.'[25] Looking at things this way, we could argue that the ad connotes a double—or even a triple—negative in which the otherness of race and the otherness of gender are intertwined to equate what the white majority has mythologized and, as Griffin maintains, many non-white people have been at pains to disavow: sexual perversion and black culture. According to Freud, as well as to nineteenth-century sexologists such as Richard Burton and Havelock Ellis, same-sex partnerships were endemic in many 'savage' and 'primitive' races.[26] But looking at things from the opposite end of the telescope, we could also argue that the marginal sexuality of the black transvestite/transsexual in the ad is an opportunity to traduce the 'master-codes of dominant culture' and 'decentre, destabilise and carnivalise' them through a process of mimicry.[27] In this way, s/he enacts the disruption of and resistance to what the white—and in this case also black—norm is expected to be. As Homi Bhabha has contended: 'In occupying two places at once . . . the depersonalized, dislocated colonial subject can become an incalculable object, quite literally difficult to place. The demand of authority cannot unify its messages nor simply identify its subjects.'[28] Thus it is not until the 'she' who rides in the taxi checks 'her' chin for stray stubble that the driver's—and our—doubts are raised about the identity of his passenger and that we encounter what Julia Kristeva crystallizes as 'the presence of the "other scene" within us'.[29] Otherwise, much like Dil in *The Crying Game*, 'he' convincingly passes as a glamorous and feminine black woman. Finally, his cross-dressing also troubles the closing caption, 'Cut for men since 1850', which takes on a double meaning: literally, that 501s are worn only by men, and metaphorically, that they are worn (by whomever) for the pleasure of men.

Notes

1   M. Wilson, 'Admen's Colour Problem', *Ad Weekly* (12 December 1969), 36–7.
2   Quoted in *Guardian* (2 March 1987).
3   W. Collins, 'Capturing the Black Market', *Adweek* (13 July 1973), 24. The respective 2000 equivalents of £1,500 and £3,000 were £16,200 and £32,400.
4   Campaign for Racial Equality, *The Irish in Britain* (London: Belmont Press), 1. Although this study is not the place to debate in close detail the relationship between race and class inequalities, or indeed how racial difference is an ideological construct that capitalist societies can rely on to cover up the disparity between the rich and poor, Barbara J Fields, 'Slavery, Race and Ideology in the United States of America', *New Left Review* 1:181 (1990), 95–118, proffers a compelling argument about these issues in American society and culture.

5 'Cheap Jeans War Hots Up', *Men's Wear* (28 May 1981), 7. The respective 2000 equivalents of £8.50 and £18.50 were £25.50 and £55.60.

6 *Independent* (27 March 1997); S. Pook, 'Tesco Loses Fight to Sell Levi's at American Prices', *Daily Telegraph* (27 November 2001). The import of discounted Levi's from the European Union was, however, not banned.

7 'Special Agents', *Look-In Fashion Model Annual* (London: Independent Television Publications, 1971), 49–55.

8 George Wayne, *Male Super Models: The Men of Boss Models* (New York: D.A.P., 1996), 30–1, 96–7, 124–5, and 133.

9 Quoted in *Sunday Times Magazine* (23 April 1972), 33. On the 'sexual danger' of modelling, see also Joanna Entwistle, 'From Catwalk to Catalogue: Male Models, Masculinity and Identity', in H. Thomas and J. Ahmed (eds), *Cultural Bodies: Ethnography and Theory* (Cambridge: Wiley-Blackwell, 2004), 55–75.

10 Horace Griffin, *And Their Own Receive Them Not: African American Lesbians and Gays in Black Churches* (Cleveland, OH: Pilgrim Press, 2006). Griffin, a gay African-American seminarian, traces black homophobia and the emphasis of heteronormativity in the church across a complex intersection of relevant issues such as class, age, family and profession.

11 Ann Chubb, 'Who's a Pretty Boy, Then?', *Sunday Times Magazine* (3 April 1977), 26. The models, all over 30 years old, were Michael Edwards, who at the time was reputedly the world's highest paid male model, earning a minimum of £500 a day; Michael Balsa; Graham Rogers, who had appeared in Dormeuil's 'Tonik for men' ads between 1976 and 1977, and who quipped, 'There are probably as many homosexuals in the mines as there are in modelling'; Fred Henrick, an underwear model; and Tuty, who replied, 'Homosexuality? That's a very old fashioned question. Life is short—you have to enjoy it the best way you can.'

12 Kobena Mercer, 'Reading Racial Fetishism: The Photographs of Robert Mapplethorpe', in *Welcome to the Jungle* (London: Routledge, 1984), 177.

13 Frantz Fanon, *The Wretched of the Earth* [1963], trans. C. Farrington (New York: Grove Press, 1985), 40.

14 *Men's Wear* (2 April 1981), 9. See *Sunday Times Magazine* (30 April 1967). Other examples of white sportsmen and presenters in menswear advertising include Innes Ireland, Peter West, Ted Dexter and Danny Blanchflower for Peter England shirts' 1963 television and press campaign (*Men's Wear*, 26 January 1963, xxx); cricketer Ted Dexter in Daks Simpson press publicity in May and October 1968 (*Men's Wear*, 4 July 1968: 10); and Jackie Charlton for Leeds-based Maple Clothing in 1974 ('Jackie OBE is more than just a name to Maple', *Men's Wear,* 4 July 1974, 33); and George Best (then playing for Hibernian) modelled suits for Scottish outfitter Tom Martin in the *Daily Record* in 1979 (*Campaign,* 4 January 1980, 2).

15 Anne McClintock, 'Soft-soaping Empire: Commodity Racism and Imperial Advertising', in G. Robertson et al. (eds), *Travellers' Tales: Narratives of Home and Displacement* (London: Routledge, 1994), 131–55.

16 bell hooks, 'Doing it for Daddy', in M. Berger, B. Wallis and S. Watson (eds), *Constructing Masculinity* (London: Routledge, 1995), 101.

17 Susan Willis, 'I Want the Black One: Is There a Place for Afro-American Culture in Commodity Culture?', *New Formations* (Spring 1990), 77–97.

18   *Campaign* (11 March 1994).

19   Bourke-White had been employed as a staff photographer on *Life* and during the Depression had also collaborated with Erskine Caldwell on the photo-documentary book *You Have Seen Their Faces* (1937). See Paula Rabinowitz, *They Must Be Represented: The Politics of Documentary* (London: Verso, 1994), chapter 3.

20   *Campaign* (10 February 1995), 2.

21   Françoise Meltzer, *Salome and the Dance of Writing: Portraits of Mimesis in Literature* (Chicago: University of Chicago Press, 1987), 21. Ekphrasis is commonly defined as the verbal representation of visual representation. See James Heffernan, 'Ekphrasis and Representation', *New Literary History* 22:2 (Spring 1991), 297–316.

22   *Campaign* (16 December 1994), 31.

23   Eila Rantonen, 'A Game of Chess: Race, Gender and Nation in Neil Jordan's *The Crying Game*', in J. Nyman and J. A. Stotesbury (eds), *Postcolonialism and Cultural Resistance* (Joensuu: University of Joentsuu, 1999), 198.

24   Homi K. Bhabha, *The Location of Culture* (London: Routledge, 1994), 86–9.

25   Rantonen, 'A Game of Chess', 198.

26   Sigmund Freud, 'Three Essays on the Theory of Sexuality' [1905], *On Sexuality,* J. Strachey (ed.), Penguin Freud Library, Vol. 7 (Harmondsworth: Penguin, 1977), 49–50; Richard Burton, *The Book of a Thousand Nights and A Night,* Vol. 10 [1885] (Boston: Milford House, 1973) and Havelock Ellis, *Sexual Inversion: Studies in the Psychology of Sex*, Vol. 2 [1897] (New York: Random House, 1936), 64.

27   Kobena Mercer, 'Diaspora Culture and the Dialogic Imagination', in M. M. Cham and C. Andrade-Watkins (eds), *Blackframes: Critical Perspectives on Black Independent Cinema* (Cambridge, MA: MIT Press, 1988), 57.

28   Homi K. Bhabha, 'Remembering Fanon', foreword to Frantz Fanon, *Black Skin, White Masks* [1952] (London: Pluto Press, 1986), xxii.

29   Julia Kristeva, *Strangers to Ourselves*, trans. A. Roudiez (New York: Columbia University Press, 1991), 181.

28
FROM 'MOTHERS' TO 'FLAT ERIC'

RACE, GENDER, AGE AND GENERATION

It is more than 50 years since Frantz Fanon wrote that 'not only must the black man be black; he must be black in relation to the white man',[1] and yet the tendency to co-opt black identities has persisted in much jeans—and menswear—advertising. Simultaneously, however, there have also been some campaigns that have attempted to represent black subjects uncompromisingly on their own terms, or at least to mobilize mimicry 'as one of the most elusive and effective strategies of colonial power and knowledge'.[2] Indeed, one of the most cogent challenges to white hegemony in the visual and verbal rhetoric of several advertising campaigns for clothing has been the destabilizing mimicry of street-smart black youths, which sequestrates and exaggerates the stereotypical traits of their own culture in order to parody and rehabilitate them. Simons Palmer was one of the first agencies to realize the potential of this strategy with its monochrome television and cinema ad for Wrangler in 1991. The ad starred Bronx rapper K Bazz playing the part of a libidinous pirate radio DJ in Los Angeles who fantasizes about a girl in her underwear.[3] But in 1997, a cluster of menswear ads added critical mass to black mimicry. These ads included, 'A man should be judged by the colour of his shirt' for the cult youth brand Ben Sherman that had been trading since 1963,[4] featuring a photograph by Jack Bankhead of a black male, arms crossed and staring at us defiantly; and 'Hush Puppies used to be worn by fathers. Now they're worn by mothers' (Figures 39 and 40).

The latter, one of a series of ads in a £1 million campaign by Delaney Fletcher Bozell, was a blatant attempt by the ad agency to transcend the staid identity that the brand, founded in 1958, had gained for its comfortable suede crepe-soled casuals.[5] With copy by Pete Kew and documentary-style photography by Jake Chessum, the ads represented cool young Americans wearing shoes in different colours in urban settings.[6] In this instance, we observe an insouciant

Figure 39 Ben Sherman, 'A man should be judged by the colour of his shirt', double-page colour press advertisement, 1997. Permission of Grey London.

Figure 40 'Hush Puppies used to be worn by fathers. Now they're worn by mothers', double-page colour press advertisement, 1997. Permission of Wolverine World Wide Inc.

black youth sitting on the steps of a tenement block wearing a pair of red Hush Puppies and copy that sublates the pejorative slang of American black culture — 'mothers' being shorthand here for 'mother fuckers', a term that literally refers to the Oedipal taboo of incest but that is a broader metaphorical form of abuse, used frequently as a putdown by black actor Samuel L. Jackson in the film *Pulp Fiction* (1994) and rapper Snoop Dogg in his song 'Down 4 My Niggas'.[7] By comparison, a 1997 press ad for Lee's original denim jacket by Grey advertising, with a grainy photograph of a black male taken from behind and surrounded by a halo of light, pays more than a passing resemblance to 'Feel me', a 1993 press campaign for Häagen-Dazs, and in the process transforms an image that Anoop Nayak insists is one of victimhood and slavery into one of auratic strength.[8] In the latter, the man's back is naked and bears the imprint of a hand in the dripping vanilla ice cream; in the Lee ad the jacket the man wears not only underscores the copy that states, 'h.d. Lee helped millions of Americans get into shape', but also emphasizes his muscular torso.

BBH likewise exploited the trend for mimicry, but with an additional twist, in its print campaign of autumn 1996 for different styles of Levi's that appeared in *The Face*. The advertisements featured colour photographs of male and female models, all over 60 years of age, by the celebrated fashion photographer Nick Knight. One of them, Alonzo, was 86 and at the time the oldest black cowboy in Colorado still to ride in the rodeo. We are a far cry here from Wrangler's 'Ranching Out' television campaign of 1993–96 or Levi's ads such as 'Pick Up' (1989) and 'Camera' and 'Pool Hall' (1991) for that matter, all of which ridicule older or more conservative men by pitching them against virile young bucks. Rather, as Knight explained, his warts-and-all approach was intended to transcend the fashion industry's aversion to ageing by making the models 'look sexy and heroic, so you don't just look at these people and say: "Oh, look at that old person"'.[9] Although, like Wrangler's publicity, the aim of 'Oldies' was to make Levis' hip with the core market of 16- to 24-year-olds by reminding it of the brand's heritage, the fact that jeans were also worn by older people suggests that the campaign would have resonated with them as well.[10] Mintel's report, *Men 2000*, for instance, had recorded that 51 per cent of men bought a pair of jeans in 1993,[11] with the biggest increase among the group of 45- to 54-year-olds, while another contemporaneous report on jeans retailing by the advertising agency DMB & B revealed that 56 per cent of the group of 15- to 65-year-olds expressed Levi's as their brand of choice.[12] These market figures contest the reckoning with 'epidermic self-awareness' that Umberto Eco argued makes wearing jeans fraught with anxiety for corpulent men and those past their prime.[13]

In any case, the favouritism that Levi's had enjoyed with either young or old consumers began to diminish within the space of two years. As part of a downturn in the overall sale of jeans, the brand had suffered a 15 per cent decline in annual sales, from $7.1 billion in 1996 to $6 billion by 1998.[14] At this time Levi's was being flatfooted by the rising popularity of The Gap and the paradigm shift to baggy jeans by designer labels such as Polo, Hilfiger, Boss and Diesel. More than ever, this decline in sales emphasized the need to promote its product through inventive publicity and thus it is hardly surprising that Levi's advertising budget remained constant. Data by Media Monitoring for fashion advertising between August 1996 and July 1997, for instance, put Levi's as top for cinema publicity, with expenditure of £1,284,555, and third in regard to television, with a sum of £3,040,538 (Wrangler was second and fourth in these categories, with respective figures of £658,211 and £2,186,848).[15] The change of fortune in the jeans market, therefore, resulted in a shift toward more experimental moving image advertisements, a cluster of which first appeared in spring 1996.

One of the first was the 'Cheat' ad for Guess jeans, directed by Andy Morahan for Paul Marciano Advertising. The campaign was shot in black and white in California and starred well-known Hollywood actors Harry Dean Stanton, Juliette Lewis, Traci Lords and Peter Horton. Its story, concerning infidelity, double-dealing and entrapment, was somewhat predictable: a rich heiress (Lords) employs a private eye (Stanton), who uses a hired hand (Lewis), to find out if her fiancé (Horton) is cheating on her. However, the creative filmic editing of the ad by John Smith was much more original: 'I wanted to give the viewer a lot of information but not in a conventional way.'[16] Hence, on one level, he combined sequences in which the narrative unfolds with others of Stanton talking to the ads' spectators as he drives his car and used overdubbed dialogue to explain why Lewis was prepared to act as a professional decoy: 'Julie's trying to get through college, I'm gonna make sure she does it.' And on another, he used a mixture of video and Super 8 footage to introduce a neorealist parallel story of surveillance, interlarding shots of Horton picking up Lewis in a bar with those of Lords' reaction as she listens to the deceit unfold in Stanton's tape recording. The campaign was a one-off but it did raise the bar regarding the relationship of creativity and complexity in jeans advertising.

Levi's initial response in 1996 came in the form of two campaigns that were targeted ostensibly at its female market: 'Planet', directed by Vaughan and Anthea, and 'Washroom', directed by Simon Robinson, which was a gold winner in the clothing category of the British Television Advertising Awards of 1996.[17] The former, with 'Spaceman' by Babylon Zoo as its soundtrack, had an overt—albeit weak—science-fiction plot as Russian supermodel Kristina Semonovskia emerges from a space ship wearing 501s. (The theme was also evident in a much more sexualized way one year later in Grey's £5 million television and press campaign for Lee, 'The first pair of jeans in space', directed by Adrian Moat. As a male and female astronaut weightlessly float around, she takes control of the situation and anchors him to her body by threading the waist button on her jeans through the fly of his.)[18] In contrast, 'Washroom', directed by Simon Robinson and with 'Falling Elevators' by MC 900ft Jesus as the soundtrack, was set in the real world. Filmed in Los Angeles, the plot dealt with a female gangster, who is dropped off by a man in a car at the bathrooms of a service station. She enters the male toilet and proceeds to change her appearance, removing her blonde wig and red lipstick. As she does so, a black man wearing dark glasses and holding a walking stick sits in the corner of the bathroom. Understanding him to be blind, she strips off her clothing without any hesitation and puts on a pair of jeans, standing in front of his face as she buttons up the flies on her 501s. Suddenly, a toilet flushes and as another black man opens the door the punchline of the ad is revealed: the seated man is not blind at all but has been holding the stick for his friend. Although the plots of both 'Planet' and 'Washroom' are ostensibly concerned with female empowerment, their subtext is nonetheless similar to 'Taxi' insofar as it implies that the ultimate beneficiary of women wearing jeans is the (even putatively blind) male spectator.

BBH's next campaign for 501s, directed by Michel Gondry and first screened on television in February 1997, once more made an overt appeal to male consumers. The ad was shot in a large marine tank in Malta and unfurls the story of a drowning handsome sailor being rescued by mermaids.[19] At first, they apply mouth-to-mouth resuscitation to him before trying to remove his jeans, which will not budge because he is wearing shrink-to-fit 501s. The ad won gold in *Campaign*'s Television Advertising Awards, but while its creative treatment was remarkable, essentially its plot and soundtrack, 'Underwater Love' by Smoke City, resorted to Levi's staple boy-meets-girl plot in which the man becomes an object of desire but manages to retain the upper hand.[20] Furthermore, the male fantasy it portrays very much overlaps with the rise in chauvinistic—and frequently leery and boorish—advertising imagery targeted at so-called new lad.

In January 1991 a press release for *GQ* announced that 'New Man has officially been laid to rest', while Sean O'Hagan, writing in *Arena* in the same year, was one of the first to use the moniker 'new lad' to describe his replacement.[21] It was, however, the launch of *loaded* in 1994 that started to capsize what John Robb called the 'fake "new man" crap' of the 1980s.[22] While it is arguable whether 'laddism' itself had ever gone away (after all, 'new men' were a minority), some of the overtly juvenile and reactionary attitudes of mainstream masculinity had at least been tempered by the way much fashion advertising in the period 1985–95 had ushered men's bodies into an ornamental realm of desire. As Rosalind Gill has argued, new man and new lad are discursive entities and 'rather than one displacing the other, they *coexist* as alternative formulations of masculinity'.[23] Given that there could be considerable seepage between one and the other (notably, a shared interest in women, cars, grooming, going to the gym and sport), it is not surprising that a residue of new man's interest in style and fashion survived into new lad culture; indeed, it was embraced by it. Certainly, from 1991 onwards there was a detectable shift toward more sexist imagery in *GQ* and *Arena* and what Sean Nixon summarizes as the 'assertive articulation of post permissive heterosexual masculine scripts'.[24] But at the same time, both titles still contained advertising for the likes of Versace, Calvin Klein and Yves Saint Laurent that queered straightness (Figure 45), which I address in the epilogue, and publicity for Ben Sherman that also appeared in the gay men's monthly *Attitude* (founded 1994). The significant differences between new man advertising and that aimed at new lad, therefore, were that the latter was never feminized, nor was there any suggestion that men were or should be interested in feminism, and most serious of all, a pathological disavowal of homoeroticism (paradoxically, even when it was targeted at a gay clientele). The key reason for the success of laddism, then, as Tim Edwards describes it, lay in the way that it 'reconciled, at least artificially, the tension of the Playboy and the Narcissist'.[25] This amalgam of identities is evident in publicity from Base shoes, 'No guts, no glory', depicting a bare-chested lad drinking his female partner under the table,[26] to Ben Sherman's 'Mum, wash me shirt', part of a £1 million print and poster advertising campaign by Grey, with a muscle-bound male photographed from behind as he cheekily throws the garment over his shoulder (Figure 41).[27]

In turn, both campaigns validated the masculinity of young working-class males, something that Levi's also achieved in its typologizing of new lad, though in a curiously inventive way, with 'Flat Eric' in 1999, the last of its campaigns to target jeans exclusively at male consumers. Rather than 501s, the three

Figure 41 Ben Sherman, 'Mum, wash me shirt', double-page colour press advertisement, 1997. Permission of Grey London.

television and cinema advertisements promoted Sta-prest trousers and denims, which had first been publicized in 1971,[28] and were backed up with a complementary campaign in the style press with photographs by Nadav Kander. The ads—featuring the eponymous furry yellow puppet and his human sidekick Angel—were directed in Los Angeles by Quentin Dupieux of Partizan Midi Minuit, who also produced the theme tune 'Flat Beat' and under the alias Mr Oizo had made a pop video in 1998 with dancing sock puppets to promote his techno EP. From these origins, Flat Eric was created specially for the ad campaign by Janet Knechtel of Jim Henson's *Muppets* workshop, and was the second animated creature to appear in Levi's publicity, following Mike Mort's and Deiniol Morris's 'Clayman' of 1995. Each of the three ads picked up on the insouciant attitude of new lad to life. 'Dancing', for example, shows the pair driving their battered American motorcar while they listen to the techno beat booming out of the car stereo. In 'ID' they are seen driving through suburbia, when they are pulled over by a cop who wants to see their papers, at which point Flat Eric changes the soundtrack from techno to country and western. Finally, in 'Fly', Angel is dozing as Flat Eric nods his head enthusiastically to the techno music and sips his 'Wizz' soda through a straw. Charlotte Raven has rightly argued that the surprising thing about the advertisements was 'the fact they are about friendship rather than sex' and, thus, they provided a departure from the chauvinistic message prevalent in much publicity aimed at new lad.[29] However, another key message of the 'Flat Eric' campaign was the intense interest that new lad took in his personal appearance and clothes, even if he did not seem to care about anything else. In 'ID', for example, the cop also invites Angel to open the boot, where we see he keeps his pristine clothes folded in neat piles, while in 'Fly' sartorial catastrophe beckons: as Flat Eric squats an insect that has landed on the impeccable knife-edge cease of Angel's Sta-prest trousers.

After the critically panned 'Kevin the Hamster' television campaign of 1998, therefore, 'Flat Eric' rehabilitated Levi's advertising to cultural prominence, in the process winning *Campaign*'s ad of the year award and receiving silver in the clothing category of the British Television Advertising awards of 1999. At the same time, 5 million copies of its 'Flat beat' techno soundtrack were sold across Europe and fans began to create their own Flat Eric websites, while an editorial in *Campaign* declared that BBH 'had successfully thrown off the "boy meets girl" theme . . . and discovered a contemporary classic'.[30] Hence, 'Flat Eric' brings us full circle in this analysis of jeans publicity, from the heady optimism of the 1970s to the new man iconography of 'Bath' and 'Laundrette' in the 1980s, and from the creative high spots of 'Creek' and 'Drugstore', aimed at Generation X in the mid 1990s, to the impact of new lad by the late 1990s and early 2000s. In my epilogue, therefore, I want to take stock of the implication of this turning point in jeans advertising as well as to trace some common threads and themes in menswear publicity in Britain since the Second World War.

Notes

1 Frantz Fanon, *Black Skin, White Masks* [1952], trans. by C. L. Markmann (London: Pluto Press, 1986), 110.

2 Homi K. Bhabha, 'Of Mimicry and Man: The Ambivalence of Colonial Discourse', *October* 28 (Spring 1984), 126.

3 *Campaign* (1 November 1991), 27.

4 Ben Sherman's first shop was opened in Brighton in 1963, with its Carnaby Street outlet following on in 1964. The brand accrued cult status with various youth movements such as the Mods in the 1960s and the Punks in the 1970s, and in the early 1990s was re-popularized by Britpop bands Oasis and Blur.

5 During the 1970s, Hush Puppies had also been promoted as a forward-looking brand. See, for example, the advertisement, 'We've changed because you've changed', *Sunday Times Magazine* (26 March 1972). While the styles of shoes advertised were called 'trend-setting', the ad copy dwelt also on 'the built-in comfort you expect from Hush Puppies'.

6 *Campaign* (4 April 1997), 6.

7 See J. Dawson, *The Compleat Motherfucker: A History of the Mother of All Dirty Words* (Port Townsend, WA: Feral House, 2009).

8 Anoop Nayak, in his illuminating article, 'Frozen Bodies: Disclosing Whiteness in Häagen-Dazs Advertising', *Body & Society* 3:3 (1997), 51–71, contends among other things, that the handprint is a form of slave branding: 'The mark signifies the absent presence of whiteness' and 'brings to the surface the taboo of cross-racial sex' (55).

9 Quoted by Karl Plewka, 'Jeans Genius', *Observer Life* (12 May 1996), 40.

10 Ibid.; *Campaign* (31 July 1992), 29.

11 *Men's Wear* (3 March 1994), 4.

12 *Campaign* (21 December 1995), 1. The report also revealed the following popularity figures: Wrangler (13 per cent), Lee (5 per cent) and Pepe (3 per cent).

13 Umberto Eco, 'Lumbar Thought', in *Faith in Fakes: Travels in Hyperreality* (London: Minerva, 1995), 194. Wrangler's national poster campaign of 1992, 'W fronts' with a photograph by Malcolm Venville of an older man wearing only his underwear, socks and suspenders and smoking a pipe, plays on a similar sense of ridicule.

14 E. Espen, 'Coming Apart at the Seams', *Observer Review* (28 March 1999), 1. See also *Men's Wear* (5 February 1998), 1, which cites a 13 per cent fall in jeans sales in the eight-week period leading up to 22 November 1998.

15 'Fashion Report—Who Spends What and Where', *Campaign* (19 September 1997), 6–7.

16 Quoted in C. Marshall, 'Guess Editor Defies Convention to Leave His Mark', *Campaign* (31 May 1996), 37.

17 *Campaign (supplement)* (15 March 1996), 21 and 23. 'Washroom' was also gold winner in the European advertising category.

18 *Campaign* (31 January 1997), 8. The ad's soundtrack was 'Legends' by Sacred Spirits and because of raunchy content it was not screened on television until after the 7.30 p.m. watershed.

19 This television ad may be viewed in the Arrows Archive at the History of Advertising Trust website: www.hatads.org.uk.

20 *Campaign* (14 March 1997), 22.

21 Sean O'Hagan, 'Here Comes the New Lad', *Arena* (May 1991), 22–3. There is an illuminating and diverse assessment of new lad in Beth Benwell (ed.), *Masculinity and Men's Lifestyle Magazines* (Oxford: Blackwell, 2003).

22 Cited in John Beynon, *Masculinities and Culture* (Milton Keynes: Oxford University Press, 2002), 110.

23 Rosalind Gill, 'Power and the Production of Subjects: A Genealogy of the New Man and the New Lad', in Beth Benwell (ed.), *Masculinity and Men's Lifestyle Magazines* (Oxford: Blackwell, 2003), 38, italics in the original.

24 Sean Nixon, *Hard Looks: Masculinities, Spectatorship and Contemporary Consumption* (London: University College Press, 1996), 203.

25 Tim Edwards, 'Sex, Booze and Gags: Masculinity, Style and Men's Magazines', in Beth Benwell (ed.), *Masculinity and Men's Lifestyle Magazines* (Oxford: Blackwell, 2003), 144.

26 The Base brand was launched in 1995. It coincided, therefore, with the rise of lad mags such as *FHM* and *loaded*, which according to Base, 'provided the perfect platform to talk directly to the target audience' (http://www.baselondon.com).

27 *Campaign* (14 February 1997), 7. The ads appeared in *The Face*, *loaded* and *Attitude*.

28 *Ad Weekly* (16 July 1971), 24. The editorial chose Levi's Sta-prest campaign, 'Relax. They'll still keep their crease', as its ad of the week. One ad featured nine photographs of a man in different yoga positions; another had a black male doing a limbo dance. The ads appeared in the *Daily Mirror*, *Sun*, and *Reveille*. The agency was Young and Rubicam, the creative director Dennis Auton, the copywriter Dolores Beashel, the art director Rodney Jeffs, and the photographer Hiroshi Yoda.

29 Charlotte Raven, 'How a Furry Yellow Muppet Restored My Faith in Culture', *Guardian* (9 March 1999), 5. These television ads may be viewed in the Arrows Archive at the History of Advertising Trust website: www.hatads.org.uk.

30 *Campaign* (14 January 2000), 35; *Campaign* (10 March 2000), 27.

EPILOGUE

GETTING THE RIGHT FIT—OBJECTS/ IMAGES/READERS

In the period of 60 or so years that this book has covered, publicity for menswear underwent significant transformations in its form and content, not least of which were the introduction of television advertising and the orientation towards a youth market in the 1950s. What, then, in the final analysis are the common threads—if any—that might unify a study concerning the production, circulation and interpretation of such publicity? And what, if anything, does it contribute to our understanding of the history of advertising and masculine identities in post-war Britain?

From the very outset, advertising was clearly considered a potent socio-economic force by the majority of menswear retailers, and in particular popular multiple tailors such as Burton's, Austin Reed and the Fifty Shilling Tailors, rechristened John Collier in spring 1954, dedicated sizeable publicity budgets to promoting their wares. For instance, throughout the post-war period of austerity and material deprivation that entailed rationing, which lasted until May 1949, and the Utility clothing scheme, which ran until 1952, men of all classes were still demonstrating a keen wish to own a new suit and advertisers were simultaneously spending huge amounts to encourage them not to lose sight of the object of their desire. Between January and March 1951 the press and poster publicity budget for tailors was £35,923 and for underwear brands it was £35,458 (both amounts equivalent to some £670,000 in 2000), while for the same period in 1952 it was £98,608 for tailors and £45,790 for underwear (equivalent to £1.7 million and £730,924 respectively in 2000). With the dawning of affluence and the teenage market this upward trend in print advertising continued unabated until the turn of the millennium. Multiple tailors Hector Powe spent £23,000 in 1960 and £100,000 in 1970 (equivalent to £314,448 and £839,781 respectively in 2000), while Burton's spent £90,000 in autumn 1985 (or £162,000 in 2000) on just one campaign in the *Daily Mirror* and *Daily Express*. But so too did several menswear advertisers resort to advertising on television. Rael Brook shirts, for example, was one of the first retailers to realize the potential of the medium, spending some £50,000 in 1959 (equivalent to £690,444 in 2000), while Burton's was spending £216,000 (or £2.6 million in 2000) on both press and television publicity by the close of 1963. After 1978, when television and cinema publicity became the principal media for jeans, advertising expenditure hit stratospheric heights with the likes of Levi's splashing out £4 million in 1985 on its 'Bath' and 'Laundrette' campaigns alone.

In general terms, since the Second World War there was also a correlation between the class and age markets for certain menswear products and the periodicals and newspapers in which publicity for them appeared. So, for instance, at the cheaper end of the market advertising for Bata shoes appeared in C1 and C2 titles such as *Picture Post* and the *Daily Mirror* in the late 1940s and 1950s, while at the same time middle-market retailers such as Austin Reed veered towards advertising in class A and B titles such as *Punch* and the *Sphere*. But there was class permeability in menswear advertising and campaigns for Austin Reed appeared in *Picture Post* as well between 1946 and 1948, while Burton's publicity appeared in both the *Daily Mirror* and *Sunday Times Magazine* in the 1960s and 1970s. It was the latter, along with the other newspaper colour supplements and magazines such as *Weekend*, *Town* and *Men in Vogue*, that by the early 1960s began to exploit both the new colour web-offset printing technologies and the youth culture zeitgeist. Thus they challenged advertising on television as well as introducing publicity that one critic regarded as 'the understated, the elegant, the urbane, the witty, the pleasantest advertising of all to look at and read'.[1]

A useful starting point to consider the production of advertising, therefore, might appear to be the issue of period style, and yet even a cursory survey of the formal aspects of the campaigns included here contests any attempt at straightforward classification; apart, that is, from the broad stylistic binaries of modernism and postmodernism. Certainly, between 1945 and 1960, hand-drawn illustration held sway in press and poster publicity for a wide spectrum of retailers and brands—from Austin Reed to Simpson and from Radiac shirts to Lyle and Scott y-fronts—and, in the form of animated dancing shirts, it even encroached on early television campaigns for Rael Brook. However, illustrators as diverse as Alexis Delmar, Ashley Havinden, Max Hoff and Poul Sprøgøe tended to have a signature style of their own rather than conforming to a common graphic language. Furthermore, as we have seen, there was considerable variation in the letterforms that different advertisers used: both Austin Reed and Burton's, for example, preferred serif typefaces in their publicity (Bodoni and Walbaum respectively), while Daks Simpson and Wolsey relied on Gill Sans as well as Havinden's singular Ashley brush script. When it comes to photographic forms of advertising between 1955 and 1975, a clearer picture emerges of a neo-modernist aesthetic. After 1958 this was singularly inspired by the so-called Swiss School precepts of white or unprinted space, simple (usually sanserif) type forms, and crisp pop-influenced images with a stark monochromatic contrast or, between 1962 and 1975, in vibrant colour as well. To one degree or another all of these formal devices are evident in publicity for Burton's, Austin Reed, Clarks, Sumrie wool, Tern shirts and synthetics such as Terylene, C-Nylon and Acrilan (Figures 7, 19 and 23). Simultaneously, however, these ads vied for attention with the likes of Alan Aldridge's psychedelic-inspired campaign for Austin Reed Cue Man and the eclectic historicism apparent in Dormeuil's 'Cloth for Men', the latter ranging respectively across the Gothic Revival, aestheticism and art deco styles (Figures 17 and 26–8). Not only did this eclecticism persist into the 1990s but the reliance on historicist imagery was also heightened in much jeans publicity. It is pointless, therefore, to speak of menswear advertising since 1945 in crude terms as a series of uniform decade styles, and more productive instead to realize that styles of advertising varied within any given decade, as much as changes in fashion and clothing did.

By extension, the alpha-pictorial content of menswear publicity was as dependent on external social and cultural forces as it was on the internal mechanisms of the advertising and fashion industries. Until rationing and Utility came to an end, therefore, the key message of campaigns for menswear was one of delayed gratification and the promise of better things to come, as poetically exemplified in publicity for Austin Reed (Figure 5). With the onset of affluence in the early 1950s and until the turn of the millennium, however, the leitmotiv of advertising rhetoric for the majority of retailers and brands responded to the lifestyles of youth culture and the male peacock, in which the emphasis was on freedom, hedonism and sexual desire. By spring 1983 Jack Bridges had quipped, 'Leaving aside advertising for jeans, men's wear advertising in the consumer press usually seems to sit in an asexual vacuum . . . the average men's wear advert positively avoids any suggestion that the other sex even exists.'[2] Yet even the quickest glance through the campaigns included in this book reveals that this was not the case, and well before jeans advertising in the 1980s, the male body was not only on display—as in a 1947 poster for Baracuta or print ads for y-fronts in 1954 and Austin Reed in 1962 (Figures 3, 9 and 19)—but, often, was also represented as a sex object, as in publicity for Bri Nylon and Van Heusen shirts, and Guards trousers in the 1960s (Figures 15 and 25). The issue here is not just one of making men visible as sex objects, but also how visible and what type of sex object they should be. In this sense, it is undeniable that the verbal and visual rhetoric of menswear publicity progressively became more daring and subversive after 1960. Of particular interest in this regard is men's underwear advertising.

In the interwar period, the 1940s and the 1950s illustrations of men in vests and pants had been common; witness the promotions for Celanese and Lyle and Scott (Figures 9 and 37). By the early 1960s photography had begun to take over in such publicity and, although they featured images of men wearing underwear, the overall message of press ads, such as those for Activity string underwear, tended to harp on the product's practical and critical valorizations (Figure 42). Thus the copy and graph in the Activity ad informed the potential purchaser that the product would keep him cool in summer but warm in winter and cost only 8s. 6d. (the equivalent of £5.62 in 2000), while the comfortableness of string underwear was reinforced in the photograph of a man, smiling as he relaxes in his pants and vest. Yet at the same time, the way that copy and image emphasize the phenomenological pleasure of not only experiencing fabric against the skin but also being seen enjoying the material experience of it betrays another tendency in several of the menswear campaigns—from underwear to sweaters and jeans—addressed in this study: that is, the idea of haptic visuality and the dialectic of looking good and feeling good that involves, as Maurice Merleau-Ponty has argued, 'an inscription of the touching in the visible, of the seeing in the tangible—and the converse'.[3] In photographic advertising from the 1970s onwards this imbrication of the senses was conveyed in a candid, sexualized fashion, such as the print ad 'What the best undressed men are wearing' for y-fronts in 1972 (Figure 10). Here, we observe a man wearing only colour underpants and slippers standing in an art deco-styled living room as he reads a newspaper. Nonetheless, he is portrayed as being comfortable on show in his own skin as he is in the y-fronts he wears, while any sexual ambiguity concerning the display of the semi-nude male body is dispelled by the female shoes and garments that have been casually discarded around the place to suggest either a pre- or post-coital conquest.

From these beginnings, both print and television publicity for men's underwear resorted more and more to two strategies in making products appeal to the male and female spectator/purchaser. Sometimes they fell back on copy based on double entendre, such as 'What women look for in men's underpants' in Cogent Elliott's 1983 press ad for Wolsey, and 'As recommended by a pair of nuts' in Brass Monkey's 1995 VH1 television campaign for figure-hugging Lycra trunks, which according to Mintel had become the most popular style of male underwear—with both men and women—by 1993.[4] Otherwise, they relied on images that emphasized the pleasure of looking at the genital bulge or packet, as is the case with publicity for Jockey's colour ribbed cotton collection, restyled by Douglas McLennan to commemorate the firm's fiftieth anniversary in 1988 (Figure 43); Steven Meisel's infamous photograph of Marky Mark wearing CK stretch boxers in 1992; 2xist, which had become a cult brand with gay men from the 1990s; and Emporio Armani since 1995 (Figure 44). In 2008 Armani signed up footballer David Beckham for a three-year publicity deal worth some £10 million to promote tight briefs in press and billboard monochrome photographs by Mert Alas and Marcus Piggott that caused his wife, Victoria, to comment she was 'proud to see his penis 25ft tall. It's enormous. Massive'.[5]

The ads led to a 30 percent surge in sales of the brand in Selfridges, London, and, according to the store's underwear buyer Mithun Ramanandi, straight

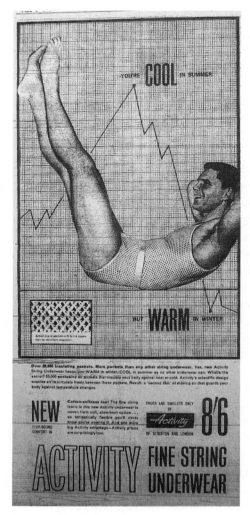

Figure 42 Activity fine string underwear, monochrome half-page press advertisement, 1960s. Private collection.

men were unabashed in buying tighter underwear.[6] Danny Hughes, the brand manager of Jockey, also stated that, according to his own company research for 1989, 60 per cent of men were prepared to buy their own underwear, and in 1993 Marks & Spencer's own label accounted for the same percentage of men's underwear sales.[7] In one of its press ads, which appeared in *Elle*, *Marie Claire*, *GQ* and *Esquire*, the agency BMP4 exploited the dual appeal of cotton-Lycra blend underpants for men and women alike, representing a parade of models

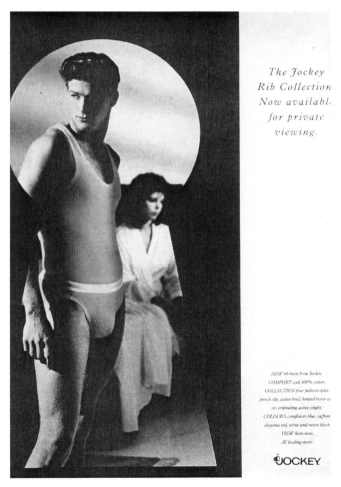

Figure 43 The Jockey Rib Collection, full-page colour press advertisement, 1988. Permission of Lyle and Scott Ltd.

wearing them on the catwalk for an adoring female audience. Nevertheless, the blatant portrayal of men's underwear did not go entirely unopposed. In 1979, for example, Patricia Scott, an employee in Shenton Smith's Kampus boutique in Cambridge, reported its owner to the police because she found the display of underpants on dummies in the shop 'vulgar, nasty, and not at all nice'.[8] Smith was subsequently fined £150 and found guilty on three charges of public indecency.[9] Equally, the objectification of men's bodies in underwear advertising was the cause of consternation for some male critics. Commenting on Lyle and Scott's 'What the best undressed men are wearing' publicity in spring 1972, T. Johnstone-Cristall protested, 'You can see what a disturbing effect this advertisement will

Figure 44 David Beckham, Emporio Armani underwear, monochrome poster on façade of Selfridges, London, autumn 2008.
Permission of Getty Images.

have on your average consumer of pants', while in 1978 Francis Harmar-Brown
remarked that an (unnamed) underwear ad on the London Underground was
troubling since it showed a 'man of heroic endowment' and this caused him to
overlook the name of the brand being promoted.[10]

Such criticism is revealing of the unease many men (and women for that
matter) have in viewing the male body in a state of undress, if not entirely naked.
But for many men also the display of male genitals—whether concealed by
underwear or not—signalled a deep-seated psychological fear of two further
things. First, it compromises the illusion of male power that Lacan propounds

in 'The Signification of the Phallus', whereby men confuse the penis and the phallus. As he argues, in patriarchal societies the phallus can only 'play its role when veiled', and 'virile display', therefore, always feminizes the phallus.[11] The fear of not measuring up to what Lehman calls the 'phallic spectacle'[12] was very much the concern of surrealist André Breton, who wrote that he and Benjamin Péret would never be seen nude in front of a woman without an erection, 'since this seemed undignified to us'.[13] Moreover, the fear of not measuring up is as evident in the regular Internet publicity for penile enlargement as it is in the blog consultations of psychosocial researcher Dr Petra Boynton[14] and is something that fashion designer Tom Ford also went on to address in his editorial for a special issue about the male nude of *GQ Style* in Spring/Summer 2008. Unable to persuade any of the male models to be photographed in a full-frontal pose, he lamented: 'Perhaps we are uncomfortable with male nudity because, in a culture where we never see anyone else's cock than in a porn film, we have a simple fear that our dicks are not as big as the next guy's.'[15] This phallocentrism was satirized in a 1999 press ad for Van Heusen shirts, depicting three men at a urinal with copy that states, '15 and a half inches and no wrinkles (every man's dream . . . and every woman's)'. But Ford also highlighted a second misconception concerning the male nude: that is, for many straight men full-frontal nudity has 'gay connotations'. If this is the case, it is tempting to ponder whether such sexual anxiety would also lead the same men to scotomize those ads that turned the tables completely by representing the male nude from behind.[16] These include 'Undress in Bermuda' for Burton in 1985, 'What's a suit without Dormeuil?' in 1989 (Figure 31), and Mario Testino's image of a naked model for Gucci underwear in 1995 that depicted a male model holding a pair of pants and bathed him in seductive lighting to emphasize the rounded contours of his pert buttocks.

At any rate, these advertisements are not a matter of representing gay men per se or publicity that was aimed exclusively at a gay audience. It is worth noting, for instance, that between the 1967 Sexual Offences Act, which had decriminalized male homosexual activities in private for adults aged 21 and over, and the 2001 amendment to the act that reduced the age of consent for gays to 16, gay men appeared overtly in British mainstream publicity only in the sexual health campaigns concerning HIV/AIDS after 1990, and in a more compromised sense in 'Chance Encounter', a television and cinema ad by Ogilvy and Mather for Impulse body spray.[17] To put things in perspective, however, the renaissance in advertising of new man by 1984 and of new lad by 1991 did not capsize the homoerotic charge of menswear publicity and the queering of masculinities it implies, as David Beckham avowed when he admitted to loving his gay following.[18] In fact, not only did some of the most sexually subversive menswear advertising appear under the new man and the new lad, but it was also published in magazines as disparate as *Arena* and *FHM*, *GQ* and *The Face*. This invites us to consider Sally Robinson's contention that such display of the male body proffers 'a different kind of empowerment'; that is, one based on equality and liberation rather than fear and domination.[19] Consequently, to bring *Advertising Menswear* to its own fitting end, I want to illustrate how the rhetoric of a 1998 pan-European ad for Yves Saint Laurent Rive Gauche crystallizes both the duality of empowerment and liberation in masculine identities to which Robinson refers as well as the relationship between form and content in menswear publicity that I have addressed throughout this study (Figure 45).

Masterminded by French ad agency Wolkoff et Arnodin, styled by Katie Grand, and photographed by Mario Sorrenti, the ad cribs Edouard Manet's controversial painting *Olympia* (1863), but with some significant changes. Hence, Victorine Meurend, the female model whom Manet depicted lying on a divan, naked save for a pair of Japanese slippers, bracelet, earrings and choker, and shielding her genitalia with a flexed left hand, has been transformed into a male model—Scott Barnhill, who had appeared formerly in publicity for Guess jeans—dressed in shirt and trousers designed by Hedi Slimane but with his feet bare. Similarly, the black female servant appears nude in the ad, whereas in Manet's painting she is fully clothed, and she carries a bouquet of stargazer lilies instead of mixed flowers, while the black cat at the bottom of Olympia's bed has disappeared entirely. In common with much postmodern menswear campaigns, therefore, the YSL Rive Gauche promotion is a hyperreal image based on another image and, like them,

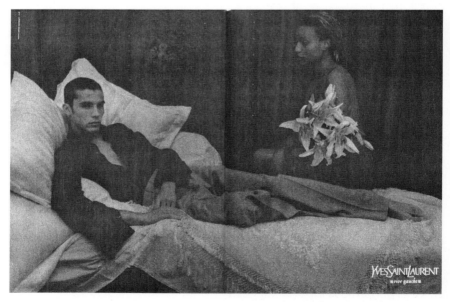

Figure 45 Yves Saint Laurent Rive Gauche, double-page colour press advertisement, photograph by Mario Sorrenti, 1998. Permission of Saint Laurent, France, Mario Sorrenti, and Wolkoff et Arnodin, Paris.

we need to interrogate whether there are any meaningful correspondences between the form and content of the original artwork and the ad, or whether the YSL campaign is nothing more than a case of vacuous postmodern style raiding.

As Roland Barthes has argued, not only is advertising a form of myth or metalanguage but also myth 'is speech stolen and restored'.[20] Furthermore, mythical speech is dynamic and motivational, its complexity difficult to unravel since it is prone to ambiguous signification, whereby 'the reader lives the myth as a story at once true and unreal'.[21] Focussing on the YSL ad in this way, therefore, we end up simultaneously approving and disapproving of the fact that it has bowdlerized an iconic painting for commercial gain in order to connote the myth that French fashion is the art form of the late twentieth century. More specifically, armed with some knowledge of the debates surrounding the production and reception of Manet's *Olympia*, we can begin to appreciate better the diffuse photographic style of the ad and the indeterminate sexual status of the male model represented in it. Crucially, *Olympia* itself has often been seen as a case of pouring old wine into new bottles insofar as Manet transformed the convention of the female nude in paintings such as Titian's *Venus of Urbino* (1538) and Goya's *Maja Unclothed* (1800/5). In addition, according to Gerald Needham, the relaxed pose and insubordinate gaze of Olympia mimic not so much high art but the brutal and vulgar style of pornographic photographs from the mid-nineteenth century.[22] Thus, along with the motif of the hissing black cat (a symbol for irresponsible love[23]), and the black woman who delivers a bouquet to Olympia (ostensibly from an 'absent' male client, referred to as 'Monsieur Arthur' by Postwer[24]), the painting was regarded both as 'indecipherable' by some critics and attacked by others on the grounds of morality.[25] As Tim Clark argues, however, 'sexuality did appear in the critics' writing but mostly in displaced form: they talked of violence . . . uncleanliness . . . a general air of death and decomposition.'[26] Paul de Saint-Victor, for instance, commented in *La Presse* (28 May 1865) that 'art sunk so low doesn't even deserve reproach', while Ernest Chesneau stated in *Le Constitutionnel* (16 May 1865) that Manet 'succeeds in provoking almost scandalous laughter'.[27] Critics of the time were likewise opposed to *Olympia* on the grounds of the artist's proto-Impressionist technique; the painting had stirred up a storm at the Salon in 1865, and Thoré had remonstrated with Manet for the clumsiness of his brushwork. But, as John A. Smith and Chris Jenks have been keen to point out, '*Olympia* is . . . a reverberant image'; its meaning hinges on complexity and hence, as they insist, 'Seeing *Olympia* as the first modernist painting does not foreclose other possibilities.'[28]

Taking up this hermeneutic challenge, we can see how the painting invites a series of polysemous responses or interpretations concerning its subject matter and style of representation and how these subtend the form and content of the YSL ad as well. First, in its rejection of high finish, *Olympia* is more often than not regarded as an entirely modern form of painting and yet Manet also owes much to the chiaroscuro style of the seventeenth-century Spanish art he had studied.[29] Likewise, the YSL ad is technically a liminal image and a rather old-fashioned one as well: a photograph whose muted palette and soft tonalism make it look like a painting, much like Photo Secessionists such as Alfred Stieglitz had attempted to do with their hand-manipulated photographs in the early twentieth century.[30] Even the Yves Saint Laurent Rive Gauche brand name is situated where we would expect to see the artist's signature, while the name of the photographer appears vertically in small print at top left. As Sorrenti himself has admitted about the style of this work, 'I was exploring colour photography and doing a lot of experimentation . . . These photographs were given a really hard time at the beginning because they were really dark, painterly and rich.'[31] And second, in the way that *Olympia* unashamedly puts the naked female body on public display and staring defiantly at the spectator, we can regard it alternately as the candid portrait of a working-class prostitute in 1860s Paris, as Clark has insisted (in his extended and trenchant analysis of the work he refers to her as such, rather than relying on the indiscriminate terms *cocotte* or courtesan), or the complex negotiation of a painterly act of seeing between the artist and his model at that point in time, as both Georges Bataille and Smith and Jenks have proposed: 'the subject, whose meaning was cancelled out, was no more than a pretext for the act—the *gamble* of painting.'[32] It is the dual sense of focus *Olympia* enacts that Barthes argues is the quintessence of ambiguous signification and that, I feel, is equally the concern of the YSL ad; indeed it helps explain why its producers resorted to such a controversial painting in the first place in order to objectify the slipperiness of queer masculine identities in the late 1990s. Thus, in comparison to its retro technical style, the Latino-styled male model in the YSL image proffers altogether more contemporary subject matter in simultaneously representing a fashionable turn-of-the-millennium dandy with his admiring black female partner and a gigolo or rent boy with his slave, the stargazer lilies she holds a tribute from an off-scene client (who may be a woman or a man).[33]

In tracing such parallels between a painting executed in 1863 and an ad in 1998 it has not been my intention to argue that they can simply be traduced as equivalents. To begin with, the painting has only a single author and the ad several—Sorrenti and Yves Saint Laurent, whose names appear in the ad, and Grand and Wolkoff and Arnodin, who are not credited—and by implication the fulcrum of the French avant-garde is transported from the Grands Boulevards, the stamping ground of Manet and the Impressionists, to the Left Bank of Paris, home of the Yves Saint Laurent atelier. But of more significance is the fact that, whether or not Manet objectified Olympia as a prostitute and hence the female body as a commodity, the main focus of the ad is unequivocally commodification—if not of the male body then certainly of male clothing. Accordingly, it elaborates the tension between the critical and utopian valorizations of Rive Gauche menswear, connoting both the quality of the product and its nexus to 'existential' factors such as lifestyle and identity. In the final analysis, the publicity represents the excellence and uniqueness of the brand by drawing mythological associations between it and art, and as such, the YSL ad shares much in common with campaigns such as Dormeuil's 'Cloth for Men' and Levi's 'Settlers Creek'. It is on this level, therefore, that menswear advertising is concerned with the 'great liberation of images' that Barthes describes in 'The Advertising Message' and that he insists, 'transforms . . . simple use into an experience of the mind'.[34] By the same measure, the transformative potential of clothing portended in menswear publicity since 1945 also reminds us that—regardless of class, age, sexuality or race—we can all, to borrow the rhetoric of advertising copy itself, 'Be.Some.Body'.[35]

Notes

1   R. Taylor, '25 Years of the Creative Circle', *Ad Weekly* (30 October 1970), 40.

2   Jack Bridges, 'Sexism in Advertising', *Men's Wear* (8 January 1981), 24.

3   Maurice Merleau-Ponty, *The Visible and the Invisible,* trans. A. Lingis (Evanston, IL: Northwestern University Press, 1968), 143.

4   *Men's Wear* (31 March 1994), 5. Mintel's report revealed that in 1993 the men's underwear sector was worth £50 million.

5   Alice Fisher, 'Beckham Factor Boost Briefs as Men Tighten Up', *The Observer* (6 July 2008), 16.

6   Ibid.

7   M. Billet and S. Lynn, 'Below the Belt', *Men's Wear* (7 June 1990), 5.

8   Quoted in *Men's Wear* (15 March 1979), 11.

9   Ibid.

10 *Adweek* (28 April 1972), 36, and F. Harmar-Brown, 'Why Oldies Are Goodies', *Campaign* (13 January 1978), 21 and 23.

11 Jacques Lacan, 'The Signification of the Phallus', in *Écrits: A Selection*, trans. A. Sheridan (London: Tavistock, 1977), 288 and 291.

12 P. Lehman, 'You and the Voyeurweb: Illustrating the Shifting Representation of the Penis on the Internet with User-generated Content', *Cinema Journal* 46: 4 (2007), 114.

13 André Breton, *The Communicating Vessels* [1932], trans. M. A. Caws and G. T. Harris (Lincoln: University of Nebraska Press, 1990), 49.

14 Lehman, 'You and the Voyeurweb'. Dr Boynton is lecturer in International Health Care Research at University College London. Her blog address is www.drpetra. co.uk.

15 Tom Ford, 'Masculinity Stripped Bare', *GQ Style* (Spring/Summer 2008), 277.

16 Freud referred to scotomization as the process whereby 'perception is entirely wiped out' in 'Fetishism' [1928], *On Sexuality*, J. Strachey (ed.), Penguin Freud Library, Vol. 7 (Harmondsworth: Penguin, 1977), 353. The term was subsequently

taken up and expanded by French psychoanalysts in the 1920s, such as Réné Laforgue, to describe how a person develops a blind spot as a form of defence mechanism against anything that would induce anxiety or conflict in one's ego. See Jan Dirk Blom, *A Dictionary of Hallucinations* (New York: Springer 2010), 464–5.

17 See Paul Jobling, 'Keeping Mrs Dawson Busy: Safe Sex, Gender and Pleasure in Condom Advertising Since 1970', in M. Nava et al (eds), *Buy This Book: Studies in Advertising and Consumption* (London: Routledge, 1996), and Kaye Wellings and Becky Field, *Stopping AIDS: AIDS/HIV, Public Education and the Mass Media in Europe* (London: Longman, 1996). The 40-second Impulse ad cost £6.5 million to produce and air, and its narrative, orchestrated to 'The Female of the Species' by Space, centred on a young woman walking along a street in Soho, who drops a bag of groceries after bumping into two gay men. One of them helps her to pick them up and as he does so he also picks up the scent of the Impulse spray, they touch hands and their eyes meet. In the next shot his male partner taps him on the shoulder and possessively beckons him to leave her. They walk away arm in arm from the woman, but at the close of the ad the implication that Impulse may turn— even momentarily—a gay guy straight is compounded by the way he turns around to smile at her and shrug apologetically.

18 Mark Simpson, 'Becks, Look What You Started', *The Times 2* (28 July 2008), 17.

19 Sally Robinson, *Marked Men: White Masculinity in Crisis* (London: Columbia University Press, 2000), 2.

20 Roland Barthes, 'Myth Today', *Mythologies*, trans. A. Lavers (London: Paladin, 1973), 136.

21 Ibid., 39.

22 Gerald Needham, 'Manet, Olympia, and Pornographic Photography', in T. B. Hess and L. Nochlin (eds), *Woman as Sex Object* (New York: Newsweek, 1972), 81–9.

23 Champfleury, *Les Chats*, J. Rothschild (ed.) (Paris, 1869).

24 Timothy J. Clark, *The Painting of Modern Life. Paris in the Art of Manet and His Followers* (London: Thames and Hudson, 1985), 87.

25 They included Clément and Gille. Ibid., n.49: 287.

26 Ibid., 96.

27 Cited in G. H. Hamilton, *Manet and his Critics* (New York: Norton, 1969), 71 and 72.

28 J. A. Smith and C. Jenks, 'Manet's *Olympia*', *Visual Studies* 21:2 (October 2006), 59. Another example of the polysemy of Manet's painting and how it can be used, therefore, to connote the ambiguity of sexual identities is George Chakravarthi's performative video, 'Olympia' (2003). In this, the artist poses on a divan as Olympia does, naked and with one hand flexed over his genitalia, but the servant delivering flowers is now male.

29 See G. Tinterow, *Manet/Velazquez: The French Taste for Spanish Painting* (New York: Metropolitian Museum of Art, 2003).

30 See W. I. Homer and C. Johnson, *Stieglitz and the Photo-Secession 1902* (New York: Viking Press, 2002).

31 Quoted in Charlotte Cotton, *Imperfect Beauty: The Making of Contemporary Fashion Photographs* (London: V & A Publications, 2000), 115.

2

32 G. Bataille, *Manet* (1955) as cited in A. C. Hanson, *Manet and Modern Tradition* (New Haven: Yale University Press, 1977), 52. Smith and Jenks, 'Manet's *Olympia*', 163.

33 I am thinking here also of the way that footballer David Beckham adopted homoerotic poses in two fashion shoots—one by Nick Knight for *Arena Homme Plus* (Summer 2000), and 'Captain Fantastic' by David Lachapelle for British *GQ* (June 2002)—and his avowal in the former that he is comfortable with being a gay icon.

34 Roland Barthes, 'The Advertising Message' [1964], in *The Semiotic Challenge,* trans. R. Howard (Berkeley: University of California Press, 1994), 178.

35 *Campaign* (20 June 1986), 12. The slogan was coined by Graham Woodall of TBWA for a 1986 poster campaign for the upmarket French leisurewear brand, Le Coq Sportif.

APPENDIX I

ADVERTISING AGENTS AND MENSWEAR ACCOUNTS, 1945–2000 (EXCLUDING LEVI'S)

Account	Agency	Date
Activity Textiles Ltd	Graham and Gillies Ltd	1958
Aertex	Osborne-Peacock Co. Ltd	1953–55
Aquascutum	SH Benson	1950–51
Austin Reed	FC Pritchard Wood & Partners	1932–54
	Clifford Bloxham & Partners Ltd	1954–61
	Pritchard, Wood	1962–67
	Davidson, Pearce, Berry and Tuck	1967–75
Baracuta	WH Emmett	1947–54
	Lovell and Rupert Curtis Ltd	1954
Barney's	Caplin Advertising	1947
Barratt Shoes	WS Crawford	1933–50
Ben Sherman	Grey	1997
Braemar Knitwear	JWT	1950
Brilon Knitwear	Notley Advertising	1961–66
Brutus Jeans	London Advertising	1972–75
	Saatchi	1976–79
	WCRS	1979–80
Burton's	WS Crawford	1954–62
	Hobson, Bates and Partners	1962–72
	Masius, Wynne, Williams	1972–73
	McCormick Richards	1973–78
	Chuter Morgenthau Hogg & Mitchell	1985

Account	Agency	Date
Catesby and Sons	Clifford Bloxham & Partners	1952
Clarks Shoes	C. D. Notley Advertising Ltd	1941–52
	Priestleys	1967
John Collier (formerly Fifty Shilling Tailors)	Greenlys Ltd	1954–66
	Lonsdale, Crowther	1967
Cooper Y-front	Colman, Prentis & Varley	1944
	Legget Nicholson and Partners	1948–59
Lee Cooper	KMP	1969
Denson Shoes	RS Caplin Ltd	1951
Dormeuil	Michael Robinson Associates	1968–80s
Double Two Shirts	Hausman Advertising Ltd	1958
Eminence Underwear	Allardyce Palmer Ltd	1966
Peter England	CR Casson Ltd	1959
Fifty Shillings Tailors	Rumble, Crowther & Nicholas Ltd	1937–54
Fingerflex Shoes	Charles Hobson	1958
Fred Perry	Wiscombe Baptie Norris	1986
Freeman, Hardy & Willis	Pictorial Publicity Ltd	1954
Cecil Gee	John Westwood Ltd	1964
Guards Menswear	Alfred Pemberton Ltd	1951–64
	Bell & Cole Publicity Ltd	1965
Guess Jeans	Paul Marciano Advertising	1996
Hepworths	United Kingdom Advertising Ltd	1966
	Gold Abbott	1974
Hush Puppies	London Press Exchange	1966–68
	Young & Rubicam	1968
ICI Terylene	Mather and Crowther	1954–56
International Wool Secretariat	Dorland	1947
	Davidson Pearce Berry Spottiswoode	1977
Jackson the Tailor	Garland-Compton	1972
	Redhead Advertising	1972
Jaeger	Colman Prentis & Varley Ltd	1930s–58
	W.S. Crawford	1958

Account	Agency	Date
	Ogilvy & Mather	1958–61
	Stratton Wolsey Advertising Ltd	1964
Lee Jeans	Yellowhammer	1986–91
	Grey	1991–97
Lee Cooper	Zetland	1980–81
Lightning Zips	Pritchard, Wood	1955
Lilley & Skinner	Everetts Advertising	1941
Lyle and Scott	Legget Nicholson	1954–55
McGregor Dressing Gowns	Elliot Advertising Ltd	1955
Maenson Overcoats	Design Advertising Ltd	1942–49
Mattamac Ltd	FC Pritchard Wood	1942–48
Mekay Shirts	GS Royds Ltd	1957–61
	Scott-Turner & Associates	1961
Mentor Shirts	Colman, Prentis & Varley Ltd	1955–58
	John Hobson and Partners	1958
Meridian Underwear	Willing's Press Service Ltd	1939–54
	SH Benson	1954
	Cogent Elliott	1969
Moss Bros	TB Browne	1950–67
Old England Shirt	CR Casson Ltd	1952–53
Hector Powe	Pritchard, Wood	1961–67
	Davis Page	1967–70
	Haddons	1970–73
Radiac Shirts and Collars	Lintas	1951
Rael Brook Shirts	Lucien Advertising	1955–59
	Hobson, Bates and Partners	1969
	Ogilvy Benson and Mather	1970
Rego Clothiers	JWT	1940–51
Rocola	Garratt Baulcombe Associates	1967–74
Saxon Hawk	Osborne-Peacock Ltd	1959
J Sears & Co Shoes	Pictorial Publicity Ltd	1954
Simpson DAKS	W. S. Crawford	1945–
Sumrie	Norman Davis Ltd	1950
Swallow Raincoats	Mundy, Gilbert & Troman	1955
Tern Shirts	Doyle Dane & Bernbach	1966

Account	Agency	Date
Terylene Trousers	Mather & Crowther	1955–66
Tootal Socks, Shirts & Ties	W. S. Crawford	1955–66
University Tailors Ltd	Charles Higham	1947
Van Heusen Collars	Willing's Press Service Ltd	1951–58
	Lovell & Rupert Curtis Ltd	1958–65
Viyella	Garratt Baulcombe Associates	1963
Weatherlux	Dudley, Turner & Vincent	1958
Weaver and Wearer	Pritchard, Wood	1963
John White Shoes	Notley Advertising	1969
Willerby Tailors	Rumble, Crowther & Nicholas Ltd	1954
	Foote, Cone and Belding	1967
Wolsey Cardinal Socks	Charles Higham	1945
	W. S. Crawford	1946–49
	C. D. Notley	1952
Wolsey Underwear	W. S. Crawford	1938–49
Wolsey x-fronts	Cecil D Notley	1951
Wrangler jeans	JWT	1970–73
	Doyle Dane Bernbach	1973–76
	Wasey Campbell-Ewald	1976–78
	Collett Dickinson and Pearce	1980–87
	BBDO	1988–90
	Simons Palmer Denton Clemmow	1990–91
	TBWA Holmes Knight Ritchie	1992–96
	Abbott Mead Vickers BBDO	1997
Yves Saint Laurent	Havas Publicis	1998

Data compiled by the author.

APPENDIX II

MENSWEAR ADVERTISING, 1945–80S: ILLUSTRATORS AND PHOTOGRAPHERS

Name	Agency	Advertiser	Date
Alan Aldridge	Pritchard, Wood	Austin Reed Cue	1966
Anton	F. C. Pritchard Wood and Partners	Saxone Shoes	1947
BW Bays	F. C. Pritchard Wood	Austin Reed	1942–48
Nicholas Bentley	W. S. Crawford	Wolsey	1941
Oscar Berger	W. S. Crawford	Wolsey	1944
Eric Bird	F. C. Pritchard Wood	Mattamac	1942–48
Carlton Studios	Rex Osborne-Peacock	Aertex	1955
F. Whitby-Cox	W. H. Emmett & Co.	Baracuta	1947–48
Alexis Delmar	Artist Partners Ltd		1952
	Clifford, Bloxham	Austin Reed	1957
Tom Eckersley	W. S. Crawford	Tootal Socks and ties	1955
Fougasse	F. C. Pritchard Wood	Austin Reed	1937–48
Ashley Havinden	W. S. Crawford	Simpson DAKS	1933–48
	W. S. Crawford	Kangol berets	1950s
FHK Henrion	W. S. Crawford	Simpson DAKS Xmas poster	1950s
Barbara Hulanicki	Helen Jardine		1958
Keith Inman	John Westwood Ltd	Cecil Gee	1964
Andrew Kim (P)	Garratt Baulcombe	Viyella	1970
Lucien Productions		Rael Brook	1953
Francis Marshall	Colman Prentis & Varley	Jaeger (men's wear)	1951–52

Name	Agency	Advertiser	Date
Raymond Meylan		M&S; Sound Boots Ltd	1954
Foster Morgan	Caplin Advertising	Barneys Kentish Town	1947
Philip Moysey	F. C. Pritchard Wood	Austin Reed	1949
Helmut Newton (P)	Pritchard, Wood	Austin Reed Cue	1965
David Olins (P)	W. S. Crawford	Tootal shirt	1962
John Parsons	W. S. Crawford	Wolsey	1942–48
Bob Peak	Lovell & Rupert Curtis	Van Heusen	1965
Tom Piesakowski	W. S. Crawford	Tootal ties	1956
Brian Robb	W. S. Crawford	Tootal cravats	1956
		Westcot Jeans	1959
Poul Sprøgøe	Helen Jardine	Y-front	1957
Eric Stemp	W. S. Crawford	Simpson DAKS	1962
Vernon Stratton		Jaeger	1961
	W. S. Crawford	Simpson DAKS	Late 1960s
Feliks Topolski	Stewart Alexander Advertising	Lotus shoes	1947
Albert Watson (P)		Simpson DAKS advertorials	1980s
Tage Werner	Aquascutum		1942–48
Hans Wilde (P)	W. S. Crawford	Dannimac	1950–52

Data compiled by the author. Photographers = (P).

APPENDIX III

TELEVISION, FILM AND RADIO ADVERTISEMENTS FOR MENSWEAR IN BRITAIN, 1955–2000 (EXCLUDING LEVI'S—SEE APPENDIX IV)

Retailer/Brand	Date	Media
Acrilan Slacks	Autumn 1960	TV
Activity Underwear	Summer 1961	TV
Advertising Films Ltd (filmlet for John Collier, Two Steeples, Unwin sportswear, Invicta underwear)	1957	TV
Adidas	May/June 1982	TV
	Summer 1985	TV
	Spring–summer 1986	TV
	Summer 1992	TV
Aertex, 'Uncle Jeff'	June 1957	Cinema
Brass Monkeys Underwear	December 1995	TV
Bucks Trousers	May 1973	TV
Brutus Jeans	22 October 1972	Cinema
	June 1974	TV
	Sept–October 1974	TV
	June 1975	TV
	Sept–October 1975	TV
	1976	TV and cinema
	1977	TV and cinema
	1978	TV and cinema
	June 1979	TV

Retailer/Brand	Date	Media
	Autumn 1979	Cinema and radio
	Summer 1980	TV
	Spring 1981	TV
	Spring 1982	TV
	May 1985	TV
Burton's	Autumn 1955–58	TV
	1968, 1969, 1977–79	TV
	March 1973	Cinema
	Autumn 1983	TV
	October 1995	TV
Burton Burtex Slacks	Spring 1958	TV
C&A	1968, 1969–75, 1977	TV
	1978–85	TV and cinema
Top Rank magazine (Clarks shoes)	January 1960	Cinema
John Collier	1957–67	TV
Lee Cooper Casuals	December 1969	Cinema
Lee Cooper Jeans	Sept–December 1979	Cinema
	Autumn 1982	Cinema
	July 1997	TV
Crimplene/Terylene	Spring 1973	TV
	March 1974	Cinema
Dingo Jeans	May 1972	TV
Double 2 Shirts	November 1959	TV
	November 1960	TV
	August 1961	TV
	November 1963	TV
	Feb–March 1972	TV
	Autumn 1983	TV
Dunlop Shoes	Spring 1979	TV
	April 1985	TV
Falmer Jeans	1977	Cinema
	Spring 1979	TV
	Spring 1985	TV
	Spring 1988	Cinema

Retailer/Brand	Date	Media
Farah Slacks	April 1982	TV
	April 1983	TV
Fingerflex Shoes	Spring 1958	TV
Gaunson Yorkers	Spring 1979	TV
Hector Powe	Oct–December 1973	Radio
Hepworth	Autumn 1976	TV
	Spring 1978	TV
	Autumn 1978	TV
Hom Underwear	December 1994	Cinema
Hush Puppies Shoes	1966	TV
	Summer 1985	TV
ICI Terylene/Cotton shirt	Autumn 1966	TV
IWS Trousers	May 1973	TV
	Spring 1977	TV
	Spring 1978	TV
	1982	TV
	October 1989	TV
	Feb/March 1990	TV
Jockey Y-fronts	Spring 1983	TV and radio
Kangol Caps	Oct/November 1960	TV
Knowsley Raincoat	February 1958	TV
Le Coq Sportif	Spring 1979	Cinema
Lee Jeans	Autumn 1978	TV
	Spring 1981	TV and cinema
	Autumn 1986	TV
	Autumn 1987	TV
	Spring 1988	TV and cinema
	Spring 1990	TV and cinema
	Autumn 1991	TV and cinema
	Autumn 1992	TV and cinema
	November 1993	TV and cinema
	February 1995	TV and cinema
	February 1996	TV and cinema
	January 1997	TV
Lois Jeans	October 1986	Radio

Retailer/Brand	Date	Media
Lord Anthony	May 1979	TV
Lybro Jeans	March 1972	TV
Lyle & Scott Y-front	Spring 1958	TV
McGregor Dressing Gown	Nov/December 1956	TV
	Oct–December 1957	TV
Mekay Non-iron Shirt	Oct–December 1957	TV
Mentor Shirts	October 1957	TV
Morley, 'Captain' Socks	Autumn 1955	TV
Nike	Spring 1984	TV
Palm Beach shirts	October 1957	TV
Pepe Jeans	February 1993	TV and cinema
	March 1995	TV and cinema
Peter England shirts	April–June 1959	TV
	January 1963	TV
Mark Powell	May 1996	Independent cinema
Rael Brook Toplin Shirt	July 1956	Cinema
Rael Brook Shirts	Spring 1958	TV
	Nov/December 1969	TV
	November 1972	TV
Radiac Shirts	December 1957	TV
Simon Shirt Co.	November 1978	TV
Swallow Raincoats	August 1955	TV
	February 1979	TV
John Temple	October 1971	Cinema
Tenbra Underwear	Spring 1957	TV
Tern Shirts	March 1961	TV and cinema
Top Man	Winter 1987–88	TV
Van Heusen Shirts	April 1976	TV
	October 1988	TV
Vidal Sassoon Jeans	Spring 1982	TV
Weatherlux Dhobi Raincoat	April 1958	TV
Wescot Texun Jeans	Summer 1957	TV
John White Shoes	March–June 1972	Cinema
	Aug–December 1972	Cinema

Retailer/Brand	Date	Media
Willerby Tailors	Jan–April 1967	TV
	June 1970	TV
	January 1972	Cinema
Wrangler Jeans	1976	TV and cinema
	1977	TV
	1978	TV
	Autumn 1980	TV
	Spring 1982	TV
	Autumn 1982	TV
	April 1987	TV
	Spring 1988	TV and cinema
	Spring 1989	TV and cinema
	Spring 1990	TV and cinema
	October 1990	TV
	Winter 1991/92	TV and cinema
	September 1993	TV and cinema
	August 1994	TV and cinema
	February 1996	TV and cinema
	March 1997	TV
	April 1998	TV and cinema
Yorkers Suits	September 1979	TV

APPENDIX IV

LEVI'S PRESS, POSTER, CINEMA, RADIO AND TELEVISION ADVERTISING CAMPAIGNS IN BRITAIN, 1968–2000

Campaign/Soundtrack/ Awards	Media & Date	Agency/ Producers	Cost
No title	A, D/1968	Young & Rubicam	
Sta-prest, 'Relax'	A/1971	Young & Rubicam/ (I) Dennis Auton and Rodney Jeffs; (II) Dolores Beashal; (III) Hitoshi Yoda	
Better to have had Levi's and lost 'em'	C/1972	Young & Rubicam	
'Bottoms'/'Tutti Frutti', Little Richard	C/1972	Young & Rubicam/ (III) John Alcott	
'Leader of the Pack'/'Leader of the Pack', Shangri-Las/ D&AD Silver; Gold Lion, Cannes	E/1976	McCann Erickson/ (I) Ridley Scott; (II) Derek Apps	
'The word is Levis'	A, B, E/1977	McCann Erickson/ (I) Adrian Lyne; (III) David Montgomery	
'Right on the button'; 'Not a patch'	B/1978	McCann Erickson/ (I) Roger Manton; (III) Jack Bankhead	
'Route 66'/Cannes Bronze Medal	B, C/1978	McCann Erickson	£650,000*
'It's written on your body'	C, E/1980	McCann Erickson	
'Talk as you walk'	A, E/1982	McCann Erickson	£1 million*

Campaign/Soundtrack/ Awards	Media & Date	Agency/ Producers	Cost
'When the world zigs, zag'	B/1982	Bartle, Bogle and Hegarty (BBH)/ (II) Barbara Noakes	£180,000
Red Tab 501s (David Bowie Tour)	B/1983	BBH	
'Rivets'; 'Stitching'	A, C, E/1983–84	BBH/ (I) Mike Cozens and Graham Watson; (III) Nick Lewin	£1.7 million
'Airport'	B, C, E/1985	BBH	
'Bath'/'Wonderful World', Sam Cooke	A, E/1985–86	BBH/ (I) Roger Lyons and John Hegarty; (II) Barbara Noakes	£4 million
'Laundrette'/'I Heard It Through the Grapevine', Marvin Gaye/Gold Lion, Cannes	A, E/1985–86	BBH/ (I) Roger Lyons and John Hegarty; (II) Barbara Noakes	£4 million
'501s Designers'	A/1996	BBH/ (II) Chris Palmer; (III) Stak	
'Parting'/'When a Man Loves a Woman', Percy Sledge/Gold Medal, NYC Film & TV Festival	C, E/1987	BBH/ (I) Steve Hopper and Dennis Lewis	£3 million
'Entrance'/'Stand By Me', Ben E King/Gold Medal, NYC Film & TV Festival	C, E/1987	BBH/ (I) Steve Hopper and Dennis Lewis	£3 million
'Refrigerator'/'Manish Boy', Muddy Waters	C, E/1988	BBH/ (I) Roger Lyons and Marcus Vinton; (II) Pete Russell	£5 million*
'New Year's Eve'/'C'mon Everybody', Eddie Cochrane	E/1988	BBH/ (I) Graham Watson; (II) Chris Herring	
'Pick Up'/'Be My Baby', Ronettes	C, E/1989	BBH/ (I) Paul Weiland	
'Stunt'	B/1989	BBH	
'Pawnbroker'/'Ain't Nobody Home', BB King	C, E/1989	BBH/ (I) John Hegarty and Robert Jansen; (II) Tom Hudson; (III) Richard Loncraine	

Campaign/Soundtrack/ Awards	Media & Date	Agency/ Producers	Cost
'Surfer'/'Can't Get Enough', Bad Company	C, E/1990	BBH/ (I) Tony Scott; (II) Barbara Noakes	
'Great Deal'/'The Joker', Steve Miller	C, E/1990	BBH/ (I) Hugh Johnson and Rosie Arnold; (II) Chas Hendley	£4 million*
	A/1990	BBH/ (III) Herb Ritts	
'Best'/*Campaign* Gold and Silver Awards	A/1990	BBH/ (III) Richard Avedon	
'Pool Hall'/'Should I Stay', Clash	C, E/1991	BBH	£7 million*
'Camera'/'20th Century Boy', T. Rex	C, E/1991	BBH/ (I) Warren Brown; (II) John McCabe	
'The Swimmer'/'Mad About the Boy', Dinah Washington	C, E/1991	BBH/ (I) Tarsem and Larry Barker; (II) Rooney Caruthers	
'The older they get'	D/1991	BBH	
'Cinderella'/'A Piece of My Heart', Irma Franklin	C, E/1992	BBH/ (I) Tarsem and Graham Watson; (II) Bruce Crouch	
'Four Stages of Life'	E/1992	BBH	
'Procession'/'Heart Attack and Vine', Screamin' Jay Hawkins	C, E/1993	BBH/ (I) Tarsem and Martin Galton; (II) Will Awdry	
'Nudes'/*Campaign* Best Poster Award	A, B/1993	BBH/ (III) Bill Brandt	
'Campfire'/'Ring of Fire', Johnny Cash	C, E/1993	BBH/ (I) Tarsem	
'Tackle'/ BTA Silver Award	C, E/1993	BBH/ (I) Carlton Chase	
'Americans'/*Campaign* Gold Press Award	A/1993	BBH/ (II) Chas Hendley; (III) Mary Ellen Mark	
'Marx'/*Campaign* Silver Award	A/1993	BBH/ (I) Graham Watson; (II) Bruce Crouch	
'Settlers Creek'/'Inside', Stiltskin/D&AD Silver Award; RSA Grand Prix	C, E/1994	BBH/ (I) Vaughan and Anthea and John Gorse; (II) Nick Worthington	

Campaign/Soundtrack/ Awards	Media & Date	Agency/ Producers	Cost
'Drugstore'/'Novelty Waves', Biosphere/Gold Lion, Cannes; BTA Best Ad Award	C, E/1994	BBH/ (I) Michel Gondry and John Gorse; (II) Nick Worthington	
'Fall'	C, E/1994	BBH/ (I) Paul Arden; (II) John O'Keefe	
'Taxi'/'Turn On, Tune In, Cop Out', Freakpower	C, E/1995	BBH/ (I) Baillie Walsh and Andy Smart; (II) Roger Beckett	£7.63 million*
'Clay man'/'Boombastic', Shaggy	C, E/1995	BBH/ (I) John McCabe; (IV) Mike Mort and Deiniol Morris	
'White Tab'/*Campaign* Best Press Award	A/1995	BBH/ (I) Tiger Savage; (II) Paul Silburn; (III) Stock Shots	
'Washroom'/'Falling Elevators', MC 900ft Jesus/*Campaign* Gold Award	C, E/1996	BBH/ (I) Simon Robinson; (II) Jo Moore	
'Planet'/'Spaceman', Babylon Zoo	C, E/1996	BBH/ (I) Vaughn and Anthea, and Andy Smart; (II) Roger Beckett	
'Pensioners'	A/1996	BBH/ (III) Nick Knight	
'Riveted together'	C, E/1996	BBH/ (I) Steve Ramser and Russell Ramsey; (II) John O'Keefe	
'Mermaids'/'Underwater Love', Smoke City/ *Campaign* Gold Winner	C, E/1997	BBH/ (I) Michel Gondry and Steve Hudson; (II) Victoria Fallon	
'Kung Fu'	C, E/1997	BBH/ (I) Jonathan Glazer and Tony McTear; (II) Jeremy Carr	£9 million*
'Sculpture'	A/1997	BBH/ (I) Adam Chiappe; (II) Matthew Saunby; (III) Kevin Summers	
'Shrink to fit'/*Campaign* Gold Award	B/1997	BBH/ (I) Rosie Arnold; (II) Will Awdry; (III) Nadav Kander	

Campaign/Soundtrack/ Awards	Media & Date	Agency/ Producers	Cost
'Earthquake'/'Whine and Grine', Prince Buster	C, E/1998	BBH/ (I) Doug Liman and Rosie Arnold; (II) Will Awdry	
'Kevin the Hamster'	C, E/1998	BBH/ (I) Gore Verbinski and Doug Nichol; (II) Rob Jack and Roger Beckett	
'Flat Eric'/'Flat Beat'/ *Campaign* Ad of the Year	C, E/1999	BBH/ (I) Quentin Dupieux and Tony Davidson; (II) Kim Papworth; (III) Nadav Kander	
'Dolls'	C, E/2000	BBH/ (I) Dante Ariola	
'Undressed'	C, E/2000	BBH/ (I) Dom and Nic for Outsider	
'Legs'	C, E/2000	BBH/ (I) Brian Beletic	

* Denotes expenditure on all advertising throughout the year. Media Codes: A (Press); B (Poster); Cinema (C); Radio (D); Television (E). Producer Codes: I (Director/Designer); II (Copy/Script); III (Photographer); IV (Illustrator). Data compiled by the author.

BIBLIOGRAPHY

Periodical Sources

The dates of the chief periodical sources consulted for this study are listed as follows. Any anonymous and untitled articles cited in the main text are not listed here, but their details are included in the endnotes.

Advertiser's Weekly (1945–70)
Ad Weekly (1970–2)
Adweek (1972–5)
Arena (1986–2000)
Campaign (1968–2000)
The Face (1980–2000)
Man About Town (1953–60)
Man and His Clothes (1945–58)
Men in Vogue (1965–8)
Men's Wear (1945–2000)
Outdoor Advertising (1965–7)
Picture Post (1945–57)
Reveille (1940–70)
Statistical Review of Advertising. London: Legion Publishing (1950–76, retitled *Statistical Review of Press and TV Advertising* by 1966)
Sunday Times Magazine (1962–85)
Weekend (1957–70)

Moving Image Sources

Readers may view the following Levi's television ad campaigns in the Arrows Archive at the History of Advertising Trust website, http://www.hatads.org. uk: 'Settler's Creek' (1984), 'Stitching' (1985), 'Laundrette' (1985), 'Parting' (1987), 'Entrance' (1987), 'Refrigerator' (1988), 'Pick Up' (1989), 'Fall' (1994), 'Drugstore' (1994), 'Kevin the Hamster' (1998), Sta-Prest 'I.d.' and 'Dancing' (1999) and 'Crew' (2000).

Alternatively, all of these ad campaigns and many of the other Levi's and jeans ads listed in Appendix IV are available on YouTube.

Abrams, Mark. 'Selling to the Teenager'. *Advertiser's Weekly*, 23 January 1959: 31–2.

Abrams, Mark. 'Selling to the Teenager'. *Advertiser's Weekly*, 12 February 1960: 31–2.

Adburgham, Alison. 'Renaissance of the Dandy'. *Observer*, 9 April 1961.

Addison, Paul. *Now the War Is Over: A Social History of Britain 1945–51*. London: BBC, 1985.

Advertiser's Weekly. '1957 Press Spending Hit New Peak'. 7 March 1958: 5.

Advertiser's Weekly. '£5 Million a Month Average on Press Ads'. 27 August 1953: 350.

Advertiser's Weekly. 'Advertising Aid for Small-town Men's Wear Retailers'. 14 January 1954: 74.

Advertiser's Weekly. 'All the Profits Went Into Ads—and He's Made a Million'. 3 April 1959: 26 and 28.

Advertiser's Weekly. 'Candid Comment on Press Rate Rises'. 4 January 1951: 3.

Advertiser's Weekly. 'Current Advertising'. 4 December 1947: 510.

Advertiser's Weekly. 'Current Advertising'. 29 April 1954: 241.

Advertiser's Weekly. 'Current Advertising'. 30 June 1957: 54.

Advertiser's Weekly. 'Current Advertising'. 13 December 1957: 64.

Advertiser's Weekly. 'Current Advertising'. 2 April 1958: 48.

Advertiser's Weekly. 'Current Advertising'. 14 January 1961: 3.

Advertiser's Weekly. 'Current Advertising'. 27 January 1967: 40.

Advertiser's Weekly. 'Current Advertising'. 10 March 1967: 53.

Advertiser's Weekly. 'Express Group Publishes Its Accounts'. 12 February 1948: 278.

Advertiser's Weekly. 'Fashion Post at McCann'. 4 September 1959: 9.

Advertiser's Weekly. 'How Newsprint Cuts and Raised Costs Hit Press Advertising'. 6 November 1947: 262.

Advertiser's Weekly. 'How Use of Provincials Solved Men's Clothes Maker's Branding Problem'. 27 March 1952: 506.

Advertiser's Weekly. 'Impact of Cinema Ads Is Surveyed'. 30 January 1958: 32.

Advertiser's Weekly. 'I.S.B.A. Research Converts "Circulation" into "Spending Power"'. 27 August 1936: 276–7, 282 and 284.

Advertiser's Weekly. 'The Layton Annual Awards'. 17 March 1955: 649.

Advertiser's Weekly. 'Magazines Take Lion's Share of Press Advertising Revenue'. 31 May 1951: 371.

Advertiser's Weekly. 'Men's Wear Trade Readership Survey'. 17 June 1948: 526.

Advertiser's Weekly. 'Newspaper Space'. 21 March 1948: 504.

Advertiser's Weekly. 'Over £42 Million on Press Ads'. 28 February 1952: 321–5.

Advertiser's Weekly. 'Over £22 Million on Press Ads'. 28 August 1952: 369.

Advertiser's Weekly. 'Press Ad Spending'. 29 May 1952: 399.

Advertiser's Weekly. 'Press Plus Window Display Made Aertex Week a Success'. 30 July 1953: 206.

Advertiser's Weekly. 'Schwerin's Findings on "Short" TV Commercials'. 12 June 1959: 4.

Advertiser's Weekly. 'A Shirt Campaign That Was Aimed at Women'. 20 July 1956: 24.

Advertiser's Weekly. '"Style for Men" Launches 1951 Campaign'. 8 February 1951: 229.

Advertiser's Weekly. 'Talking to Teenagers in Their Own Language'. 29 January 1960: 38.

Advertiser's Weekly. 'Top Young Minds Read the *Daily Mirror*'. 12 April 1963: 1.

Advertiser's Weekly. 'Vogue Announces the Winners of Its Second Annual Advertising Awards'. 24 November 1949: 345.

Advertiser's Weekly. 'What Is Spent on Advertising in Relation to Total Sales and National Income'. 22 July 1954: 156–7.

Advertiser's Weekly. 'What Is Spent on Advertising in Relation to Total Sales and National Income'. 22 July 1954: 156–7

Adweek. 'The Loss Makers'. 27 June 1975: 12–13.

Adweek. 'The Men's Wear Sales Battle Looms'. 7 February 1975: 11.

Adweek. 'Newsprint Crisis Worsens'. 5 October 1973: 4.

Ad Weekly. 'The Young Ones—What Are They Worth?' 19 November 1971: 33–4.

Alinder, James, and Szarkowski, John. *Ansel Adams: Classic Images*. Boston: Little, Brown, 1987.

Allport, Alan. *Demobbed: Coming Home After the Second World War*. New Haven: Yale University Press, 2009.

Amber, G. 'Oh Dear, I've Seen This Movie'. *Adweek*, 3 November 1972: 16.

Amies, Hardy. *Just So Far*. London: Collins, 1954.

Archives of Advertising. *Pete Hawley The Jantzen Ads: A Survey, 1942–1960*. Hartford: McBride, 2005.

Armstrong, Stephen. 'Boys in the Brand'. *Guardian (Media)*, 11 May 1998: 8–9.

Art and Industry. 'Advertising That Advertises'. December 1952: 182–9.

Art and Industry. 'Alfred Pemberton Limited'. August 1953: 51–5.

Art and Industry. 'British Poster Designers Know Their Job'. February 1948: 42–51.

Art and Industry. 'Colman Prentis & Varley Ltd'. May 1952: 146–53.

Art and Industry. 'C. R. Casson Ltd'. May 1953: 149.

Art and Industry. 'Greenlys Limited'. January 1953: 2–9.

Art and Industry. 'The London Press Exchange'. March 1953: 74–81.

Art and Industry. 'Pearl Falconer'. November 1941: 133–6.

Art and Industry. 'Stuart Advertising Agency Ltd'. November 1952: 152–9.

Atterbury, Paul, and Wainwright, Clive (eds). *Pugin: A Gothic Passion*. New Haven: Yale University Press, 1994.

Avedon, Richard. *In the American West 1979–1984*. New York: Harry N. Abrams, 1985.

Bacon, C. W. 'Scraperboard in Advertising'. *Art and Industry*, November 1951: 168–73.

Bakhtin, Mikhail. 'Forms of Time and of the Chronotope in the Novel', in M. Holquist (ed.), *The Dialogic Imagination: Four Essays by M. M. Bakhtin*, trans. by C. Emerson and M. Holquist. Austin: University of Texas Press, 1981: 84–258.

Ballam, Harry. 'Mary Gowing'. *Art and Industry*, May 1958: 168–72.

Barbey D'Aurevilly, Jules. *Of Dandyism and of George Brummell* [1844], trans. by D. Ainslie. New York: PAJ, 1988.

Barthes, Roland. 'The Advertising Message' [1964], in *The Semiotic Challenge*, trans. by R. Howard. Berkeley: University of California Press, 1994: 173–8.

Barthes, Roland. 'Blue Is in Fashion This Year' [1960], in *The Language of Fashion*. Sydney: Power, 2006: 41–58.

Barthes, Roland. 'Fashion: A Strategy of Desire' [1966], in *The Language of Fashion*. Sydney: Power, 2006: 86–90.

Barthes, Roland. *The Fashion System* [1967], trans. by M. Ward and R. Howard. Berkeley: University of California Press, 1990.

Barthes, Roland. 'From Work to Text', in *Image Music Text*. London: Fontana, 1977: 155–64.

Barthes, Roland. *Image Music Text*, trans. by S. Heath. London: Fontana, 1977.

Barthes, Roland. 'Myth Today', in *Mythologies*, trans. by A. Lavers. London: Paladin, 1973: 117–74.

Baudrillard, Jean. 'The Precession of Simulacra', in *Simulacra and Simulation*, trans. by S. F. Glaser. Ann Arbor: University of Michigan Press, 1994: 1–42.

Beard, J. S. 'Filmlet Survey Measures Impact of Screen Advertising in Three Cities'. *Advertiser's Weekly*, 6 May 1954: 268 and 270.

Benwell, Beth (ed.). *Masculinity and Men's Lifestyle Magazines*. Oxford: Blackwell, 2003.

Betjeman, John. 'Current Advertising—A Commentary'. *Penrose Annual* (1940): 17–20.

Beyfus, Drusilla. 'How to Tell a Boy From a Girl'. *Sunday Times Magazine*, 20 September 1964: 46–7.

Beynon, John. *Masculinities and Culture*. Milton Keynes: Oxford University Press, 2002.

Bhabha, Homi K. *The Location of Culture.* London: Routledge, 1994.

Bhabha, Homi K. 'Of Mimicry and Man: The Ambivalence of Colonial Discourse'. *October* 28 (Spring 1984): 25–33.

Bhabha, Homi K. 'Remembering Fanon', foreword to Frantz Fanon, *Black Skin, White Masks* [1952]. London: Pluto Press, 1986: vii–xxv.

Billet, M., and Lynn, S. 'Below the Belt'. *Men's Wear*, 7 June 1990: 12–13.

Bishop, F. P. *The Ethics of Advertising*. London: Robert Hale, 1949.

Blom, Jan Dirk. *A Dictionary of Hallucinations*. New York: Springer, 2010.

Booker, Christopher. *The Neophiliacs*. London: Pimlico, 1969.

Bordo, Susan. 'Gay Men's Revenge'. *Journal of Aesthetics and Art Criticism* 57:1 (Winter 1999): 21–5.

Bourdieu, Pierre. *Distinction*. London: Routledge, 1992.

Bowen-Jones, C. 'Adman Finds a New Woman'. *The Times*, 16 March 1988: 26.

Brake, Michael. *The Sociology of Youth Culture and Youth Subcultures*. London: Routledge and Kegan Paul, 1980.

Breton, André. *The Communicating Vessels* [1932], trans. by M. A. Caws and G. T. Harris. Lincoln: University of Nebraska Press, 1990.

Breward, Christopher. *Fashioning London—Clothing and the Modern Metropolis*. Oxford: Berg, 2004.

Breward, Christopher. 'Style and Subversion: Postwar Poses and the Neo-Edwardian Suit in Mid-Twentieth Century Britain'. *Gender and History* 14:3 (November 2002): 560–83.

Bridges, Jack. 'Sexism in Advertising'. *Men's Wear*, 8 January 1981: 24.

Burton, Richard. *The Book of a Thousand Nights and A Night,* Vol. 10 [1885]. Boston: Milford House, 1973.

Butler, W. Harold. 'The Types We Use'. *Advertiser's Weekly*, 1 March 1945: 290–1.

Butler, W. Harold. 'The Types We Use'. *Advertiser's Weekly*, 9 October 1947: 56 and 60.

Butler, W. Harold. 'The Types We Use'. *Advertiser's Weekly*, 23 October 1947: 170 and 172.

Butler, W. Harold. 'The Types We Use'. *Advertiser's Weekly*, 6 October 1949: 10 and 18.

Butler, W. Harold. 'The Types We Use'. *Advertiser's Weekly*, 12 December 1958: 40, 44 and 48.

Butler, W. Harold. 'The Types We Use'. *Advertiser's Weekly*, 30 December 1960: 12 and 14.

Butler, W. Harold. 'The Types We Use'. *Advertiser's Weekly*, 7 February 1964: 26 and 28.

Campaign. 'Fashion Report—Who Spends What and Where'. 19 September 1997: 6–7.

Campaign. 'Levi's—the Golden Decade'. 5 February 1993: 36–7.

Campaign. 'Top 300 Agencies Report'. 28 February 1992: 27.

Campaign. 'Wranglers Looks Around From DDB'. 4 February 1976: 1.

Campaign for Racial Equality. *The Irish in Britain*. London: Belmont Press, 1997.

Central Statistical Office. *The Treasury Blue Book*. London: HMSO, 1953.

Champfleury. *Les Chats*, J. Rothschild (ed.). Paris: 1869.

Chapman, Rowena. 'The Great Pretender: Variations on the New Man Theme', in R. Chapman and J. Rutherford (eds), *Male Order: Unwrapping Masculinity.* London: Lawrence and Wishart, 1988: 225–48.

Chapman, Rowena, and Rutherford, Jonathan (eds). *Male Order: Unwrapping Masculinity*. London: Lawrence and Wishart, 1988.

Cheskin, Louis. *How to Predict What People Will Buy*. New York: Liveright, 1957.

Chubb, Ann. 'Who's a Pretty Boy Then?' *Sunday Times Magazine*, 3 April 1977: 26.

Claridge, J. 'Agency of 1986. BBH: A Flair Hard to Beat'. *Campaign*, 9 January 1987: 32.

Clark, Danae. 'Commodity Lesbianism', in H. Abelove, M. A. Brale and D. M. Halperin (eds), *The Lesbian and Gay Studies Reader*. New York and London: Routledge, 1993: 186–201.

Clark, Timothy J. *The Painting of Modern Life: Paris in the Art of Manet and His Followers*. London: Thames and Hudson, 1985.

Cobbett, William. *Advice to Young Men and (Incidentally) to Young Women in the Middle and Higher Ranks of Life in a Series of Letters, Addressed to a Youth, a Bachelor, a Lover, a Husband, a Father, a Citizen or a Subject*. London: 1829.

Cockburn, M. 'Selling Sports Wear With a Difference'. *Men's Wear*, 14 August 1980: 24–5.

Cohn, Nik. *Today They Are No Gentlemen: The Changes in Englishmen's Clothes Since the War*. London: Weidenfeld and Nicholson, 1971.

Cole, Shaun. *Don We Now Our Gay Apparel*. Oxford: Berg, 2000.

Collins, W. 'Capturing the Black Market'. *Adweek*, 13 July 1973: 24.

Compton, N. 'Campaign Trail'. *Men's Wear*, 29 October 1992: 15.

Connell, Robert W. *Masculinities*. Oxford: Polity, 1995.

Cooper, Austin. *Making a Poster*. London and New York: Studio Publications, 1945.

Cotton, Charlotte. *Imperfect Beauty: The Making of Contemporary Fashion Photographs*. London: V & A Publications, 2000.

Coward, Noel. 'Shadow Play: A Musical Fantasy' [1935]. London: Samuel French Trade, 2010.

Crome, Erica. 'Durable Press Trousers'. *Men's Wear*, 4 April 1968: viii, x, xiii and xv.

Crome, Erica. 'Underwear Circus'. *Men's Wear*, 22 July 1971: 12.

Daily Express. 'The Party-girl of 15 Who Grew Up Too Fast'. 16 September 1961: 4.

Daniels, M. 'Chasing the "Brand Vulnerable" Motorists'. *Ad Weekly,* 10 April 1970: 41.

Darcy, R. 'Bodoni Would Be Amazed'. *Advertiser's Weekly,* 3 September 1953: 398.

David, H. 'In the Pink'. *The Times Saturday Review*, 13 June 1992: 10–11.

Davies, A. H. 'The Youth Market. The Media: This Is What They Look At'. *Advertiser's Weekly*, 21 February 1958: 28, 30 and 32.

Davies, Jim. 'Campaign Craft: Profile'. *Campaign*, 18 October 1996: 22–3.

Dawson, J. *The Compleat Motherfucker: A History of the Mother of All Dirty Words.* Port Townsend, WA: Feral House, 2009.

de Holden Stone, James, and Gray, Milner. 'In the Case of Art v. Advertising: A Summing Up'. *Penrose Annual* (1953): 61–4.

Dennis, P. *Daring Hearts: Lesbian and Gay Lives of 50s and 60s Brighton*. Brighton: Queenspark, 1992.

Dichter, Ernest. *The Strategy of Desire*. New York: T. V. Boardman & Co, 1960.

Dijkstra, Bram. *Idols of Perversity: Fantasies of Feminine Evil in Fin-de-Siecle Culture*. Oxford: Oxford University Press, 1986.

Douglas, T. 'Why Jeans Manufacturers Are Enjoying Record Sales'. *Campaign,* 6 August 1976: 9.

Eco, Umberto. *Faith in Fakes: Travels in Hyperreality*. London: Minerva, 1995.

Edwards, Tim. *Men in the Mirror: Men's Fashion, Masculinity and Consumer Society*. London: Cassell, 1997.

Edwards, Tim. 'Sex, Booze and Gags: Masculinity, Style and Men's Magazines', in B. Benwell (ed.), *Masculinity and Men's Lifestyle Magazines*. Oxford: Blackwell, 2003: 144.

Ellis, Havelock. *Sexual Inversion: Studies in the Psychology of Sex,* Vol. 2 [1897]. New York: Random House, 1936.

Entwistle, Joanne. 'From Catwalk to Catalogue: Male Models, Masculinity and Identity', in H. Thomas and J. Ahmed (eds), *Cultural Bodies: Ethnography and Theory*. Oxford: Blackwell, 2004: 55–75.

Espen, H. 'Coming Apart at the Seams'. *Observer Review*, 28 March 1999: 1–2.

The Face. 'Review of 1986'. January 1987: 68.

Fanon, Frantz. *Black Skin, White Masks* [1952], trans. by C.L. Markmann. London: Pluto Press, 1986.

Fanon, Frantz. *The Wretched of the Earth* [1963], trans. by C. Farrington. New York: Grove Press, 1985.

Fieldhouse, Shirley. 'The Cost of a Shining Image'. *Daily Telegraph*, 31 December 1962: 7.

Fields, Barbara, J. 'Slavery, Race and Ideology in the United States of America'. *New Left Review* 1:181 (1990): 95–118.

Fillin-Yeh, Susan (ed.). *Dandies: Fashion and Finesse in Art and Culture*. New York: New York University Press, 2001.

Fisher, Alice. 'Beckham Factor Boost Briefs as Men Tighten Up'. *The Observer*, 6 July 2008: 16.

Floch, Jean-Marie. *Semiotics, Marketing and Communication: Beneath the Signs, the Strategies*, trans. by R.O. Bodkin. London: Palgrave, 2001.

Forbes, C. 'Advertising Review'. *Advertiser's Weekly,* 30 September 1966: 34–5.

Forbes, C. 'So Similar It Hertz!' *Advertiser's Weekly,* 6 May 1966: 34–5.

Ford, Tom. 'Masculinity Stripped Bare'. *GQ Style* (Spring/Summer 2008): 277.

Frankel, Henryk, and Ady, Peter. 'The Wartime Clothing Budget'. *Advertiser's Weekly*, 21 June 1945: 26–28, 30, 32, 36, 38 and 40.

Friedan, Betty. *The Feminine Mystique*. London: Victor Gollancz, 1971.

Freud, Sigmund. 'Fetishism' [1927], in J. Strachey (ed.), *On Sexuality*, Penguin Freud Library, Vol. 7. Harmondsworth: Penguin, 1977: 345–57.

Freud, Sigmund. *On Metapsychology*, J. Strachey (ed.). Harmondsworth: Penguin, 1991.

Freud, Sigmund. 'Three Essays on the Theory of Sexuality' [1905], in J. Strachey (ed.), *On Sexuality*, Penguin Freud Library, Vol. 7. Harmondsworth: Penguin, 1977: 31–169.

Fyvel, T.R. *The Insecure Offenders: Rebellious Youth in the Welfare State*. London: Pelican, 1961.

Gaines, Jane. 'The Queen Christina Tie-Ups: Convergence of Show Window and Screen'. *Quarterly Review of Film and Video* II (1989): 35–60.

Games, Abram. 'Approach to the Poster'. *Art and Industry*, July 1948: 24–9.

Garber, Marjorie. *Vested Interests: Cross-dressing and Cultural Anxiety*. New York: Harper Collins, 1993.

Gardener, Anne. 'Fashion Retailing 1946–86', in P. Sparke (ed.), *Did Britain Make It? British Design in Context 1946–86*. London: Design Council, 1986: 117–27.

Garfield, Simon. *Our Hidden Lives: The Everyday Diaries of a Forgotten Britain 1945– 1948*. London: Ebury Press, 2004.

Garland, Sidney T. 'Advertising Causes an Evolution in Men's Wear'. *Advertiser's Weekly*, 4 July 1919: 5–6.

Garrett, A. 'New York Taxi Driver Blues'. *Campaign*, 19 January 1990: 30.

Garrett, James. 'Commercial Production', in B. Henry (ed.), *British Television Advertising: The First Thirty Years*. London: Century Bantam, 1986.

Gaskell, Jane. '3 in 5—The Mortality Rate in Teenage *Marriage*'. *Daily Express*, 11 September 1961: 12.

Gaskell, Jane. 'Does a Baby Inhibit Teenage Marriage?' *Daily Express*, 12 September 1961: 10.

Gilbert, Geoffrey M. 'Meet the New Man'. *Man and His Clothes*, August 1953: 26–7.

Gill, Rosalind. 'Power and the Production of Subjects: A Genealogy of the New Man and the New Lad', in B. Benwell (ed.), *Masculinity and Men's Lifestyle Magazines*. Oxford: Blackwell, 2003: 38.

Gillman, Peter. 'The Unofficial Poor'. *Sunday Times Magazine*, 27 February 1972: 36–9, 41 and 43.

Goldhill, Christine. 'Under-wares'. *Men's Wear*, 4 January 1973: 13.

Goldman, Robert. *Reading Ads Socially*. London: Routledge, 1992.

Goldthorpe, J.K. 'Fifty Years of Advertising'. *Art and Industry*, January 1951: 16–21.

Goodman, Nelson. *Languages of Art*. Indianapolis: Hackett, 1976.

Gowing, Mary. 'Arpad Elfer'. *Art and Industry*, March 1957: 82–7.

Gowing, Mary. 'Can Good Art Be Bad Propaganda?' *Art and Industry*, July 1947: 8–13.

Gowing, Mary. 'Harry Ballam'. *Art and Industry*, April 1957: 119–25.

Gowing, Mary. 'Ruth Gill'. *Art and Industry*, September 1957: 84–9.

Gowing, Mary. 'Tom Eckersley'. *Art and Industry*, November 1957: 159–62 and 180.

Gregory, B. 'Now More Than Ever a Page Is a Page'. *Adweek*, 4 January 1974: 12–13.

Green, H. 'How Creative Minds Work'. *Campaign*, 20 September 1996: 23.

Griffin, H. *And Their Own Receive Them Not: African American Lesbians and Gays in Black Churches*. Cleveland, OH: Pilgrim Press, 2006.

Guardian. 'Shopping New Man'. 20 January 1998: 14.

Halpern, Joseph. 'Decadent Narrative. *A Rebours*'. *Stanford French Review* (Spring 1978): 91–102.

Hamilton, George H. *Manet and His Critics*. New York: Norton, 1969.

Handley, Susannah. *Nylon: The Story of a Fashion Revolution*. Baltimore: John Hopkins University Press, 1999.

Hanson, Anne C. *Manet and the Modern Tradition*. New Haven: Yale University Press, 1977.

Harmar-Brown, F. 'Why Oldies Are Goodies'. *Campaign*, 13 January 1978: 21 and 23.

Havinden, Ashley. *Advertising and the Artist*. London: Studio Publications, 1956.

Havinden, Ashley. 'The Importance of "Company Handwriting"'. *Penrose Annual* (1955): 58–61.

Heath, Ashley. 'Kitsch 'n' Pink'. *The Face*, July 1993: 58–9.

Hebdige, Dick. 'The Bottom Line on Planet One—Squaring up to THE FACE'. *Ten.8* 19 (1985): 40–9.

Hebdige, Dick. *Subculture: The Meaning of Style*. London: Methuen, 1974.

Heffernan, James. 'Ekphrasis and Representation'. *New Literary History* 22:2 (Spring 1991): 297–316.

Hegarty, John. 'Why Creativity Must Lose Its Straightjacket'. *Campaign*, 30 March 1979: 45.

Hegarty, John. 'Why Levi's Proved to Be Such a Good Fit for BBH'. *Campaign*, 23 July 2010: 11.

Henley, Charlotte. *The Butch Manual: The Current Drag and How to Do It*. New York, 1982.

Hennessy, Peter. *Having It So Good: Britain in the Fifties*. London: Allen Lane, 2006.

Hennessy, Peter. *Never Again, Britain 1945–1951*. London: Vintage, 1992.

Henry, Brian (ed.). *British Television Advertising: The First Thirty Years*. London: Century Benham, 1986.

Henry, Harry. 'Motivation Research?—It's out of the Swaddling Clothes'. *Advertiser's Weekly*, 5 July 1957: 24 and 26.

Hewitt, John. *The Commercial Art of Tom Purvis*. Manchester: Manchester Metropolitan University Press, 1996.

Hobson, John. *The Selection of Advertising*. London: Business Publications, 1961.

Hoggart, Richard. *The Uses of Literacy*. Harmondsworth: Penguin, 1957.

Holden, Anthony. 'This Year's Models'. *Guardian*, 20 August 1990: 31.

Hollander, Anne. 'The Great Emancipator, Chanel'. *Connoisseur* 213 (February 1983).

Homer, W. I., and Johnson, C. *Stieglitz and the Photo-Secession 1902.* New York: Viking Press, 2002.

Honigsbaum, M. 'Blitz—No Time to Grow Up'. *The Guardian Media*, 2 September 1991: 23.

hooks, bell. 'Doing it for Daddy', in M. Berger, B. Wallis and S. Watson (eds), *Constructing Masculinity.* London: Routledge, 1995: 98–106.

Hopcraft, Arthur. 'Grimsby: The Men in Wide-Bottomed Suits'. *Sunday Times Magazine*, 28 November 1965: 35.

Hopkins, Harry. *The New Look: A Social History of the Forties and Fifties*. London: Secker and Warburg, 1963.

Horwell, Veronica. ' "King of Carnaby Street" Who Changed Attitudes to Male Fashion'. *Guardian*, 9 February 2004.

Howarth, T.E.B. *Prospect and Reality: Great Britain 1945–1955*. London: Collins, 1985.

Hughes, David. 'The Spivs', in M. Sissons and P. French (eds), *Age of Austerity*. London: Hodder and Stoughton, 1963: 69–88.

Hughes, Ted. *Tales From Ovid*. London: Faber and Faber, 1997.

Huysmans, Joris-Karl. *Against Nature* [1884]. Harmondsworth: Penguin, 1977.

Irigaray, Luce. 'The Speculum of the Other Woman', in M. Whitford (ed.), *The Irigaray Reader*. Oxford: Blackwell, 1991: 65–6.

Jackson, Stanley. *The Indiscreet Guide to Soho*. London: Muse Arts Ltd, 1946.

Jacobson, Sydney. 'The Problem of the Demobbed Officer'. *Picture Post*, 26 January 1946: 26–7.

Jobling, Paul. *Fashion Spreads: Word and Image in Fashion Photography Since 1980*. Oxford: Berg, 1999.

Jobling, Paul. 'Keeping Mrs Dawson Busy: Safe Sex, Gender and Pleasure in Condom Advertising Since 1970', in M. Nava, A. Blake, I. MacRury and B. Richards (eds), *Buy This Book: Studies in Advertising and Consumption*. London: Routledge, 1996: 157–77.

Jobling, Paul. *Man Appeal: Advertising, Modernism and Menswear*. Oxford: Berg, 2005.

Jobling, Paul, and Crowley, David. *Graphic Design: Reproduction and Representation Since 1800*. Manchester: Manchester University Press, 1996.

Johnson, R. 'Bona Fide Desert Boot That Enjoys a New Cult Status'. *Campaign*, 15 May 1987.

Johnstone-Cristall, T. 'From Sunny Sublime to Dreary Stereotype'. *Ad Weekly*, 4 June 1971: 34–5.

Johnstone-Cristall, T. 'Getting Too Clever by Half'. *Ad Weekly*, 8 January 1971: 35.

Johnstone-Cristall, T. 'Keep Your Feet on the Ground'. *Ad Weekly*, 16 April 1971: 30–1.
Johnstone-Cristall, T. 'A Matter of Models'. *Ad Weekly*, 5 May 1972: 32–3.
Johnstone-Cristall, T. 'Tailors Don't Need Ad Dummies'. *Ad Weekly*, 9 April 1971: 26–7.
Johnstone-Cristall, T. 'Venture into Fantasy Land'. *Ad Weekly*, 28 April 1972: 36.
Johnstone-Cristall, T. 'What a Good Picture. What a Lousy Ad'. *Ad Weekly*, 17 July
    1970: 34–5.
Johnstone-Cristall, T. 'When Expense Is No Object'. *Ad Weekly,* 6 November 1970:
    38–9.
Jones, H. 'Crawford's Genius of Good Taste'. *Adweek*, 15 June 1973: 28.
Kee, Robert. 'Can the Wage-Freeze Hold For Them?' *Picture Post*, 3 June 1950: 37–41.
Kimmel, M. S. *Manhood in America: A Cultural History*. Oxford: Oxford University Press,
    2006.
King, J. J. 'Borrowed Bottoms Invite Criticism'. *Adweek*, 24 November 1972: 16.
King, J. 'This Burton Experience Is Quite Something'. *Adweek*, 23 March 1973: 16.
King, S. editorial. *Adweek*, 20 April 1973: 18–19.
Klein, Donna. *Women in Advertising, Ten Years On*. London: IPA, 2000.
Klein, M. 'Little Big Man: Hustling, Gender Narcissism and Body-building Culture', in
    M. A. Messner and D. F. Sabo (eds), *Sport, Men and the Gender Order.* Champaign,
    IL: Human Kinetic Books, 1990: 127–40.
Knight, India. 'The Teenage Rebel Is Dead'. *Campaign*, 13 May 1988: 58–9.
Koski, John. 'Ad of the Week'. *Campaign*, 11 May 1979: 24.
Koski, John. 'Menswear Market Faces a Big Strategy Shake-up'. *Campaign*, 5 May
    1978: 20.
Kosofsky Sedgwick, Eve. *The Epistemology of the Closet*. Harmondsworth: Penguin
    1990.
Kristeva, Julia. *Strangers to Ourselves*, trans. by A. Roudiez. New York: Columbia
    University Press, 1991.
Kynaston, David. *Austerity Britain 1945–51*. London: Bloomsbury, 2007.
La Bar, Elizabeth. 'Conversation with Mary Ellen Mark'. *Photographer's Forum* 2
    (February/March 1980): 5–12.
Lacan, Jacques. *The Seminar of Jacques Lacan, Book 1*. Cambridge: Cambridge
    University Press, 1988.
Lacan, Jacques. 'The Signification of the Phallus', in *Écrits: A Selection*, trans. by
    A. Sheridan. London: Tavistock, 1977: 288 and 291.
Lacey, Robert. 'The Richest Shopkeepers in the World'. *Sunday Times Magazine*, 17
    December 1972: 27, 30, 32 and 34.
Lacey, Robert. 'Their Weekly Bread'. *Sunday Times Magazine*, 1 October 1972: 56–7,
    59, 61 and 63.
Laurie, Peter. *The Teenage Revolution*. London: Anthony Blond, 1965.
Lehman, P. 'In an Imperfect World Men with Small Penises Are Unforgiven: The
    Representation of the Penis/Phallus in American Films of the 1990s'. *Men and
    Masculinities* 1:2 (1998): 123–37.
Lehman, P. 'You and the Voyeurweb: Illustrating the Shifting Representation of the Penis
    on the Internet with User-generated Content'. *Cinema Journal* 46: 4 (2007): 108–16.
Lever, A. E. 'What Advertising Costs'. *Advertiser's Weekly*, 23 January 1947: 160
    and 164.
Lewis, Patricia. 'Wide-Eyed Appeal in Tush's Violet Gaze'. *Daily Express*, 7 September
    1961: 10.
Lewis, Paul. *The Fifties*. London: William Heinemann, 1978.

Lomas, Claire. ' "Men Don't Wear Velvet You Know!" Fashionable Gay Masculinity and the Shopping Experience, London, 1950–Early 1970s'. *Oral History* 35:1 (Spring 2007): 82–90.

Look-In Fashion Model Annual. 'Special Agents'. London: Independent Television, 1971: 49–55.

MacIntyre, C.F. *Selected Poems*. Berkeley: University of California Press, 1970.

Mallows, J. 'Do You Want the Power of Sunday Colour Behind You?' *Campaign*, 2 July 1982.

Marchant, Hilde. 'The Making of Boy Gangsters'. *Picture Post*, 10 October 1953: 16–18, 42 and 11.

Marks, Laura. *The Skin of the Film*. Durham, NC: Duke University Press, 2000.

Marquis, S. 'The Publishing Conundrum: How to Reach the "New Man" '. *Campaign*, 26 July 1985: 39.

Marshall, A. 'Guess Editor Defies Convention to Leave His Mark'. *Campaign,* 31 May 1996: 37.

Martin, Michele. 'Why Fashion Shuns Adland'. *Campaign*, 23 May 1997: 36–7.

Martin, Richard. ' "Feel Like A Million!": The Propitious Epoch in Men's Underwear Imagery, 1939–1952'. *Journal of American Culture* 18:2 (1995): 51–8.

Martin, Richard, and Koda, Harold. *Jocks and Nerds*. New York: Rizzoli, 1988.

Marwick, Arthur. *British Society Since 1945*. Harmondsworth: Pelican, 1982.

Marwick, Arthur. *The Sixties—Cultural Revolution in the United Kingdom c.1958–c.1974*. Oxford: Oxford University Press, 1998.

Mass Observation. *The Press and Its Readers*. London: Art and Technics, 1949.

Mawer, N. 'Supplementary Benefits and Drawbacks'. *Campaign*, 13 January 1978: 16–17.

McClintock, Anne. 'Soft-soaping Empire: Commodity Racism and Imperial Advertising', in G. Robertson, M. Mash, L. Tickner, J. Bird, B. Curtis and T. Putnam (eds), *Travellers' Tales: Narratives of Home and Displacement*. London: Routledge, 1994: 131–55.

McSharry, Deirdre. 'The Young Peacock Cult'. *Daily Express*, 3 April 1965: 14.

Media Week. '*The Face* That Launched a Hundred'. 22 July 1988: 29.

Meltzer, Françoise. *Salome and the Dance of Writing: Portraits of Mimesis in Literature*. Chicago: University of Chicago Press, 1987.

Mendelssohn, John. 'David Bowie? Pantomime Rock?' *Rolling Stone*, 1 April 1971: www.rollingstone.com/archives, accessed 26 September 2010.

Men's Wear. 'A £100 Loan Launched Burton's Fifty Years Ago'. 4 March 1950: 18–19.

Men's Wear. '18 Per Cent Bought Knitwear and 15 Per Cent Shirts from Marks and Spencer'. 1 December 1962: 11.

Men's Wear. '19 Manchester Bespoke Tailors Launch Combined Advertising'. 6 March 1954: 15–16.

Men's Wear. 'Big Men's Wear TV Programme'. 25 April 1959: 11.

Men's Wear. 'Cheap Jeans War Hots Up'. 28 May 1981: 7.

Men's Wear. 'Clothes Advertising Campaigns Are Educating Public'. 16 October 1954: 17.

Men's Wear. 'The Facts Behind the Theories'. 27 November 1986: 9.

Men's Wear. 'Get Wise to Publicity'. 12 March 1960: 19–20.

Men's Wear. 'The Influence of the Woman Shopper'. 12 May 1956: 18–20.

Men's Wear. 'Jeans Continue Their Climb up the Fashion Ladder'. 4 July 1964: 20–1.

Men's Wear. 'Jeans Importer Explains His Problem'. 1 February 1968: 12.

Men's Wear. 'Men's Underwear Prices Heads Clothing Price-Rise Chart'. 5 August 1976: 5.

Men's Wear. 'Mr. Average Now Buys More Underwear'. 21 April 1956: 34.

Men's Wear. 'Plea for the Peacock Look'. 25 May 1963: 9.

Men's Wear. 'Sleek Line Cruise Clothes for Mr. Armstrong Jones'. 7 May 1960: 13.

Men's Wear. 'Teen Man Market Surprises'. 1 December 1962: 11.

Men's Wear. 'Television Vindicated'. 17 December 1960: 15.

Men's Wear. 'Today's Teenage Male'. 7 April 1951: 20.

Men's Wear. 'Woman's Influence: Burton's Plot It'. 9 January 1965: 7.

Men's Wear. 'Zip Goes a Million on Men's Wear Ads'. 28 March 1964: 9.

Mercer, Kobena. 'Diaspora Culture and the Dialogic Imagination', in M. M. Cham and C. Andrade-Watkins (eds), *Blackframes: Critical Perspectives on Black Independent Cinema*. Cambridge, MA: MIT Press, 1988: 50–61.

Mercer, Kobena. 'Reading Racial Fetishism: The Photographs of Robert Mapplethorpe', in *Welcome to the Jungle*. London: Routledge, 1984: 177–220.

Merleau-Ponty, Maurice. *The Visible and the Invisible*, trans. by A. Lingis. Evanston, IL: Northwestern University Press, 1968.

Miller, David A. *Bringing out Roland Barthes.* Berkeley: University of California Press, 1992.

Mills, G.H.S. 'Advertising is Largely a Matter of Words'. *Art and Industry*, December 1948: 211.

Mills, G.H.S. 'The New Idea in Advertising'. *Commercial Art*, November 1923: 298.

Mintel. *Clothing and Footwear Retailing Report.* London: Mintel, 1991.

Mintel. *Men 2000.* London: Mintel, 1993.

Mirza, K. 'Dominic Dormeuil'. *Draper's*, 24 January 2009.

Mort, Frank. 'The Commercial Domain: Advertising and the Cultural Management of Demand', in B. Conekin, F. Mort and C. Waters (eds), *Moments of Modernity: Reconstructing Britain 1945–1964*. New York: Rivers Oram, 1999: 55–75.

Mort, Frank. *Cultures of Consumption—Masculinities and Social Space in Late Twentieth-Century Britain*. London: Routledge, 1997.

Mulvey, Laura. *Visual and Other Pleasures*. Basingstoke: Macmillan, 1989.

Myerson, Jeremy, and Vickers, Graham. *Rewind: Forty Years of Design and Advertising*. London: Phaidon, 2002.

Nash, R. *Wilderness and the American Mind*. New Haven: Yale University Press, 1979.

National Galleries of Scotland. *Advertising and the Artist: The Work and Collection of Ashley Havinden*. Edinburgh: National Galleries of Scotland, 2003.

Nayak, Anoop. 'Frozen Bodies: Disclosing Whiteness in Häagen-Dazs Advertising'. *Body & Society* 3:3 (1997): 51–71.

Needham, Gerald. 'Manet, Olympia, and Pornographic Photography', in T. B. Hess and L. Nochlin (eds), *Woman as Sex Object*. New York: Newsweek, 1972: 81–9.

Nevett, T. R. *Advertising in Britain*. London: Heinemann, 1982.

Newman, Joseph N. *Motivation Research and Marketing Management*. Boston: Harvard Business School, 1957.

Nixon, Sean. *Advertising Cultures*. London: Sage, 2003.

Nixon, Sean. *Hard Looks: Masculinities, Spectatorship and Contemporary Consumption*. London: University College Press, 1996.

Nixon, Sean. 'In Pursuit of the Professional Ideal: Advertising in the Construction of Commercial Expertise in Britain 1953–1964', in P. Jackson, M. Lowe, D. Miller and F. Mort (eds), *Commercial Cultures: Economies, Practices, Spaces*. London: Sage, 2000: 55–74.

O'Hagan, Sean. 'Here Comes the New Lad'. *Arena*, May 1991: 22–3.

O'Kelly, L. 'Levi 501s: Why Hegarty Knew the Time Was Right for a Denim Revival'. *Campaign*, 25 April 1986: 16.

O'Neill, Alistair. 'John Stephen: A Carnaby Street Presentation of Masculinity 1957–1975'. *Fashion Theory* 4:4 (2000): 487–506.

O'Neill, Alistair. *London—After a Fashion*. London: Reaktion, 2007.

Orwell, George. *The Collected Essays, Journalism and Letters, 1943–1945*, Vol. 3. Harmondsworth: Penguin, 1978.

Orwell, Stanley. 'Selling to the 16–24 Market'. *Advertiser's Weekly*, 3 February 1961: 25.

Orwell, Stanley. 'Survey of the Youth Market'. *Advertiser's Weekly*, 21 February 1958: 23 and 26.

Osborne, Roger. *40 Years of NME Charts*. London: Boxtree, 1992.

Outdoor Advertising. 'The First Audience Survey Carried out by an Outdoor Advertising Contractor for the Purpose of Describing to Advertisers the Audiences Which His Sites Offer'. February 1965: 4–7.

Outdoor Advertising. 'Planning and Posters'. September/October 1966: 13–15.

Packard, Vance. *The Hidden Persuaders*. Harmondsworth: Penguin, 1991.

Pajaczkowska, Clare. 'On Stuff and Nonsense'. *Textile* 3:3 (2005).

Pelican [pseud.]. 'The Month on the Hoardings'. *Advertiser's Weekly*, 5 October 1923: 25.

Plewka, Karl. 'Jeans Genius'. *Observer Life*, 12 May 1996: 40.

Pook, S. 'Tesco Loses Fight to Sell Levi's at American Prices'. *Daily Telegraph*, 27 November 2001.

Powe, Hector. 'What is Advertising? Science or Sympathy?' *Commercial Art* 6 (January–June 1929): 200–4.

Powell, Anthony. *The Military Philosophers*. London: William Heinemann, 1968.

Priestley, J. B., and Hawkes, Jacquetta. *Journey Down a Rainbow*. London: Heinemann Cresset, 1955.

Quant, Mary. 'A Design for Personal Living'. *The Listener*, December 1974: 816.

Rabinowitz, Paula. *They Must Be Represented: The Politics of Documentary*. London: Verso, 1994.

Rantonen, Eila. 'A Game of Chess: Race, Gender and Nation in Neil Jordan's *The Crying Game*', in J. Nyman and J. A. Stotesbury (eds), *Postcolonialism and Cultural Resistance*. Joensuu: University of Joensuu, 1999: 192–204.

Raven, Charlotte. 'How a Furry Yellow Muppet Restored My Faith in Culture'. *Guardian*, 9 March 1999: 5.

Raynor, William. 'One Man's Porn . . . Another Man's Pleasure'. *Ad Weekly*, 14 January 1972: 28–30.

Reed, John R. *Decadent Style*. Athens, OH: Ohio University Press, 1985.

Rice, R. 'Young, Trendy and Bland?' *Campaign*, 11 April 1991: 12.

Ritchie, B. *A Touch of Class: The Story of Austin Reed*. London: James and James, 1991.

Robins, Jane. 'Generation X Advertising'. *The Money Programme* [report] BBC2, 2 April 1995.

Robinson, Sally. *Marked Men: White Masculinity in Crisis*. London: Columbia University Press, 2000.

Roter, Ronnie. 'Wrangler: The Real Reason for Our Split with Waseys'. *Campaign,* 15 August 1980: 20.

Samuel, Lawrence R. *Freud on Madison Avenue: Motivation Research and Subliminal Advertising*. Philadelphia: University of Pennsylvania Press, 2010.

Sargeant, Amy. 'The Man in the White Suit: New Textiles and the Social Fabric'. *Visual Culture in Britain* 9:1 (Summer 2008): 27–54.

The Scanner. 'Triple Suit Attack by Colliers'. *Men's Wear*, 10 April 1969: 41.

Schuster, George. 'Are We TOO Few for the Job?' *Picture Post*, 19 April 1947.

Selby, H. L. 'In Eight Years—'. *Advertiser's Weekly*, 12 December 1930: 416 and 430.

Settle, Alison. 'The Fashion Artist in Advertising'. *Art and Industry*, December 1948: 212–18.

Sharman, H. 'The Ups and Downs of Consumer Spending'. *Campaign*, 10 February 1978: 11.

Simpson, Mark. 'Becks, Look What You Started'. *The Times 2*, 28 July 2008: 17.

Sinfield, Alan. 'Private Lives/Public Theatre: Noel Coward and the Politics of Homosexual Representation'. *Representations* 36 (1991): 43–63.

Sinfield, Alan. *The Wilde Century*. London: Cassell, 1994.

Sked, Alan, and Cook, Chris. *Post-War Britain, A Political History*. Harmondsworth: Pelican, 1984.

Smith, David. 'Shirts, Volkswagen and Christmas Pudding'. *Ad Weekly*, 13 March 1970: 32.

Smith, George Horseley. *Motivation Research in Advertising and Marketing*. London: Advertising Research Foundation, 1954.

Smith, John A., and Jenks, Chris. 'Manet's *Olympia*'. *Visual Studies* 21:2 (October 2006): 157–66.

Sontag, Susan. 'Notes on "Camp"' [1964], in *Against Interpretation and Other Essays*. London: Picador, 2001: 275–92.

Sparke, Penny (ed.) *Did Britain Make It? British Design in Context 1946–86*. London: Design Council, 1986.

Sreenivasan, S. 'Extraneous Lattice in Regenerated Cellulose'. *Textile Research Journal* 54:2 (1984): 119–22.

Stein, S. 'The Good, the Bad and the Ugly . . . Mostly Good'. *Ad Weekly*, 21 April 1972.

Stern, B. B. 'The Importance of Being Ernest: Commemorating Dichter's Contribution to Advertising Research'. *Journal of Advertising Research* (June 2004): 165–9.

Stokes, C. W. 'Modern Publicity'. *Art and Industry*, January 1949: 30–2.

Sugden, A. V., and Edmondson, J. L. *A History of English Wallpaper, 1509–1914*. London, 1926.

Sunday Pictorial. 'Wanted: 100 Families to Speak for Britain'. 7 July 1946: 4–5.

Sunday Times. 'A Step Back in Fashion'. 20 November 1988.

Sunday Times Magazine. 'Tern's Bid to End White Supremacy'. 22 October 1967.

Sunday Times Magazine. 'Tern Shirts: Further Deflationary Measures'. 1 December 1968.

Sunday Times Magazine. 'Why Should Girls Get All the Fun?' 25 November 1973.

Sunday Times Magazine. 'Will It Ever Come to This?' 21 May 1967.

Symes, A. 'Man About Chelsea'. *Men's Wear*, 4 April 1959: 14.

Tailor and Cutter. 'Meet the Spiv'. 15 August 1947: 561.

Taylor, B. 'Do Style Shows Sell More Clothes?' *Men's Wear*, 22 December 1951: 14–15.

Taylor, John. 'Wide Scope for Improving the Masculine Approach'. *Advertiser's Weekly*, 4 March 1960: 38.

Taylor, John. 'What the Well-Dressed Man Is Flaunting'. *Sunday Times Magazine*, 26 October 1975: 32–4.

Taylor, R. '25 Years of the Creative Circle'. *Ad Weekly*, 30 October 1970: 37–8 and 40.

Ten.8. 23 (1986) colour supplement living.

Thau Heyman, Therese (ed.). *Seeing Straight, Group f.64*. Oakland, CA: Oakland Museum, 1992.

Thumin, Janet. 'The 'Popular', Cash and Culture in Postwar British Cinema'. *Screen* 32:3 (1991): 245–71.

Tinterow, G. *Manet/Velazquez: The French Taste for Spanish Painting*. New York: Metropolitan Museum of Art, 2003.

Tomalin, N. 'When All the Beautiful People Came to the Aid of the Party'. *Sunday Times Magazine*, 14 June 1970: 24–6.

Treasure, J. 'What 1974 Holds in Store for the Ad Business'. *Adweek*, 4 January 1974: 11.

van der Haag, Ernest, and Ross, Ralph. *The Fabric of Society*. New York: Harcourt Brace, 1957.

Vassie, Michael. '. . . and the Joke Is on Men'. *Ad Weekly*, 1 September 1972: 20–3.

Vassie, Michael. 'Where the Outsider Scores'. *Adweek*, 1 June 1973: 18.

Wainwright, Clive. 'Pre-Raphaelite Furniture', in J. M. Crook (ed.), *The Strange Genius of William Burges, 'Art-Architect', 1827–1881*. Cardiff: National Museum of Wales, 1981.

Wainwright, David. *The British Tradition: Simpson, A World of Style*. London: Quiller Press, 1996.

Wayne, George. *Male Super Models: The Men of Boss Models*. New York: DAP, 1996.

Weeks, Jeffrey. *Sex, Politics and Society*. London: Longman, 1989.

Wellings, Kaye, and Field, Becky. *Stopping AIDS: AIDS/HIV, Public Education and the Mass Media in Europe*. London: Longman, 1996.

White, Ian. 'The Jeans Phenomenon'. *Campaign*, 27 April 1979: 49.

White, Ian. 'The Underlying Appeal of Jeans Is That They Are Classless'. *Campaign*, 27 April 1979: 47.

Williams, Melanie. 'Women in Prison and Women in Dressing Gowns'. *Journal of Gender Studies* 11:2 (2002): 5–16.

Williamson, Judith. *Decoding Advertisements: Ideology and Meaning in Advertising*. London: Marion Boyars, 1978.

Williamson, Judith. 'Short Circuit of the New Man'. *New Statesman*, 20 May 1988: 28.

Wilkinson, Helen. 'The "New Heraldry": Stock Photography, Visual Literacy and Advertising in 1930s Britain'. *Journal of Design History* 10:1 (1997): 23–38.

Willis, Susan. 'I Want the Black One: Is There a Place for Afro-American Culture in Commodity Culture?' *New Formations* (Spring 1990): 77–97.

Wilson, Elizabeth. *Adorned in Dreams: Fashion and Modernity*. London: Virago, 1985.

Wilson, Michael. 'Admen's Colour Problem'. *Ad Weekly*, 12 December 1969: 36–7.

Winship, Janice. 'Back to the Future—A Style for the Eighties'. *New Socialist* (July/August 1986): 48–9.

Witt, E. 'The Personal Adman'. *Reporter*, 14 May 1959: 36–7.

Wollheim, Richard. *Art and Its Objects*. Harmondsworth: Peregrine, 1975.

Wood, D. 'Who Will Watch the Most Television Later Tonight?' *Campaign*, 30 April 1982: 31.

Wood, Gaby. 'Western Hero'. *Observer Review*, 30 June 2002: 5.

Woman' Readers Buy for Men. London: Odhams Press, 1953.

Wray, Margaret. *The Women's Outerwear Industry*. London: Gerald Duckworth, 1957.

Wyndham, Francis. 'Gee, but It's Great to Be Gee!' *Sunday Times Magazine*, 19 January 1969: 16–19 and 21.

Zweig, Stefan. *Mental Healers: Hans Mesmer, Mary Baker Eddy, Sigmund Freud*, trans. by Eden and Cedar Paul. London: Cassell and Co., 1933.

INDEX